THE RELIGION OF *Israel*

THE RELIGION OF
Israel

by HENRY RENCKENS, S.J.

Translated by N. B. Smith

SHEED AND WARD: *New York*

© Sheed and Ward, 1966

Originally published as *De Godsdienst van Israel*,
J. J. Romen & Zonen (1962), The Netherlands

Nihil Obstat
   W. John Fradet
   Censor Deputatus

Imprimatur
   Robert F. Joyce
   Bishop of Burlington

December 14, 1965

The Nihil Obstat and Imprimatur are official declarations
that a book or pamphlet is considered to be free of
doctrinal or moral error. No implication is contained
therein that those who have granted the Nihil Obstat and
Imprimatur agree with the contents, opinions, or statements expressed.

Library of Congress Catalog Card Number: 66–12261

Manufactured in the United States of America

Foreword

IF THE WORD ISRAEL is considered in its broadest sense, it is at once
evident that Israel's long history is divided by the rise of Christianity into two distinct parts. For the Christian, these two parts are
of unequal interest since it is the pre-Christian period of Israel's
religion which constitutes the prehistory of the Christian faith. The
Rabbi Jesus of Nazareth, whose career formed the point of departure for the Christian religion, was not simply the bud (or the
offspring) of Yahweh, but also the "fruit of the earth" (Isa. 4:2); in
other words, a fruit which ripened, under the special blessing of
the God of Israel, in human soil. The new religion of Christianity
broke through at a definite point in human history. That point was
found in Israel. The fertility of the earth was concentrated, by a
special providence on God's part, in the promised land, and the
separate existence of Christianity was clearly the continuation of a
separate existence which already had its roots in Israel. God's preoccupation with man was thus concentrated within one point, and
Israel's religion of the pre-Christian period was the direct result of
this divine concentration.

For this reason, the religion of Israel, together with Christianity,
occupies a unique place among the other religions of mankind. The
religion of "ancient" Israel is in a very special sense a revealed
religion, or rather, it is preeminently a revealed religion, forming

an integral part of the Christian mystery. This is why those literary works which form the written legacy of pre-Christian Israel—the collection of books comprising the Old Testament—must be regarded, in the Christian religion, as standard or canonical works.

The Christian attitude towards the post-Christian or post-biblical Israel is, however, quite different. True, this period of Israel's history merits the Christian's closest attention, since it can still provide much of what he needs to know concerning the Christian religion. But the historical and literary tradition which linked ancient Israel and the Israel of the post-biblical period has given the Jew, ideally speaking, an enviable and irreplaceable feeling for the way in which the Old Testament writings and institutions came into being and developed. Christian exegetes frequently find data in the study of Jewish texts of the later period which they would otherwise have discovered only with great difficulty. Furthermore, this literary and historical tradition was both the vehicle and the expression of a living and unbroken religious tradition which connected post-biblical Israel with the Bible and, in a special sense, connected it with the Bible as the source of revelation. The religious Jew possessed a living faith which was kept in a constant state of alertness and readiness by the God who had been, and still was, his God, and who spoke to him through the medium of Holy Scripture. The Jew thus had an insight into faith which was founded upon a certain special privilege and was therefore able to lead to an admirable understanding of the special value of the Old Testament—an understanding which is, at times, somewhat denied to the Christian mind. The Israel of this period not only preserved the Hebrew text of the Old Testament, but even retained, for a certain time, the revised and enlarged Greek edition of the Hebrew text which was to become the Bible of the ancient Church. It also produced a literature which offers many points of contact with the cultural environment in which Holy Scripture came into being and the events of the Bible were enacted. It is therefore important for Christians to remember that God still speaks to them through this "cast off" Israel, the miracle of whose continued existence can be regarded as an enduring sign that God has not yet given up his last secret (Rom. 9-11).

In a word, since both religions sprang from the same soil, it is still possible for Christianity to learn from the Israel of the post-biblical period, and acquire not only a deeper knowledge of the origin and essence of Christianity and a better insight into certain aspects of the Christian repository of faith, but also a more precise understanding of the concrete, historical forms in which revelation has been expressed and which have subsequently continued to play a diverse part in the formation of the Church.

Yet in spite of this, it remains true that Israel has also perpetuated a tradition of disbelief, since first reacting against the gospel of Christ, and has allowed its Old Testament inheritance to develop along quite different lines, which can have no binding value for Christians. The religion of Israel's post-Christian period is dealt with in another volume in the present series: *Het Nabijbels Joden-dom*. Here, the Jewish world in the centuries before and at the time of Christ is taken into consideration, insofar as it provides any definite indications of the Judaism of the post-biblical period. In the present volume, however, our aim is to outline the religion of pre-Christian Israel, with particular emphasis upon what can be learnt about it from the books of the Old Testament.

The religion of ancient Israel goes to the very heart of the Old Testament and, conversely, the whole of the Old Testament is deeply concerned with Israel's religion. It is possible that a longer period of study might have resulted in a fuller treatment of the subject, but the reader will have to make-do with this attempt—perhaps only a partial success—on the author's part, until a better and more completely successful book is written on the subject, perhaps by someone else. However, it is the author's hope that this study of Israel's religion, even in its present, incomplete form, will contribute towards a better understanding, in the reader's study of the Bible, of God's purpose in the Old Testament and, in particular, of his present purpose, in the lives of men today.

Contents

ix

I

The Mystery of Israel

THE AIM of the first chapter of this book, which can equally well be read as the last, is to find an explanation of the true nature of the religion of Israel, as well as to attempt to place this religion within the framework of the other religions of the period. At the same time, this chapter serves to correct the possible misunderstanding that the religion of Israel can simply be ranked alongside all other religions, and regarded as one among many others. If this chapter succeeds in correcting this false impression, then it will have succeeded in one of its aims, but, needless to say, it was not written principally with this in mind. It is, of course, necessary to have an almost global insight into the nature of any phenomenon, if this phenomenon is to be effectively traced through its entire historical development. If, then, any contention in this chapter seems to have been made too rashly, or any statement gives the impression of vagueness, the reader must refer to the comprehensive, historical scope of the entire series, of which this book forms a part.

1. The Dilemma: Problem or Mystery

It is impossible for any thinking person to be indifferent towards Israel. No matter what period or which aspect of Israel's constantly changing existence is considered, the same question recurs again and again—the question asked by the Assyrian general, Holofernes, when he addressed the leaders of Israel's neighbors, Moab and Ammon: "Tell me, what kind of people are they? Why are they, of all the people in the west, the only ones who have refused to come out to meet us and receive us in peace?" (see Judith 5:2f.). The answer which Achior, the chief of the Ammonites, gave amounts to this: the secret of the people of Israel was to be found in their God Yahweh; he then went on to demonstrate the validity of his answer by giving a summary of Israel's eventful history.

The aim of the author of the book of Judith in providing a graphic survey of Israel's history was to give life to the proud awareness which he and his racial and religious fellows had of their distinct and separate existence. This objective was especially neces- sary in the last centuries before Christ, when it was for the Jews a matter of vital importance to preserve their identity in a heathen environment. The vital law, the very principle of Israel's origin and continued existence, was to be different from the law of other people: "Behold, a people that shall dwell alone, and shall not be reckoned among the nations" (Num. 23:9). This ancient text, the oracle of the heathen soothsayer, Balaam, is a testimony to the im- pression which Israel, even at this period, made on her neighbors, and perhaps gives even clearer evidence of Israel's consciousness of her own status. For it is true to say that Israel was always con- scious that she was different. It is with reason that Israel was called the "chosen" people. Perhaps the term has become rather hackneyed, but it is still the only one which accurately summarizes Israel's enduring vision of her own essential role. This emerges clearly from the written legacy of Israel, the Old Testament, which is entirely based on the concept of divine election.

Thus Israel herself provides a radically superhuman interpretation of the strange phenomenon in which her origin and development were exempt from the normal laws of history, and, what is perhaps even more noteworthy, her religion did not fit into any of the normal patterns recognized by scholars of comparative religion. God took a hand in the growth and historical development of this nation. He shaped Israel in a way which far transcended the normal course of divine providence, and by so doing the Creator of heaven and earth decreed the fate of all nations and bore in his hand the hearts of kings and rulers. The main article of faith in Israel's creed stated that Yahweh, to whom the entire earth belonged, had chosen, from among all nations, the lowly people of Israel to be his people—a people consecrated to him as his special possession. The entire Old Testament is based on the paradox that the God of the world and of mankind, at a given moment and for a definite period of time, became the national God of one, single nation. That nation was pre-Christian Israel.

The Christian interpretation of the phenomenon of Israel is in complete accord with the Jewish interpretation, in acknowledging this divine factor. Israel is thus as much a mystery as the phenomenon of Christianity is a mystery, and Israel is furthermore directly implicated in this mystery. It is, however, a mystery which cannot be proved as such. It can only be substantiated when it is approached with faith, or better, when it is experienced as a living reality. It should, however, be noted at this point that it is not the author's intention to lose himself in endless argument with unshakeably convinced rationalists, in a book aimed first and foremost at believers. Having postulated, then, that this mystery is a fact of history, it is advisable to express the factuality of the mystery in all its aspects. This expression is not so much directed toward convincing those who already believe, as attempting to ascertain the exact place which the mystery of Israel occupies in Christian faith, and the precise extent to which this mystery is, both in the case of the individual and in its application to the Christian community, life of the Christian life.

Nineteenth-century rationalism broke with a long tradition, of which the Bible was the oldest and most emphatic witness. The mystery was neglected, but for a time it was not actively missed. The wealth of new data just beginning to appear resulted in the Bible becoming less interesting from the divine point of view and infinitely more fascinating as a human document. Looking back upon this period, it is now possible to say that the rationalist approach to the Bible, with its emphasis on the persons of the Bible rather than the systems, might well have been more reasonable if the "faithful" approach of that time had been more reasonable in its textual exegesis. But the reverse might equally well have applied: the acrimonious, polemical controversy between a priori conception of life led to extreme attitudes, to forced interpretations, and even to a falsification of a posteriori conclusions from the facts, the only sphere in which it might have been possible for the two sides to reach a mutual understanding. But this period is now past history. Even though an essential difference of opinion still persists at the deepest level in the ultimate interpretation of the data and in the ascertainment and reconstruction of the factual data, it is certainly true to say that a common ground does exist and that each side is willing to learn from the other.

Israel has been rediscovered as an ancient, oriental people and the Old Testament, as the national literature of that people, is a book of the ancient, oriental world. Much of what had been regarded as specifically biblical and attributable to revelation was later seen to have a more general, Semitic character. For the formulation and application of his belief in the Bible, it was necessary for man to bring out subtly variant shades of meaning, to acquire a new vision of the Bible, through thinking about it in a new way. Without doing violence in any way to the living core of its essential reality, it was necessary to free the Bible from those concepts which for centuries had grown up with it, and then to find a new mode of expression which was appropriate to the present age. This operation, of course, continues to present grave difficulties and it is one which can easily lead to critical situations. There is ample evidence today both of errors due to a rash approach and to the opposite attitude of regarding everything that is new with deep suspicion. As a result of a similar process of evolution, both the way of faith and the scientific approach have an important function to fulfill here, and it should consequently not cause any surprise, since this is undoubtedly a dramatic new turn of events, if the two are not yet fully coordinated. The Church certainly has a charisma of faith now, but, even though her knowledge can be of great service in this respect, there can be no implication here of a specifically scientific charisma. The Church has never ceased to encourage scholarly research in this direction, but she has always insisted upon extreme caution. If any of the Church's strictures at that time appear now to be excessive, they were generally not so then, although we must always be ready to scientifically and tolerantly accept the fact that the Church is inevitably a child of her time, and not necessarily the most gifted or at least the most zealous child. After some fifty years of fierce, biblical controversy, a certain degree of harmony was attained in the nineteen-thirties, by which time the new data had been sufficiently well assimilated and the new exegetical approach had reached a state of development where it could provide a coherent and comprehensive view of the whole field.

The modern approach to Israel not only preserves the supernatural element for the believer, but also enables him to see the exceptional position of Israel and her religion in more sharply defined terms. Now that we recognize more clearly the human and historical factors which were at work in Israel, it is possible for us to come much closer to an understanding of Israel's mentality. It is possible to have a firmer, imaginative grasp of Israel's outlook and to know on a deeper level the essential meaning of Israel. But again and again, both in the Bible as a whole and in individual parts of Scripture, we come up against an element of originality which either defies closer interpretation or else cannot be traced back to any evident source. All that can be said of this element is that it represents the authentic Israel. The many new perspectives of Israel, for which in particular we are indebted to the literary and archeological development of the ancient, oriental world, may have succeeded in clearing up a great deal of what was previously regarded as the wonder of Israel. But, at the same time, these recent discoveries have also restored the essential and enveloping wonder to its original position, with the result that it can once again be assessed at its true value. Now that we are no longer encumbered by meaningless little specimens of divine omnipotence, we are able to more clearly perceive the God who takes man seriously and enables him to discover that he is deeply engaged on his behalf. In addition to those whose point of view is informed by faith, and who recognize the finger of God where Israel is concerned, there are scholars whose liberal claim is that their view of the Old Testament and Israel is "different"—who stipulate a margin of intransparency, one unique occurrence, an element of a-rationality, the "religious genius" of Israel—and are certainly not apologetic about their attitude. The rationalists of the previous century, who confidently believed that they could find an explanation for everything, may have less distinguished successors in this century, but the great age of rationalism is, beyond all dispute, over. Now that we know that there is behind every individual, human existence a personal core of being which has its own secrets and cannot be traced back to general or universal, antecedent categories, it should not be too surprising that a national existence also can be rooted in one point— in a unique core of being which is postulated as datum and must be accepted as such.

2. The Mystery: Both Concealed and Revealed in the Course of Israel's History

The phenomenon of Israel appears in history as the constantly moving resultant of varying dynamic forces. Israel came into being and maintained her existence by polar tensions; characteristics of a general, oriental nature were at the same time strictly Israelitic. Elements in the normal line of historical development conflicted with elements which lay outside this line and purely human data pointed unmistakably to the superhuman factor. The God of revelation did not remain transcendent or hovering, as it were, above history. He entered human history and his presence there was not like the intrusion of a meteor from another planet. On the contrary, he penetrated into a given, factual situation and assumed a particular shape within this situation, making, in other words, a sign of it. A sign is not a mathematical formula. It does not possess any power of compulsion. It is always possible to stand still when confronted by any given, material datum and yet not "see" its significance, since the material datum must always coincide with a desire to see and personal consent on the part of the witness. All these various tensions can be traced to one single, all-embracing tension between the vertical and the horizontal, dynamic lines of history, and in the whole of the history of salvation, the result depends on which of the two lines is the more powerful. The eternal and divine element, represented by the vertical line, reveals itself in the historical and human element, represented by the horizontal line, but the eternal and divine at the same time is also concealed by the historical and human line of development.

The general course of Israel's continued existence is a striking example of this phenomenon. Israel appears to be only one of the many ancient peoples and states inhabiting the Near East, whose rise and ultimate disappearance has been historically recorded. Her history is similar to that of an entire set of racial groups in Syria and Palestine, whose way of life at first was nomadic, but eventually settled in one place, and finally at the end of either a shorter or longer period of settled existence, disappeared altogether. This historical phenomenon is due to a purely physical, geographical circumstance. The Levant was the disputed corridor which joined the powerful, ancient centers of civilization, namely Egypt, Mesopotamia, and Asia Minor. As long as one of the "great powers" prevailed in this corridor, it was not possible for any political unions of importance to be established. This happened only once, during the period between the thirteenth and the nineteenth century, when there was no real world power in existence. The sixteenth century saw the collapse of the ancient Babylonian kingdom under Hammurabi. The rise of the "maritime nations" finally put an end to the international function which Egypt had begun to fulfill, and for the time being no nation came forward to replace and carry on Egypt's international function. Various dynamic, ethnic groups, which had been struggling for an existence in the territory bordering on the corridor, now found the chance of a lifetime within their grasp. They established themselves in the fertile area which they had desired for so long—in their eyes a land of milk and honey—and formed a more organized, territorial union which, in the natural course of events, developed into the state community of a kingdom. Thus, with the rise of a new world power after the beginning of the first millennium before Christ, the Levant appeared as a dissected map of autonomous political unions, each firmly rooted in its own traditions and covering an area of unknown dimensions. Along the Mediterranean coast, the Philistines, one of the "maritime nations," had established a strong league of cities. The Phoenician city-states were also flourishing at about this time along the Syrian and Palestinian coastline. To the north, extending beyond the Upper Euphrates, were the Aramaean states, of which the most important was "Aram of Damascus." The whole of the hinterland, stretching as far as the River Jordan, formed the heart of the kingdom of David and Solomon. After the disruption of this kingdom, the larger, northern half of this territory, together with a stretch of land in the Transjordan extending farther to the south, formed the Northern Kingdom of Israel. The Southern Kingdom of Judah consisted of the smaller, southern half of the Cisjordan and the Negeb. The kingdoms of Edom, Moab, and Ammon, established shortly before Israel, were spread over this traditional territory of the twelve tribes from the southeast to as far north as the land occupied by the Aramaeans.

Even though the seventh century had marked the end of Assyrian mastery in the whole area, the world power which they had built up still persisted. In fact their power had simply passed into the hands of others. The Assyrians first gave way to the Neobabylonians (the Chaldaeans and Nebuchadnezzar). Power next fell into the hands of the Persians, from whom it was eventually wrested by the "Greeks." This Greek empire was divided on Alexander's death among the Diadochi. The territory finally came under the sway of the Romans. What happened then was that the various united states were permanently deprived of their autonomy in this part of the ancient world, at the ascension of the Assyrians to power. These earlier, political unions simply had to passively undergo all the international, political complications of this long period of history. Each state declined from its position of independence and first became a tributary nation and then a mere province within a world empire. Furthermore, the links which bound each of these peoples to their own national past were gradually loosened by a continued deportation or "exile" of the best elements of the population, and by the introduction of foreign elements into the population. Consequently, as time went by all that was left to remind these peoples of their past glory were the names and the frontiers of the various imperial provinces.

At one time, of course, the Bible was, for all intents and purposes, our only source of information and knowledge of the history of the ancient, oriental world. While this still prevailed, the overriding impression of Israel's national history must have been that it was guided by God himself along exceptional paths and that its structure was unique. Now, however, it is evident that the course of history followed a classic and inevitable plan, and we can see with far greater clarity wherein the essential core of Israel's originality really lies. For, while Israel was actually involved in these historical events in common with her neighbors, an inheritance was coming into being which survived all the vicissitudes of her history. It was this inheritance which enabled her to remain intact and indeed more truly Israel than she had ever been even *after* her eclipse as a nation, at the same time that her neighbors and companions in adversity were absorbed into the imperial union. Therefore, although at first sight the history of ancient Israel gives the impression of following a perfectly normal course, it is obvious that there was definitely something afoot, something which, equally obviously, was of a religious nature. This religious element within Israel's history enabled facts and data of the oriental world at the time to gain a totally new dimension and to have a different and larger implication than similar facts and data elsewhere. In consequence, Holy Scripture, which has a religious purport and expresses this within the material data itself, is still right when it suggests that, in the case of Israel, we are concerned with unique events. As always, all that is really required is to understand Scripture at the level at which it is speaking.

Israel did not reveal herself as a creative genius, but as a nation working her slow and laborious way up to the general level of civilization in the oriental world of her time. As a latecomer in a cultural environment which had already been established for a long time, Israel did not make an original contribution of her own and was for some time obliged to rely upon the expert knowledge and capabilities of her neighbors. Thus, it is all the more surprising that Israel should have been so much ahead of her time and environment, in her religious and national literature. Not only did Israel easily master the existing literary forms of expression (as in the case of the proverbs, the psalms, and the laws), and use these forms in a completely independent way, but she also created other forms which, if we compare them with the weak parallels to be found elsewhere, must be regarded as quite new. Among these new forms are the historiography of Israel and almost all the prophetic books. The reason is quite clear. Israel had something to say which no other people had to say. Israel spoke from an entirely new experience of God.

All the various enigmatic symptoms refer to the basic enigma. In every respect except one, Israel was at the same level as the other ancient, oriental, racial groups or even below this average level. In her religion, however, she rose to a position of solitary eminence. She succeeded in reaching this height only in spite of herself and in spite of her environment. Mysterious, dynamic forces were at work in Israel and all the persistent efforts which have been made to explain these forces have so far resulted in failure. They cannot be explained by approaching the enigma of Israel from the inside as it were, and attributing them, for example, to a natural predisposition on the part of the people, nor can they be elucidated by an approach from outside, and claiming, for example, that they were derived from other peoples. Israel was fully conscious of her exceptional position, and every page of her literature bears witness to this awareness. What made Israel were forces from above. This is, of course, the most important, single fact which the Old Testament seeks to convey and its testimony makes an immediate appeal to our faith. The frequently circumstantial account of all kinds of fascinating details merely serves to convince us of this central fact and throughout the whole of the Old Testament the inspired and unfailingly affirmative judgment of the various authors is constantly directed towards this one single fact: Yahweh is the divine reality and he has personally concerned himself with Israel.

We have been digressive for the following reason. There must still be many good people to whom it may come as a complete surprise that not everything in the Old Testament is true history, and that a great deal of the Old Testament account, which is told with such masterly attention to detail, often has a subordinate function, that of serving to communicate information which is directly related to faith. All their lives, such people may have sincerely believed many strange and improbable things, simply because they were in the Bible and therefore safeguarded by divine truth. Then, quite suddenly, they are confronted with the disturbing news that they are no longer required to believe these things. They may even feel that everything that they have believed concerning the Bible has been in vain. The question as to what we are bound to believe in the Old Testament is frequently raised, and it is usually accompanied by the subtle insinuation that if we do not assent to everything, then everything in the Old Testament rests on unstable foundations. This problem is discussed more fully in the eighth section of this chapter, and it is also hoped that this book will provide a satisfactory answer. In the meantime, it should be possible to formulate the principle, at least for the time being, in this way. The various historical details of the Old Testament do not constitute the essential object of the biblical communication of faith. Although they are extremely valuable in themselves, they are principally a means of expressing a testimony running through the Old Testament, which is directly related to the divine fact. This fact is God's entry into the world of man, his activity within history, with the patriarchs and their descendants. Our belief in the Bible is sound only so long as we ultimately surrender, through the medium of this account of God's actions in the past, to the holy conviction that God actually addresses us through the situation in which we see ourselves to be placed. For that is precisely the appeal which, coming from the various biblical accounts, was made to Israel.

3. The Application of the Dilemma to Israel's Monotheism, Messianism, and Historiography

If the evidence of the Bible is accepted, many of the problems with which ancient Israel confronts the modern exegete can be freely explained. In this connection, the three examples which follow are worthy of our attention, since they are intimately concerned with matters which demand more than a cursory examination. So many attempts have been made in recent years to provide on purely natural grounds a satisfactory explanation for the origin and development of the religion of Israel—her monotheism—and her expectation of salvation, or messianism. Various hypotheses have been hotly defended. The most ingenious evolutionary theories have been put forward. Facts and data of all kinds have been collected in great numbers by scholars of comparative religion. The purpose of all of this was to establish a natural basis for these phenomena. If these efforts were crowned by success, then nothing more would remain to be said about the specifically revelational character of Israel's religion, since both monotheism and messianism are essential features which have a most important bearing upon all the other, apparently inexplicable, elements of the religion of Israel, and above all play a decisive part in our interpretation of the mystery of Israel's historiography.

(a) Monotheism

The first point of departure in all Christian preaching to the pagan, polytheistic world has always been a strict monotheism, expressed in the first article of the Christian creed. The Christian message first implies a recognition of a God who is both one and universal, and a disavowal of all other gods in the world. Christianity did no more than simply take over this article of faith from Israel, and, in so doing, put what had previously been the most highly characteristic, national possession of Israel within the reach of all men. The immediate question which arises in connection with Israel's monotheism is how this nation ever succeeded in making such an enormous, spiritual advance. A monotheistic desert was invented, and this assumption was combined with the further assumption that the Semitic world generally had a special disposition for concentration on the one hand, but an inability for personification on the other. What is probably meant by "personification" in this instance is a tendency to personify all kinds of phenomena, especially natural phenomena. This form of personification was undoubtedly one of the factors responsible for the rise of polytheism. The personification of a given phenomenon which is too powerful for man can very easily result in the deification of that phenomenon. Unfortunately, the rest of the Semites and desert tribes were all, without exception, polytheistic, and general factors of a similar nature can scarcely be applied to provide an explanation of something which pertains in the strictest sense to Israel alone. By the same token, the approach of common factors cannot be used in an effort to trace Israel's religion back to a universal, human tendency towards monotheism. Though this tendency undoubtedly existed, it cannot be used here to explain why, only in the case of Israel, strict monotheism was the result. In striking contrast, in all other cases of the period this monotheistic tendency went no further than a kind of henotheism, in which one god was chosen for particular worship, usually by that group of the people with whom he was believed to have a special relationship (monolatry), or some form of monarchism, in which a monarchical structure was built up within the pantheon, at the head of which one of the many gods was appointed as supreme God.

Too much attention, almost exclusive attention, has been given, in nearly every consideration of the problem of monotheism and monotheistic tendencies, to the numerical factor. Far too little account, on the other hand, has been taken of the character of the one god whose existence has supposedly been discovered in various cases. A good example of this is the monotheism of Akhnaten, the remarkable pharaoh living during the fourteenth century B.C., who attempted to secure a monopoly of public worship for his god Aten. Generally speaking, a great deal of what has been said concerning Akhnaten's monotheism has been misleading. Apart from the fact that this monotheism was purely theoretical and far from being completely consistent, the god in question was also lacking in any ethical or transcendent character. All the evidence points to the fact that, although he enjoyed a uniquely privileged position, Aten was no more than a typically pagan deity. He was simply and solely a sun-god, a personification of the sun's disc, with which Akhnaten was mystically associated in a manner close to self-identification. Akhnaten's personal life and public administration demonstrate in the clearest possible way the superficial and mathematical type of reasoning whereupon comparison between this unreal monotheism and that of Israel is based, without any consideration of the effects at the moral or social level.

Israel's confession of the one God, Yahweh, was quite unambiguous, and this confession was framed in such a way that the incomparable character which Israel ascribed to Yahweh made it impossible for any other gods to hold their own beside or under him. In Israel's concept of God, then, the starting point was the character of Yahweh. The second idea, that no other gods could possibly exist beside Yahweh, simply emerged as a consequence of the first, and time was needed for this idea to wholly crystallize. If this fact is overlooked, it is easy to attribute a strictly monotheistic principle to Israel's religion either at too early or too late a stage in her history. Her monotheism, in this sense, dated essentially from the prophetic age, and was a fruit which was fully harvested for the first time during the period of Deutero-Isaiah and the exile. However, Yahweh was from the beginning always Yahweh, a God beside whom there was no room for any other god. Not only were the Israelites never permitted to worship "strange" gods (the gods of other peoples), but what is even more remarkable is that there was never at any time any trace of other Israelitic gods, either equal or subordinate to Yahweh. Nothing which even remotely resembled a pantheon ever existed in the case of Israel. In all other religions of the time, the national god was unfailingly accompanied by a female partner or *paredros*. There was no place even for a *paredros* beside Yahweh. Now that we know a little more about the Canaanite pantheon surrounding Baal and Ashtoreth, the fact that Yahweh had no partner of any kind indeed calls for an explanation. On no account is it possible, for example, to regard Yahweh as a "baptized" Baal. The archeological disclosure of the ancient, oriental world in recent years has made it abundantly clear to us exactly how solitary a God Yahweh was. His solitude was that of transcendent holiness, and this is what Israel intimately came to know. The emergence of this authentically divine element caused the supposedly divine, unauthentic element to diminish in importance in the mind of the believer. Monotheism is already established in principle whenever a real human decision is made in the matter of faith and a complete surrender to God takes place, despite the fact—or perhaps even because of the fact—that the person making this decision and this submission experiences God as his personal protector. It is possible to speak here of a monotheistic insight or understanding which had still not reached the point where it needed to be clearly and explicitly put into conceptual terms, and had certainly not reached the stage at which a hard and fast formulation or definition was necessary. By making this distinction, it is possible to avoid the risk of equating Israel's omissions in this connection with those of the other peoples of the period, since the development of her concept of God, taking place at this time, was firmly based on a fully consistent understanding of God.

(b) Messianism

Israel's hope of salvation, or messianism, is as striking a phenomenon as her monotheism. Not only did nothing elsewhere compare to the biblical figure of the Messiah, but it is impossible to find, outside Israel, any trace of a similar, eschatological perspective towards the future, a constant orientation, preserved with such clarity and in such a homogeneously developing form, throughout the whole of the people's existence. This hope of future salvation was concretized in many different ideas and certain favorite themes, each following its own particular line of development. However, in each idea and theme the mysterious driving power which seems to have been inherent in Israel is recognized. Despite this diversity of expression, Israel is recognized. Despite this diversity of expression, Israel remained a single, living, coherent whole. At best, one may say that certain vital elements peculiar to the ancient, oriental world were assimilated by Israel and played some part in filling out the picture of the future and in helping to define it more precisely. A particular case here is that of the ancient, oriental ideology concerning kings and the royal court. This does not, however, get to the heart of the matter. It is true, of course, that a certain desire for salvation is a universal experience of all men. The setbacks and disappointments of life give rise to a nostalgic longing for a golden age. Most men like to believe that such an age did exist at some time in the past, and, especially at critical moments in history, with a sometimes vague and sometimes more clearly defined hope; they look forward to the time when this golden age may return as a lasting reality. A universal factor of this kind, however, is really inadequate in the case of Israel and it would be altogether too facile to resort to a psychological interpretation of the peculiar character of her hope of salvation. From the purely psychological point of view, it might be possible to claim that Israel's special, political disappointment was transmuted into a special kind of hope for the future—but we have already noted that the tragic, national history of Israel was shared by all the peoples of Syria and Palestine. The glory of a nation's past certainly does help to shape her vision of the future, insofar as sorrow for what has been lost is transmuted into an expectation of the return of the old order in one form or another. But this provides, at the very most, a mere explanation of the concrete ideas resulting from the attempts of the disappointed people to find an outlet for their hopes for the future. The original cause of the expectation itself remains as puzzling as ever.

The Bible, however, provides us with an answer to this problem, which fits in perfectly with all the facts. The first and all-inclusive object of Israel's hope of salvation was Yahweh. From the very beginning he revealed himself as the saving God, a God promising total salvation and vouching fully for the validity of his promise. Permitting no other god beside him, he insisted absolutely upon his people's complete reliance on him. They were to expect salvation from him alone and from no other. The one, true God was to bring true salvation, and that was that. The key to the problem of Israel's messianism is, then, that here was a new experience of faith. Yahweh entered human history, took it in hand, and guided it towards a specific goal, always working according to a definite plan of salvation. His saving acts of the past guaranteed the future. Yahweh was the First and the Last. His seal marked the beginning— the historical past. In the same way, the end of history also belonged to him. The future belonged to Israel's confession of faith as much as the past. Faith in Yahweh and hope of salvation were dependent upon each other. Monotheism and messianism were not two separate doctrines in the case of Israel, but two aspects of the same basic experience of God. In revealing himself to man, Yahweh offered himself as the God of his people, since, by its very nature, divine revelation implies a concern for man's salvation. Apart from demanding the exclusion of all other gods, to be someone's god also incorporates the promise that the worshiper's salvation is assured. This, then, was how the true God became the God of Israel and how Israel, through her experience of the inconceivable greatness of her God, became aware of the unlimited possibilities of salvation.

(c) Historiography

It is a remarkable fact that, of all the various nations of the ancient, civilized world as we know it, it was only the Greeks and Israelites who produced, independently, an authentic body of historical literature. What is more, since her written history preceded that of the Greeks by several centuries, the place which Israel occupied within her own world was quite unique. The connection which has been made between the early appearance of Israel's independent, historical consciousness and her separate, religious existence is fully justified, and it is perfectly reasonable to claim that the mystery of Israel's religion is at the same time the mystery of her "historical genius." If divine intervention did indeed play a decisive part in the history of Israel—and if the evidence of the Bible is accepted, then this was certainly the case—Israel's religion must stand or fall with her history. Furthermore, if Israel's religion was also a revealed religion, then the preaching of religion in Israel must have been a preaching of facts derived from the past, and thus a preaching of past history, in the same way that the Christian message consists fundamentally, in one sense, of an enumeration of historical facts. This is not to say that other racial groups in the ancient world did not keep the memory of their past alive, either by compiling a documentary record of certain facts, in chronicles or annals, or by incorporating some elements of their historical past into their public worship. Frequently too, this history was preserved in the loose form of popular sagas and legends. It was, however, only in the case of Israel that we find a real concern for the underlying implications of the historical facts and their interrelationship. Israel's faith enabled her to see Yahweh as her redeemer, to whom she was indebted for her existence as a nation, and who not only gave meaning to her continued existence as such, but was also leading her, as a nation, towards a definite goal. It was in this way that Israel was able to preserve a unified vision despite all the different events which befell the nation, and this single vision formed, in principle, the potential basis for an authentic historiography.

It was by means of her faith too, that Israel came to see her national God as the creator of heaven and earth, the God of the world and of human kind. In this total vision, nature and history were both ruled by one and the same God. The account of the origin of the world and the human race at the same time formed the point of departure for the history of the world, since the creator of the world and of man did not abandon the work of his own hands, but rather gave to each creature its place and governed its destiny. Israel saw that Yahweh's blessing and curse, his judgment and mercy, were what determined the course of events in the world. This faith enabled Israel to situate her own "natural" history within the wider framework of "universal" history. The most that happened in the case of other nations was that there was "one God and one people," and even so it was more usual for this formula to be expressed the other way round, that is, as "one people, one God." The concept of one God, one people, was, however, not only fully applicable in the case of Israel it also gained a totally new significance and thereby enabled Israel to compile an authentic, national history. "One God, one people" also became, in this new perspective, "one God, one human race," so that Israel was able to move from a limited vision of purely national history to an insight into a worldwide historical perspective and to trace in bold lines the major developments in the progress of mankind from the creation of the

refers to this in his sermon to the gentiles: "We are . . . preaching to you to be converted from these vain things to the living God, who made heaven and earth and the sea and all things that are in them; who in times past suffered all nations to walk in their own ways. Nevertheless he left not himself without testimony, doing good from heaven, giving rains and fruitful seasons, filling our hearts with food and gladness" (Acts 14:14-16). This outward witness finds a natural sounding board in man's inner being, since this cosmic revelation was in no way Israel's monopoly, but was and still is offered to all nations and peoples, "that they should seek God, if haply they may feel after him or find him, although he be not far from every one of us. For in him we live and move and are" (Acts 17:27-28).

This universal, human religiosity, as briefly outlined in the foregoing paragraphs, was the foundation upon which religion was built. Certain, more precise ideas and conceptions developed in man, and especially within individual, human communities, from undefined, natural, religious instincts. In the same way, definite practices and conventions also gradually emerged within each community. These gave outward expression and social form to man's basic religious needs, and constituted an attempt to satisfy the religious feeling of the group by giving it concrete form and an intimate object. It is, then, possible to say that a human community or group had a definite religion whenever its theoretical ideas and living, practical forms had developed to the point where they had been systematized into an organic whole. Because there were many different social groupings in the ancient world, there were also many religions. Even though they all had their roots in the same soil— the universal need of man for religion and religious expression— these religions were, of course, by no means all of equal merit. Their relative status depended upon whether they did in fact express the objective religious truth and man's attitude towards it, or whether they impeded this truth and prevented man from reaching it. But a religion providing the complete, perfect answer to man's natural, religious disposition—in other words, a pure "natural religion"—is something which *de facto* can never be fully achieved.

The revealed religion of Israel had to make a place for itself in a world full of religions, which had grown out of man's natural instinct for religion, in answer to the universal, cosmic revelation. As nature was there for the sake of the grace which perfected it (according to Scripture, the God of salvation is the creator of heaven and earth), the "particular" revelation of Israel was, as it were, an extension of cosmic revelation. It was a new and more direct revelation, the personal, divine answer to man's religious question. It did more than simply provide the pure answer to this question. Although it was in complete accord with man's basic religious need, it also far transcended this, extending his religious aspirations infinitely beyond his humanly limited horizon. God's inward and outward approach to man by means of nature had been no more than an intimation, a gradual introduction to what was to come. Through Israel he spoke to man in an entirely new way. This demanded an entirely new response on the part of man. But God himself, speaking to man in this new way, put him in a position to make this answer, which was at the same time the answer required by pure, natural religion. The perfect answer which could not be made by pure, natural religion, the ultimate reality which no such religion could reach or become was in fact achieved by being transcended. The pure natural religion, then, no longer acted as an independent organ, but came into its own as a functional part of the total, living organism. The religious nature of man was able to attain full and harmonious development within revealed religion, because man was able to find his God in this way, even though it implied a transcendence of, but in complete accordance with, human nature.

5. The Capacity for an Assimilation of the Mystery by Means of Transformation and Purification

God's particular revelation entered human history at a definite period in time and at a definite point of contact. (The words "period" and "point of contact" are used here with special reference to biblical history for the sake of convenience. But it is equally possible to think of this as a gradual process of historical growth, rather than as a concentrated, historical phenomenon.) The social group which experienced this divine fact, in the religious sense, was in no way a completely unknown quantity. Its members followed the ideas and practices of their time and environment, and they had to give expression to their new experience as best they could within the limitations of time and place. It was perfectly possible for them to do this, in principle, though not until they had undergone a process of purification and transformation. This purification and transformation is a most important precondition if healthy, natural religiosity—fundamentally inspired by grace—is to make itself heard within the prevailing religious experience. Some form of purification is necessary if degeneration and deformation are to be avoided, and any qualitatively new, religious experience which seeks to express itself is bound to require some kind of transformation. The constant law to which divine revelation is subject is that this revelation will be translated into human terms, assimilated by its human recipients, and will assume a human form. Divine revelation is thus also exposed to a constant risk, especially as the human form, which it is bound to assume, will also inevitably be an historical form, with all the limitations of time and place implied.

In Israel, then, revealed religion assumed an ancient, oriental, general, semitic form. At first sight, and especially in its early stages, the impression made by Israel's religion is very little different from that which was made by the other religions of the period. The religion of Israel was, of course, entirely original, and essentially new in content, but the danger of its losing its own, peculiar character was ever present. It was always possible for pagan interpretation and practice to creep into the inner content of Israel's religion by way of its ancient, oriental form, which, in the case of the other religions of the environment, was always accompanied by a pagan content. But again and again the God of revelation put those who genuinely believed in him individually and collectively in a position to see his own incomparable originality. In this way, the Israelites reacted continuously against all the pagan influences inherent in their environment and thus, more and more, were able to stand aloof from those dangerous, pagan forms. They strove incessantly to achieve a more suitable form, and frequently the result of this long struggle was a new creation, though it was rare for a new form to emerge out of nothing. Israel's religion, then, was notable both because of its entirely new content and also because of its characteristically individual, outward appearance, which reflected this completely individual, inner content, a form which ultimately betrayed an affinity, merely in its most general family features, with those of the other religions of the ancient, oriental world.

Perhaps the most striking example of this "incarnation" of divine revelation is provided by Israel's conception of God himself. It would, at first sight, seem that Israel thought of God in a completely oriental way. This was, however, no more than a point of departure, from which Israel moved to that idea of God which is now so familiar to us—that of *one* God of the world and mankind. This idea had been almost completely lost until God himself began to speak. There were many gods, each of whom had a local and national character. The diversity of the sublunar world has led to an equally great diversity in the divine sphere. The phenomena of the natural world, the division of the known world into geographical and political regions, the different groupings of humanity according to race, language, areas of habitation, tribes, and families, were all faithfully reproduced in the pantheon. Gods were related by blood to particular tribes and individual gods were associated with particular, natural zones. There were private, tutelary gods and hereditary gods of family, town, or state. It is easy to see how a universal, religious instinct and a generally experienced, religious need gave rise to the development of a more explicit and concrete idea, which in turn was bound to act as a serious impediment to man's authentic religiosity. The divine element was humanized, at times even reduced to the animal level. It was almost continuously subjected to a process of particularization, nationalization, or naturalization, and suffered considerably as the result. The divine element did not succeed in drawing man up to a higher level of existence. What in fact happened was that man cut the divine down to his own measure and used it to serve his own ends.

One of the most important advances made in the field of biblical scholarship during this century has been to throw a clearer light on the subtle nuances contained in many passages in the Bible which had previously received very scant attention and had indeed been treated as if they were catechism statements made all too familiar by frequent usage. Even though biblical passages of this type do in one way or another convey the same basic religious truths as formulae in the catechism, they are at least essentially different in one important aspect. In the Old Testament, faith was still groping for a means of expression, and the words and ideas used in the Old Testament were of necessity those which the available, linguistic sources had to offer. One of the less favorable results of our greatly improved historical knowledge is that many biblical texts have become more indistinct than we should like. This frequent loss of precision, however, is more than amply compensated for by the immense gain in breadth and depth and even more in vitality and freshness which this modern approach has afforded us, by providing us, as it were, with a more sensitive nose for the unique scent of texts themselves. This scent, if we follow it faithfully, will not as a rule lead us to the minds of scholars who seek to express the faith of the Old Testament in carefully worded formulae, but will lead us to a direct experience of the faith of men who used their own language to say what was on their minds, because they had surrendered to the God whom they knew to be speaking directly to them.

6. An Example: The New Consciousness of God in Search of a Concept of God

The fact that the basic article of Israel's confession of faith—Yahweh is Israel's God and Israel is Yahweh's people—was expressed in a strictly oriental form has been repeatedly, and justifiably, stressed. Everything that the people of the ancient, oriental world expected from their gods was, for Israel, embodied in Yahweh. "For all people will walk every one in the name of his god; but we will walk in the name of Yahweh our God for ever and ever" (Mic. 4:5). Whoever pronounced the name of Israel was at the same time pronouncing the name of Yahweh. Yahweh was the national God of Israel, to whom the land and its people belonged as a possession. He was Israel's true king and lawgiver, the Israelites' commander in the holy war which never ceased, the source of their life and salvation, and the permanent guarantee of their national well-being. The popular, ancient, oriental idea of God emerges very clearly in Jephthah's statement, in which Yahweh, as the God of Israel, is apparently equated with Kemosh, the god of Moab:

So Yahweh, the God of Israel, destroyed the Amorites, his people of Israel fighting against him. And wilt thou now possess this land? Are not those things which thy god Kemosh possesseth due to thee by right? But what Yahweh, our God, hath obtained by conquest shall be our possession (Judges 11:23–24).

It is not necessary to regard this as an adaptation on Jephthah's part to the mentality of the pagans whom he was addressing, since the same idea is expressed in David's lament, that those compatriots who were hostile to him were, by preventing him from remaining in the land of Israel, virtually forcing him to seek salvation from the local gods. Not only was David unable to reach Yahweh, but also Yahweh could not come to him, with the result that were David, whose life was constantly threatened, to die, Yahweh would not even be aware of his death, let alone be able to avenge it:

If Yahweh stir thee (Saul) up against me, let him accept of sacrifice (so that his anger against me may be placated). But if the sons of men, they are cursed in the sight of Yahweh, who have cast me out this day, that I should not dwell in the inheritance of Yahweh (the land of Canaan), saying: Go, serve strange gods. And now let not my blood be shed upon the earth while I am far from the face of Yahweh (1 Sam. 26:19-20).

Uncovered ground, soaked in blood, cried to heaven for vengeance, but Yahweh did not live in the country where David was forced to stay! This close association between deity and land is powerfully expressed in Naaman's request to be allowed to take a load of Canaan's soil with him to Damascus, so that he might still be able to keep in touch with Yahweh, while he was no longer in the land of Yahweh, and set up an altar to him there:

I beseech thee, grant to me thy servant, to take from hence two mules' burden of earth. For thy servant will not henceforth offer holocaust, or victim, to other gods, but to Yahweh (2 Kings 5:17).

Israel's language, then, was the language of her time. But formulae which sounded the same did not necessarily mean the same thing in Israel as they did in her environment. It is, of course, true that the similarity which is apparent in the foregoing examples was, initially at least, evidence to the contrary, but Israel was certainly always aware, even in the earliest stages of her history, of the essential difference which existed between herself and her neighbors. Her later, explicit formulation of this distinction should, however, not be interpreted as a heterogeneous supplement or appendage, but rather as the outcome of an inward development of her original consciousness of this difference from her neighbors. Both aspects—Israel's similarity to, and her difference from her environment—can be seen to their full advantage in the passage in which Jeremiah reproaches Jerusalem for having forsaken the love of her youth when Yahweh led Israel out of the land of Egypt. No one, he laments, has looked for Yahweh. No pagan would ever treat his god in this way:

Pass over to the isles of Hittim and see, and send into Kedar and consider diligently: and see if there hath been done any thing like this. If a nation hath changed their gods, and indeed they are not gods: but my people have changed their glory into an idol (Jer. 2:10–11).

It was not part of the nature of revelation to pronounce immediate judgment upon whether the gods of other nations really existed or not. For the time being at least, the question did not arise. Yahweh did, however, reveal himself immediately as an incomparable God, beside whom all others at first sank into insignificance and finally disappeared altogether in importance. This process can be observed in the canticle of the Red Sea:

> Who is like to thee among the gods, O Yahweh,
> Who is like to thee, glorious in holiness,
> terrible and praiseworthy, doing wonders? (Exod. 15:11).

Even when the Israelites came to realize with clarity, especially as a result of the preaching of the prophets, that Yahweh was the one God of the world, they still preferred to make use of expressions which were reminiscent of the popular, oriental idea of divinity at the time, to proclaim the greatness of their God Yahweh. The following passages from Deuteronomy illustrate this tendency particularly well:

There is no other god either in heaven or earth, that is able to do thy works . . . Neither is there any other nation so great, that hath gods so nigh them as our God is present to all our petitions. Ask of the days of old, that have been before thy time from the day that God created man upon the earth, from one end of heaven to the other and thereof, if ever there was done the like thing, or it hath been known at any time, that a people should hear the voice of God speaking out of the midst of fire, as thou hast heard, and lived; if God ever did so as to go, and take to himself a nation out of the midst of nations by temptations, signs, and wonders, by fight, and a strong hand, and a stretched-out arm, and horrible visions, according to all the things that the Lord your God did for you in Egypt, before thy eyes (Deut. 3:24; 4:7, 32–34).

The writer of the Chronicles, too, draws a striking contrast between the old faith and his own, more advanced attitude in two statements which he puts into the mouth of Solomon:

The house which I desire to build is great: for our God is great above all gods. Who then can be able to build him a worthy house, if heaven, and the heaven of heavens cannot contain him? (2 Chron. 2:5, 6; *see also* 6:14, 18ff.).

Jethro's statement: "Now I know that Yahweh is great above all gods" (Exod. 18:11), is also entirely in accord with the old conception of God. Israel's deliverance from bondage in Egypt, however, implies a victory on Yahweh's part over the gods of Egypt (Exod. 12:12). The formulation has a markedly henotheistic flavor, but is used in the later psalms as a proud confession of monotheistic faith (Ps. 85:8, 88:7, 94:3, 95:4, 96:9 134:5). The phrase "the most high God," which occurs frequently in the Bible, originated in the Semitic world and was used to refer to one god in the monarchically modified, polytheistic structure. In Scripture, however, it became a literary means of expression used exclusively in a monotheistic sense. The same applies to the formula "Yahweh, the God of gods" (Deut. 10:17; Joshua 22:22; Ps. 135:2f.; Dan. 2:47, 3:90, 11:36; Apoc. 17:14, 19:16).

The Old Testament is full of purely monotheistic expressions. We have only to think of the account of the creation and of whole sections of the prophetic books. What emerges with particular clarity from the above examples is that even formulae whose outward form presupposes a henotheistic or polytheistic origin or point of departure are permeated with monotheism when used in the Bible. This is particularly so in the case of the one formula which seems to express the monotheistic attitude of the Old Testament in the most striking way: "Yahweh, the God of Israel." In Israel, a new dialogue between God and man came into being. The text which provides the classic example of this new and special relationship is: "You shall be my peculiar possession above all people, *for all the earth is mine*" (Exod. 19:5). This text at the same time reveals Israel's acute awareness of her special relationship, and her national limitations with regard to other nations. God demanded the whole of man, and was in turn experienced by him as the existential answer to the deepest human questions concerning life. In this way, all limitations were, in principle, overcome, even though the first contact with this God was still limited to a particular situation. It was possible too for this living experience to be accompanied by a defective terminology—an understanding which was still theoretically defective, and a means of expression which was similarly not complete. For Israel had still to rely on the ancient, oriental terms and conceptual language in order to express her consciousness of God and put it into words, and these terms and concepts referred to a totally different idea of what constituted divinity. The texts and examples which have been quoted in this section illustrate both sides of the question. On the one hand, Israel was still tied to her period and environment. On the other hand, the new content, meaning, and potential which she gave to these ancient, oriental forms of expression were such that the older terminology was able to overstep its limitations and emerge as a fully explicit medium for the expression of Israel's thought.

7. The Mystery as the Creative Factor in Religion and in God's People

In this section, the reality of the mystery of Israel will be approached from two sides. In the first place, contact with the God of revelation leads not only to truth in religious thought, but also to truth (in the real rather than formal sense) in religious action. Both of these aspects are of importance in the religion of Israel. The newness of this experience of God became apparent as the result of this experience. A new people came into being.

It has already been pointed out that an exclusive concern with the purely numerical factor in any consideration of monotheism is bound to lead to a one-sided view of the religion in question. Monotheism and polytheism cannot be satisfactorily differentiated simply on a basis of numbers alone. If a true assessment is to be made of the real worth of Israel's monotheism, it is of the utmost importance to consider both the character of this one God of Israel, and his relationship with the world and with man. It is probably more accurate to refer to a religion which has rejected a multiplicity of gods and in which the creature is too closely identified with the divine element, as a monistic system. Similarly, a system in which the creature and the divine element are too freely dissociated is perhaps better regarded as deistic. The decisive factor which ultimately tips the balance one way or another is whether the relationship between the one God and the created world and creature is both pure and clearly defined. If any error is made in this vital consideration, then errors will be made in any attempt to approach the question of the number of gods. The reverse is also true.

The divine element is what is holy, totally different, and infinitely elevated above the created world. Pure faith in God cannot exist without this sense of distance. But, despite this distance between them, the divine at the same time embraces and fills everything which exists, bearing it up and activating it. It is the element which is closest and most intimate to the created world, permeating everything without losing its identity in it. There can also be no pure faith in God without this sense of closeness and intimacy. The terms normally used to designate these two aspects of the divine are, of course, transcendence and immanence. They appear to be mutually exclusive and are consequently difficult to think of in the same context. It is, however, precisely this relationship—the harmony and the tension—between the transcendence and the immanence of God and the world which has provided the criterion for all the ideas concerning the divine which men have formed in the course of history. The real miracle of Israel's religion is that the hitherto vague feeling experienced by all men for this divine element was crystallized in Israel into a clear, conscious truth and a certain knowledge. This awareness and knowledge of God which Israel achieved were, however, at the same time accompanied by an abundance of subtle gradations and a wealth of illustrative forms and manifestations which would seem to have retained in full many divine attributes, which to all appearances were in conflict with each other. The total image of the divine provided by Israel is, however, a balanced and consistent one. It is an image which is hard to explain, unless we ascribe it to a special experience, of the divine reality itself, over a long period of time.

The concept which men form of the relationship between a deity and those who worship this deity is of the utmost importance, not only for their idea of God but also for their religious experience. In the pagan religions of the ancient, oriental world, the divine element was often so completely absorbed into the national interest that each nation or people was inclined to treat it as if it were private property and to play it forth at every possible opportunity like a winning card. Though the people belonged, in name at least, to their deity, the relationship was, in fact, often the very reverse—the deity belonged to the people. Not only did this have the result of reducing the divine to the level of an ineffectual agent in individual or community action, but it also frequently resulted in men using the divine for their own purposes, as if it were no more than a religious label. Thus true religiosity and moral conduct ceased to play the leading part in religion, and their functions were taken over by a closely regulated system of magic and ritualism. Those who were expert in these magic and ritual arts assumed the functions of the gods and, by using the right formula or the appropriate rite and the opportune moment, bestowed supposedly divine favors upon, or exercized judgment over their fellow believers. It was an almost automatic process—the human switchboard operator switched on either favor or judgment. One of the main tasks of this type of religious system was the training of specially chosen men in such "divine" arts and skills. To a very great extent, these skills were prescribed in ritual instructions which normally regulated the outward behavior of those who minutely practiced the religion in question. This ritualism did not, however, generally attempt to influence the personal attitude of the individual, and it was often quite possible for him to remain totally uncommitted and, in the human and personal sense, free. It is clear, then, that in systems of this kind, sin was bound to lose a great deal of its moral character. This does not mean that the idea of guilt or sin was unknown in such religions. It was, of course, frequently present, but almost always as the consequence of a belief that every disaster or calamity was the expression of divine wrath occasioned by some human transgression. The divine was quite capricious. It was a totally incalculable factor. No attempt was made to look for moral guilt in the first instance when an offence had been committed against the god or gods. It was the automatic response of the mechanical system which was at once suspected, and the first concern was to trace a possible fault in the switchboard which regulated and combined these countless factors and set definite, divine powers in operation.

Israel's religion, despite the fact that it came into being within this ancient, oriental, religious climate, stands out in complete contrast. Her religion was not merely largely adapted to the prevailing oriental idea of what was divine. This adaptation was also accompanied by a profound and positive reshaping of the existing, oriental mode of thought. Her religion was at the same time both similar to and different from those of her neighbors. Marduk was the god of Babel, and Yahweh the God of Israel. But Marduk's character was derived from Babel. Marduk was Marduk because Babel was Babel. Israel, on the other hand, was not what she was naturally disposed to be, but became what she was because Yahweh was Yahweh. Yahweh was Israel's God in this unique sense: it was not Israel which made Yahweh, but Yahweh who made Israel. Men are always disposed to create gods in their own image and likeness, a process which always entails a grave risk of multiplicity, degeneration, and corruption in religion. The fact that man was created according to the image of God, and not God according to the image of man, was of critical importance in Israel's theology of the creation. This was no empty formula, but a doctrine which was basic to Israel's theology. It is, of course, possible to discover analogies in other religions, but it was only in the case of Israel that this concept acquired a totally new, inner significance, since it was in Israel alone that the divine was continuously experienced as the decisive and formative factor in the nation's existence. Yahweh was far more than a mere reflection of Israel's national consciousness. What in fact distinguished Yahweh from other gods was not a spontaneous product on the part of Israel. Yahwism obviously grew in spite of Israel's spontaneous inclinations and had to maintain this growth by opposing these natural inclinations which were constantly striving to degrade Yahwism and bring it down to the general level of Canaanite religion, reducing it to a kind of baalism. Those who succeeded in achieving this degradation were, of course, lost not only to Yahwism but also, in the long run, to Israel as well, as it was Yahwism which was again and again responsible for creating Israel anew and for continuously restoring her to her true and unique nature and task. It is, then, only relatively true to say that Israel made her own religion. We may, with far greater justification, claim the reverse—that Israel was made by her religion.

What certainly does not happen is that a people are already in existence and that God reveals his religion to this people. Once again, the reverse is the case. The people come into existence, within a given, social environment, as a consequence of God's intervention, by means of revelation. Revelation demands a response of faith and God calls together those who believe in him. The people who are summoned in this way find a common meeting point in this God of revelation who is one and the same for all who believe in him and answer his call. The inevitable outcome of this is the formation of a community of faith, or a "church." As revelation is always adapted to and formed by the present religious environment, the resulting religious association between human beings believing in and answering this divine revelation was bound to lead, in that region and at that time (of the prevailing national idea of gods and deities) to the formation of a national community. Thus it was that Israel came to stand apart from other peoples as a separate nation. Even though it was first and foremost Yahwism which enabled the Israelites to form themselves into a nation, and to preserve their national identity intact, the fact that the people themselves had a certain innate quality of their own should not be overlooked. Israel's roots extended a long way into the ancient, oriental culture in which she had succeeded in winning a place for herself, and she was able, under favorable conditions, to prolong her independent existence, at least for a time, as a purely human, historical community, irrespective of Yahwism. A body deprived of its soul does not begin to decay immediately.

Israel's origin in history and her continued, historical existence were only possible within the framework of Yahwism, though this was also limited, of course, to a particular time and locality. But Israel's origin and survival, in its purely historical aspect, did not always coincide with her existence as an authentic, religious community. The "Israel of God" was, so to speak, assimilated by the Israel of history, and remained the constant factor in the otherwise changing life of a nation which was composed, at least in its early stages, of somewhat heterogeneous and inconstant elements. This phenomenon is best illustrated by the image of Israel which was used in the Bible itself. The tree as an image of Israel may be cut down and die as a result, but its root contains sufficient life-giving forces to produce a new trunk and branches. This image is obviously applicable to Israel's national life, during the most critical periods in her history. However, the same pattern of disintegration and regrowth is also discernible, on a smaller scale, throughout the history of the whole nation's existence, as an uninterrupted process by which new cells come into being within the living organism as old cells die off. Israel's consciousness of God, aroused by divine revelation, was the vitalizing spirit which used the available materials to build a body for itself. This spirit was then able to express itself, grow, and expand within the body which it had created. The body, however, remained dependent upon the world which surrounded it and into which it so closely fitted, the environment whose eventful history it fully shared and to whose influences it was constantly subjected. Israel, considered particularly as a human community living within history, a community which strictly speaking did not come to be known as "Israel" in the original sense of the word until the middle period of its existence, was just such a body. The external, social form, within which the authentic, religious community was able to grow and finally develop a definite shape, was in the course of human history subjected to every caprice of change and modification, because the spirit within the body, which was always creating new forms, was constantly seeking new and changing ways of expressing itself.

God's faithful community—the "church" of Yahweh—was the one constant element in the checkered history of a nation whose outward form was always changing. This national character emerges clearly from the Old Testament, which provides us with a coherent account of Israel's religious and historical development in a direct line from Abraham to Christ. The inner, religious community of Israel was obliged to organize itself socially, in order to achieve a concrete form within the historical framework which was present. With the passage of time, it frequently happened that this concrete, crystallized form, by reason of too close an affinity with its period and environment, lost its original content and meaning, with the result that it became incapable of giving pure expression to the inner, religious community. Whenever this occurred, this particular, concrete form had, sooner or later, to disappear, and its disappearance inevitably had the effect of shocking and chastening the faithful community. As a consequence, it would begin, as it were, to grow afresh within the community in its changed, historical situation, and to create a new expression for itself within this new, historical pattern. It was, then, by a process of renewal and rejuvenation that the authentic Israel of God was able to make its way through history. The Old Testament history of salvation was, therefore, essentially the history of the development and formation of a church.

8. Holy Scripture as an Attendant Phenomenon and an Essential and Integral Part of the Mystery

We can, of course, best approach Israel and the mystery of Israel through the Old Testament, in which Israel's vital experience was echoed. It is in the Old Testament, too, that we are brought face to face with the mystery. This does not mean that everything in Israel's experience was authentic, but that the mystery was expressed in the extremely human record of this ancient, oriental people. What lay behind the whole of Israel's national life was the inspiration which proceeded from this mystery, and which gave form and shape to the great diversity of material resulting from historical events and the various statements of the people. Since Israel's life as a nation was mirrored in her literature, Scripture cannot be absolutely authentic in every respect. Although, as a whole, the Old Testament must be regarded as inspired, it is important to differentiate between the entirety of Scripture and those individual parts which have to be judged according to their relative function within the whole. God spoke to Israel and formed her. For this reason, and insofar as what God said to Israel resulted in her formation, he must also be considered as being the creator of Israel's literature. Just as the constant and imperishable "Israel of God" assumed many different historical forms as the people of the Bible, so, in the same way, the eternal and authoritative word of God assumed various forms, in accordance with the changing nature of the biblical nation in whose "language" this word was expressed. The outward, empirical form of the different biblical accounts—the religious ideas, practices, and terms, all of which were determined by the spirit of the age and the environmental climate—have to be seen as signposts pointing in the direction in which we must search, if we wish to understand exactly what these particular people were really trying to say, as believers. What they were in fact attempting to say was, after all, what God himself wished to tell all men for all time, though in "language" which was restricted to that particular time and place.

The dialogue between God and Israel, opened and kept in motion by God's historical actions, was continued and finally brought to a close in the written record of this conversation. Even while it was still in the process of being written, then, Scripture was already the source of revelation for ancient Israel. It represented—in the literal sense of making present again—what God had said in the past and made this, so to speak, permanent. At the same time, it was also able to act as an entirely new statement on God's part, which could be accurately interpreted in the light of the past, with its deep and far-reaching implications. What was implied in the present became clear by reference to the past. When God spoke to the patriarchs, he was at the same time addressing their descendants. The religious tradition which had been initiated when God spoke to the patriarchs continuously brought the later generations of Israel face to face with the divine reality. Scripture may be considered not merely as part of this tradition, but as its culmination, the crystallization-point of its most intense expression. It enjoys, therefore, the privilege of being the special organ, or sacrament, of God's speaking to man.

Scripture is all too frequently regarded as a disconnected mystery, standing apart from the whole. In our introduction to the subject we have, therefore, deliberately kept one aim in view: the restoration of the mystery of Scripture to its rightful place within the total, all-embracing mystery of Israel. The Old Testament is an extension of this great mystery. It accompanied the total mystery as an attendant phenomenon. It constituted the documentary record of this mystery and its abiding monument.

A great diversity of facts and data was included in this document, because it formed the total record of an entire nation and its many experiences. It would be unreasonable to attempt to sort out the data contained in the Old Testament according to whether these constitute divine statements or not, for, generally speaking, scriptural

inspiration in the strictest sense of the word tended to let the purely
material ingredients of the Bible stand at their own relative value,
whatever their inspirational value might have been. The singular
quality of the inspiration implied in any data in the Bible is, however, to be perceived in the light in which the dedicated writers
allowed these facts to be seen. This light was the light of their faith.
They wrote in order to bear witness to their faith, to communicate
that faith to others. Faith is a sharing in the knowledge of God.
The conclusion to which the dedicated writers of the Bible came
concerning faith, had, therefore, and still has, divine authority, and
calls for faith on our part. All the material data to be found in the
Bible serve to give expression to that verdict. Each individual fact
should be judged according to its relationship with the truth which
the Bible was seeking to express in the context of faith, and it is
only within this context that any factual statement in Scripture can
be fully understood. Since the Old Testament contains so many
material facts of this kind and fully incorporates them by making
them subservient to its purpose of conveying faith, we are bound to
acknowledge the whole of Scripture to be inspired and authoritative. Every detail of a successful work of art forms an essential part
of the finished whole. In the same way, those individual parts of
Holy Scripture which do not appear to fit into the whole are of
importance, since in their own way they contribute to the total
vision which inspired the writers.

Going a little more deeply into the distinction which we have
already made between Israel's outward, empirical form and God's
actions within her history, it is reasonable to suppose that the judgment which Scripture passed on the subject of faith was not directed towards the outward history of Israel but towards the divine
actions visible within it. No certain knowledge of Israel's faith can
be gained from the scriptural accounts of the nation's military
engagements. This knowledge can, on the other hand, be derived
from what Scripture has to say about the faithful community or

"church" which acted, throughout Israel's history, as God's partner in the dialogue in which he revealed himself to his people. God's way of speaking to men is by means of facts, and the language in which these facts are presented can only be understood by men who believe. It is in this way that what we may call the "church" of the faithful came into being and continues to exist within the greater community of mankind, and it was this "church" which voiced its thoughts concerning faith in the Old Testament. There is no such thing as an abstract "church" and no abstract opinions or judgments were passed by the biblical writers of the "church" community of Israel. These inspired writers expressed their opinions in concrete form by giving an account of the history of the visible, human community within which the "church" community was actively present, though always changing its form with changing circumstances. Holy Scripture was then, and still is now, an unfailing source of knowledge for the "church." To learn what God has to say to us, we must turn, in faith, to Scripture and listen to what is said there, while taking care to penetrate to the essential meaning and deeper implications of the history related in it. The material data of the Old Testament account of historical events, however, only reflect what was known and thought about the past in the environment in which the historical account originated. The writers of the history of the various empirical forms which were successively assumed by the "church" had, it should be noted, to rely upon the information available to them at the time. When Scripture had eventually reached the point where it was in the form in which we now know it, Israel still possessed only the vaguest and most scanty facts about the earliest period of her national existence. It was, however, precisely in these early, little known stages that the faithful community had its beginnings. In order to relate this early history, the incipient "church" was given a concrete form, which was to a great extent borrowed from conditions appertaining to a later period. The resulting impression is that all kinds of elements in

Scripture of much later formation were already present in a cut and dried form in the earliest period. This is, however, not the impression which the writers of Scripture were seeking to make. What they were really aiming to do was to show how the later faith of Israel had its roots in God's revelation to the patriarchs. To achieve this, they incorporated the full, mature knowledge which they had of faith at this later stage into their account of the original experience of this faith, which was all-embracing in its scope, even at this very early stage. They wished to demonstrate the essence and vocation of Israel as a faithful community, by providing a detailed history of the origins of this community, but their judgment with regard to this early faith was grafted, in their minds, to an historical vision which was strictly limited in time. It was, in other words, a schematized and simplified vision, resulting in a view of Israel as a relatively uniform and empirical phenomenon, whose historical continuity, assumed by the dedicated writers to be self-evident, formed the principal means of expressing and affirming the continuity of the "church," which was in any case a constant factor within this changing, historical process.

Even if modern, biblical research should prove that Israel's growth (and therefore the development of her religion as well), followed a far less direct and straightforward line than is indicated in the biblical account of her history from Abraham to David, no insuperable difficulties of principle should arise as far as the infallibility of the information conveyed by the Bible is concerned. What might, in principle, have happened did not necessarily occur in fact. Israel's faith was certainly creative with regard to the past. What is more, creativeness expanded according to the remoteness of that past, in other words, the longer the material in question had formed the substance of teaching and preaching in Israel. However, a creation from nothing was a highly irregular occurrence. Historical facts and data always formed the normal point of departure. These were wholly assimilated into Scripture. The Bible consequently remained essentially historical, with the further result that it always keeps us, as it kept Israel, in vital contact with the past. This fact emerges again and again, often in the most forcible and surprising way, even in instances where the narration of particular events of past history is overloaded with dogmatic implications. It is indeed frequently very difficult to locate this historical core precisely and to be absolutely sure about the extent and exact positioning of the "primordial rock of reality" upon which the tradition which was assimilated into the biblical account was founded. But this is, after all, not such a vital question as many make it out to be.

What we have always to take into account, then, in any consideration of the earliest period, is the fact that this was shaped and even reconstructed by Israel's living tradition of faith. As far as the later period, from David onwards, is concerned, however, we are faced with a different problem—that of the *writing* of history. This writing we owe to the oldest parts of the Old Testament. Some of these later accounts form the written record of a long tradition. Others, however, are no more than hastily noted reports of events which took place in the fairly recent or even the immediate past. In one way or another, then, the history of each period was always written. At the same time, however, the need was always felt, in each successive period, to review what had already been recorded previously in the light of new experience. The inevitable consequence of this was that, as Israel's vision was enlarged with the passage of time, the older texts were added to and edited to form new editions. It was in this way that the Pentateuch came into being, in three main layers. The foundation was laid in the so-called Yahwistic account. This account bears the stamp of the religious and literary mind of the period of the earlier kings. It provided a synthesis of the whole of the preceding tradition which, as we have seen, was both religious and national, and made it permanent in the form of a written record. As a result, the national tradition was stimulated, borne up by, and became the concrete expression of the tradition of faith within Israel. The second layer, which was built on this foundation, is the account of the period of the later kings. Its religious and literary expression is different from that of the bottom layer, in that the prophetic movement was already powerfully under way by this time. The third layer, which bears all the characteristic marks of the Jewish period which began with the exile, gives the whole pentateuchal edifice its permanent form.

In addition to this vertical growth discernible in the construction of the Pentateuch, there was also a horizontal extension of the national historiography of Israel at this time. The Yahwistic account is immediately followed by and continued with two great histories. The first of these is the so-called "deuteronomic" history. The whole of Deuteronomy was inspired by the prophetic insight, and it is possible to regard this book as the greatest prologue to the prophetic age. It created the framework within which the books of Joshua, Samuel, and Kings, with their wealth of facts drawn from widely differing sources and their variety of accounts dating from the early period, were connected together to form one great, single entity, or one single, extended sermon. The second horizontal account is the so-called "priestly" history. This may be ascribed to the priestly historiography prevalent in the Jewish world during and after the exile, and includes the two books of Chronicles, which recapitulate and sometimes enlarge on the past already described in earlier books of the Bible, and the books of Ezra and Nehemiah. These two books take up the thread of Israel's history where the Chronicles leave it off, and give their own view of the origin of the restored community of Israel—the Jerusalem of the Jews.

In this way, the scope of the Bible was constantly enlarged. The facts of Israel's national life accumulated throughout the centuries, and the historical edifice grew higher and higher all the time. Each successive century produced its own written record which penetrated to the very heart of the community. These records were preserved and, with the passage of time, came to be regarded as standard works. This gradual expansion in the material scope of the Bible was a genuine growth, since the Bible, which came into being as a result of faith, grew together with the growing community of believers, as an organ within the total living organism. This process of growth culminated in and, in one sense, was brought to a close with the New Testament, which marked the fulfillment of faith, scripture, and "church." In this end-process, the Greek Bible formed the indispensable link connecting the Hebrew Bible with the writings of the apostolic Church. It represented the faithful tradition of the worldwide "church" of the Jews, expressed in the Greek language. This "church" tradition was established by the production of a new literature and by the translation of the Hebrew Bible into Greek. The Greek version of the Bible was, however, more than simply a translation. Considered in its entirety, it was at the same time a new edition and a reinterpretation of the literature which it had inherited. This inheritance was seen in the light of a new and more mature understanding of the nature of faith, and interpreted in a totally new way, according to the changed spirit of the times and the different mental and spiritual attitudes towards the literary taste and the theological conventions which prevailed.

The pure essence of the biblical message—the total religious truth which the Bible seeks to convey—is never to be found in isolation in the text, but is always assimilated into a definite, historical form, and thus remains subject to the inevitable limitations imposed by this form. Holy Scripture is a miraculous unity because it comprises the expression of faith of men who confessed exactly the same faith. Yet, at the same time, it is extraordinarily diverse in texture, because each individual believer was only able to conceive and express his faith in his own way, or rather in the way in which the period and environment in which he lived conditioned him to think about and express it. Consequently, although the faith of the Bible was expressed in many different ways, in accordance with the prevalent historical situation, it was always essentially the same faith which was confessed in every case. In this way, it was possible for this faith to display itself in a multitude of aspects and in an almost inexhaustible wealth of detail, without any loss of fundamental unity. For, against this backcloth of ever-changing form and expression, the essential features, eternally valid and never tied to any particular place or time, are always clearly discernible. For us, the Bible is an authentic picture which always remains consistent and which gradually gains in clarity and definition as it unfolds before our eyes. The fundamental authenticity of the image presented by the Bible can be assessed, in all its aspects, more and more accurately as the various lines converge, in ever increasing numbers, towards the center. In our difficult quest for what a particular Old Testament story is really trying to convey to us in terms of faith, we have to allow ourselves to be guided by the Bible as a whole and by revelation as a whole. It is only when we see, in clear perspective, the whole of God's activity with regard to man that we can learn what he is really saying to him in the Bible. It is only within this total vision that we can safely define the extent to which each separate biblical account contributes to the total expression of the divine message.

9. The Religion of Israel: Definition, Classification, and Its Value as a Sign

Just as Israel in its empirical form did not always coincide in every detail with the Israel of God, so also, all of Israel's religious ideas and practices were not authentically religious. It is possible to make a valid distinction between the religion of Israel and the religion of the Old Testament or, to put this in another way, between the religion of the people of the biblical story and the religion of the Bible itself. This book is vitally concerned with the question of authenticity in Israel's religion, as it is principally intended for the present-day believer. Nevertheless, although it is only the author's secondary aim to satisfy the curiosity of those who are mainly interested in religious history or comparative religion, such readers must inevitably realize that the problems are not unrelated. The first religion, that of the people of Israel, of which the Bible is indisputably our most important, historical source, and the second religion, that of the Old Testament itself, of which the Bible is at the same time the source of revelation, were throughout the course of history inseparably associated with each other, despite the fact that this association was not always one of close friendship. A most important consequence of this mutual relationship is that we have been able to obtain a living and historical image of the second religion—the Old Testament religion—only by way of the first, because here too the religion of the Bible was, as it were, assimilated into the popular religion of Israel and, conversely, the biblical religion expressed itself through the religion of the people and was always its constant inspiration. On the other hand, neither of the two religions ever completely concealed the other. Whenever the rank growth of the popular religion threatened to stifle the biblical religion of Israel, as it frequently did, there was always a reaction, stemming from the original, authentic religion, and taking the form of a renewal or purification. Sometimes, however, the situation had reached a point where mere reformation from within was of no avail. The only possible solution was a violent break with the historical past, a deluge which swept away all the familiar forms and washed the soil clean of all the ideas which had so firmly taken root there. Then, on the imperishable foundation of the ancient faith, a new, purified, popular religion would gradually arise. Whatever the circumstances, the biblical religion was always fully assimilated, in one way or another, into the religious experience of the people as a whole.

It is, of course, vitally necessary for this book to concern itself with the history of Israel, even if this should be principally religious history. It would not be fitting for a book of this kind to confine itself to a systematic survey of the religious concepts contained in the Bible. This is more properly the function of a work of biblical theology. The distinction must be all the more scrupulously borne in mind in any consideration in this book of the religious institutions and practices found in the Bible—a dish which used to form the staple item on the bill of fare of biblical archaeology and was generally served up under the name of *antiquitates sacrae*. At the same time, it will also be clear from the argument of the previous paragraph, that a work of this kind cannot be exclusively concerned with the provision of an outline of what might be called the orthodoxy of the Bible, perhaps in direct contradiction to the religion which in fact prevailed in Israel. It is, indeed, impossible to give a more precise definition of the subject matter of this book than that contained in the title: the religion of Israel.

It would be impossible, in any outline of Israel's religion, to avoid dealing with the secular history and politics of Israel, since the nation's religious development can be fully understood only within the context of her total development. There is, in every nation, a continual interplay between religion and history. This is especially true of Israel. Religious and national life were always merging into each other; particular religious experiences or attitudes frequently led the nation in a definite direction and, conversely, certain historical situations were the direct cause of religious movements and tendencies. As the various turning points in Israel's external history certainly marked off well defined stages in the nation's religious development, it is possible to divide the chapters which follow under these successive stages.

To restrict ourselves exclusively to the task of historical reconstruction would, however, result in a serious impoverishment of the biblical datum. We should not be primarily concerned with questions such as who the patriarchs were, what they thought or did, what occurred during the journey through the desert, and so on. It is often very difficult to find a satisfactory answer to questions of this kind. They are, in fact, of secondary importance, and though they should not be evaded, they are principally useful insofar as they can help us to find an answer to the far more important question: what we can learn from the scriptural vision of the patriarchs, the desert generation, and so on. For this reason, the historical treatment of the material is supplemented in this book by a thematic treatment of this material. The following brief survey of the chapter divisions, grouped according to the stages in Israel's religious life as defined by the turning points in her national history, should make this clear.

1. The starting point is the call of Abraham (about 1850). Abraham migrated from the region of the Euphrates estuary to Canaan, where he became the ancestor of a family or clan of nomads and seminomads. This clan eventually grew into a nameless multitude of people in Egypt (from about 1700 onwards). In addition to providing an historical outline of this period, the second chapter of this book furnishes the data necessary for the formation of a clear idea of the "patriarchal religion." It is, however, obvious that this second chapter, *The Patriarchs of Israel,* introduces a theme which extends as far as the New Testament.

2. There is also a second starting point—the call of Moses (about 1300). Moses was the founder of Israel as a nation, in the real sense of the word. He led a still amorphous group of people out of Egypt and fashioned it into a solid, national community which, after leading a wandering life in the desert, eventually secured a firm foothold in Canaan (just before 1200). If this book was concerned with providing a purely historical outline of Israel's development, a third chapter on the Mosaic religion would be perfectly adequate here. As this is not, however, the principal aim of the book, the mosaic

period is dealt with under two chapter headings: *The God of Israel* (Chapter III), and *The Worship of Israel* (Chapter IV).

3. When the transition from a nomadic existence to a settled way of life had been completed, in Canaan, the religious federation of the tribes developed into the state community of a kingdom (about 1000). The flourishing monarchy so firmly consolidated Israel into a definite political and social structure that, after the disruption of the empire (about 925), the Northern Kingdom of Israel and the smaller Southern Kingdom of Judah were able to stand on their own feet for several centuries as two relatively independent states. The religious consequences of this totally new pattern of civilization, according to which Israel's national life was directed from this time forward, are discussed in the fifth chapter under the theme of *The King of Israel.*

4. The Northern Kingdom came to an end with the Assyrian exile (721), and the Southern Kingdom with the Babylonian captivity (587). The decline of Israel formed the background to the prophetic books. In the sixth chapter, an attempt is made to provide an outline, in synthesis, of the *Prophets of Israel.*

5. Though Israel did not hand down any lasting political ideas or institutions, her spiritual wealth was inherited by subsequent generations. These later Jews, closely bound together in the first place by ethnic ties, formed a somewhat exclusively religious community. The more widely the Jews were dispersed, in the physical sense, throughout the ancient world, the more closely they tended to focus their attention, in the spiritual sense, upon the restored congregation of Jerusalem. One characteristic of this many-sided phenomenon, the religion of the Jewish world of the Old Testament, is considered in the seventh chapter, under the title of *The Remnant of Israel.*

This introductory chapter may perhaps have taxed the reader considerably by reason of its length and complexity. Its aim has been to present the whole of the history of Israel so that the reader will see it as a testimony and as a sign of the coming of God among men, of his increasingly deeper, spiritual penetration into the world of man. This history was one of constant action and reaction between God and man. In it, God revealed to man the way in which he acts and the way in which he associates with man here and now, not only his way of acting in the past. It is in incidents and scenes, strictly limited to a certain place and time in history and indeed forming part of the history of that most obdurate and capricious of nations, Israel of the Old Testament, that we encounter eternal man. We should on no account make the mistake of regarding our generation as the absolute norm, and the people of Israel as peculiar. We should never allow ourselves to be scandalized by them, for the Old Testament portrayal of man is unpleasantly close to the truth. *Tu es ille vir.* It is a full portrait, unflattering and indeed quite merciless. The eternal God revealed himself in Yahweh, the national God of Israel, and it cannot be denied that Israel's conception of God is unrivaled in its insight into the full, divine mystery. The eternally valid truth was made incarnate in a concrete, historical form.

This form had its own history and developed in its own way. It is still the sign of God's concern for us and his intervention on our behalf, a sign which sometimes conceals and sometimes reveals the divine reality and which occasionally even has a sacramental value. The entire subject of Israel's history is both important and fascinating for us because, though it was restricted to a particular period and a particular place, it is at the same time the lasting sign of the essential reality which we ourselves experience and to which we must give our consent.

II

The Patriarchs of Israel

WHENEVER GOD concerns himself in a new way with man, something quite new comes into being, in the long run, at the human level. In this sense, something new came to light in the phenomenon of Israel and reached its climax in the total newness of the Christian fact. Man does not give an empty answer to God's word when it is addressed to him. It has power to renew and to recreate. It does not consist of theoretical formulae sent down from heaven, but is incorporated into divine acts of saving history. God's word is deed and reality. Man does not usually hear heavenly voices. What generally happens is that he has experience, so to speak, of God and, through this experience discovers God in a new way. In most cases of divine intervention, God's hand is concealed behind human situations. These situations may well be striking or even miraculous, but the religious value of the signs can be fully appreciated only by the believer.

God never forces himself upon mankind and sometimes the divine traveling companion goes almost unnoticed as he accompanies humanity on its pilgrimage. He is, however, always there and he tends to fall in line with the conversation as he finds it. He joins in the pilgrims' intercourse and gives it a new slant. In this way a new principle is introduced, but one which is very gradual in its operation. A process of growth and assimilation is initiated. It takes time

for this new element to permeate the existing human condition and
perceptibly to reshape it.

1. The Distinctively Historical Character of the Patriarchal Account

In this chapter, an attempt is made to reach a deeper understanding of the first period of the new contact between God and man.
We shall endeavor to situate the first point of contact within its
historical and geographical context and, moving on from this point,
to examine how something totally new began to emerge. We shall
also try to trace the development of this new element and see how
its first, broad outlines gradually gained a sharper and more distinct
form. As this later, more clearly defined form impressed itself already on the biblical account of the earliest period, any attempt to
trace the growth of this new element must be focused on the essential and wider implication of the historical events, rather than on
their more precise details. We cannot, then, content ourselves in
this chapter with a mere retelling of the history of the patriarchs as
this appears in Genesis 12–50. Genesis is a testimony of Israel's early
faith and a witness for the later faith of Israel. All kinds of data, as
well as facts from many different sources, have been assimilated into
the book of Genesis. In order to express the belief that the national
God of the people was already taking a hand in shaping the adventures of the patriarchs, these adventures were narrated in Genesis.
What is more, they were recounted according to the recollections which were still alive among the people. The intrinsic, historical worth of these remembered adventures is in no way enhanced
simply because of the fact that they were incorporated into the
Bible. They are bound to remain an approximation of the past as
it was attainable at that time. However tentative this approximation
may have been, real facts must in the past have set in motion the

tradition from which this widespread cycle of narratives eventually emerged, and this must have come about in such a manner that the basic structure of the cycle is still capable of disclosing something of the essential disposition of the facts and their interrelationship.

In this connection, two points stand out with particular clarity. The first is that there must have been an objective starting point somewhere in the past, a first beginning for this new element which later became the incontestable fact which challenges us in the phenomenon of Israel. We may indeed claim that a new initiative on the part of God is the essential content of the constant confession which forms the keynote of all the various narratives, and unites them into one, single, great confession of faith. The second point which emerges with singular clarity is that the cycle of narratives is permeated with recollections of the distinctive character of the environment of the men in whose midst this new element came into being.

The data provided in Genesis, seen in the light of and supplemented by our present-day knowledge of the ancient, oriental world of that time, enable us to form an essentially reliable idea not only of the fact of salvation as this is confessed in the book of Genesis, but also of the historical, human framework, described in Genesis, within which this fact of salvation was accomplished. The patriarchal history is also truly historical, even though it is not historical in the superficial sense of the word. That is to say, the account in Genesis of the patriarchs does not relate in objective detail all the facts of the case in the same way that a police report, for example, provides all the details of an accident. It is historical in a better and higher sense. It gives us a deeper and purer insight into the past than the most painstaking report of material events can ever do. In a word, it typifies. Contemporary exegesis is not able to guarantee with certainty that Esau was in fact red-haired (Gen. 25:25, 30), although it certainly has the right to rule out this possibility. What it can, however, do is to affirm again and again how authentic the

Genesis accounts are within their situation. All the various elements which are difficult to ascribe to a later reconstruction point to an objective and factual foundation.

If, for example, the tradition persisted in Israel that the patriarchs enjoyed a special relationship with the Aramaeans of Mesopotamia, then there can be no other reasonable explanation for this than that this was actually the case. This link between Israel and Aram plays an important part both in the account of Abraham and in the story of Jacob. The objectivity of this recollection has recently been confirmed in the most surprising way by the Mesopotamian cuneiform documents. These documents have provided us with interesting parallels concerning proper names and the various social and juridical customs peculiar to the history of the patriarchs. The recollection of a bond with Aram also finds expression in several genealogical lists. The fact that these lists contradict each other to some extent reveals that they go back to historical rather than to genealogical relationships. In Genesis 10:22, it is stated that Aram was a son of Shem, whereas Terah, Abraham's father, was a descendant in the seventh generation from Aram's brother Arpaxad (*see* Gen. 11:12ff.). In Genesis 22:21, on the other hand, we find that Aram was a grandson of Abraham's brother Nahor, who was perhaps for this reason regarded as the father of Kesed, because it was desired to include the Chaldaeans as well (in Hebrew: *Kaśedîm*) in a genealogical system which was devised to classify all the most prominent people who played a part in a definite environment and at a certain time, under one, single heading.

If we can accept an objective link of this kind with the past as an established fact, then we can be reasonably certain that the objective data will also correspond in one way or another to the material provided in the biblical account, however difficult it may be to ascertain precisely the degree of objectivity. This may, of course, not be the only thing, nor even the first thing which we require of the texts. Although the message of the Bible must and indeed does rest firmly on historical soil, it is nonetheless possible to do full justice to this message and to approach it from every perspective, without actually digging deeply into this soil to expose the virgin rock of the original facts on which it ultimately rests. In practice, it is generally sufficient to know that the virgin rock is there.

It is here, then, that we touch upon the highest and most essential objectivity of the patriarchal history. What this history relates is God's real intervention—the origin and development of the new bond between God and a group of human beings. This bond was the objective starting point for the later covenant between Yahweh and Israel. The covenant is an historical fact which we put on record and which demands an equally historical point of departure. A new intervention on the part of God is perceived by those who believe in God, in external events, the significance of whose signs they accept. The recollection of these external events was preserved and handed down especially by virtue of the value of these signs. Thus, a varied narrative of remembered events, with all the limited possibilities of historical accuracy as the result of the handing down of narrative material over a lengthy period of time, became the embodiment and the concrete expression of a profession of faith. The direct object of this confession of faith was always the essential fact of God's intervention. We have no need, then, to be informed in every secondary detail of the way in which the facts, by which God visibly revealed his intervening hand to his believers, were enacted.

Although certain details of the patriarchal history give us very little to go on as far as the ascertainment of the material, factual situation in the past is concerned, they still retain their value insofar as they often serve to characterize the essential reality which can be seen, in the light of faith, behind the material events. If we consider the extended line produced by man's first reaction of faith, what we find is that a tradition crystallized round the first factual, objective point of departure. This tradition was one of growing, faithful insight and understanding, and it continued to make use of the narrative form of the most ancient accounts, with the result that the narrative which we find in the Bible was gradually developed in a traditional form from the original starting point. A faith which aims to bear witness enlarges on its narrative material, places certain emphases on it, gives certain nuances to various facts, and even incorporates into it facts derived from other sources. It was in this way that the extremely varied synthesis, which we admire so much in the book of Genesis, came about. Everything in Genesis contributes towards an understanding of the message of the Bible, because everything is subservient to and permeated with the deep conviction of faith which inspired the people of God. The Israelites believed that Yahweh was actively concerned with them as he was unfailingly concerned with the patriarchs. God is also actively concerned with us today, and the biblical narrative gives the present-day reader of the Bible a faithful understanding of his own human situation, so that he is able to discover the presence of God within this situation.

2. *The Situation of the Patriarchs*

The "authenticity of the situation" provided in the accounts of Genesis emerges with particular clarity from the very reliable picture given in these accounts of the way of life of the patriarchal family. We are consequently able to place the patriarchal way of life, with reasonable accuracy, within the environment of the time. That part of the Near East which has been inhabited since time immemorial is the so-called "fertile crescent," a region, semicircular in shape, which borders the centrally situated desert zone in the north. The desert is partly accessible to travelers riding on horses or camels, and in recent years it has become completely accessible with the use of the jeep. In the patriarchal age, of course, horses and camels had no part to play; the nomadic peoples of that period traveled by donkey. There were, therefore, only two possible ways of life open to these people, seminomadic or sedentary. The territory available to the seminomads was that region which is bounded by the desert on the one hand and the sedentary zone on the other; it was limited by the climate and in particular by the rainfall. This territory is not fertile enough to provide a permanent dwelling-place. The inhabitants of this area were, therefore, obliged to move periodically in order to find sufficient food throughout the whole year, or rather, suitable pasture for their cattle. There was, of course, abundant pasture during the wet season, but with the onset of the dry season the desert zone expanded and the nomadic tribes were forced more and more into the fertile, sedentary region. In this way, a distinctive pattern of life emerged. The tribes moved to and fro every year from winter grazing grounds to summer pastures. They were half-sedentary because they were sometimes able to remain long enough in one place during the early part of the year to grow a few crops and keep some larger cattle. They were also half-sedentary in another sense. Their annual journeys of a few miles were always confined within fairly strict limits and only rarely did they become truly nomadic, by moving to a completely different region. These regular, short journeys were only possible with sheep and goats. The inhabitants of this territory were, then, "small cattle" nomads.

Generally speaking, then, the nomads lived on the fringe of a fairly clearly defined sedentary zone and their presence constituted a characteristic element of the sedentary way of life. They formed part of that environment; they were the strangers who came and went. Sometimes they came to trade, sometimes to raid. It frequently happened, too, that they settled, though still as strangers, among the sedentary population for long periods, serving as slaves, mercenary soldiers, or workers. There are also established cases of their having been allocated definite places in which to live. In short, the semi-nomads formed a kind of fringe group of the more settled communities. As such, they had a special name. This name is to be found at various times in many different places and languages. In Akkadian, the language of Mesopotamia, they were known as *ḫabiru,* in Egyptian as *'apiru,* in Ugaritic, the language spoken on the Syrian coast, as *'apirim,* and finally—and most significantly—in Hebrew as *'ibherîm* (Hebrews). According to this evidence, then, the name "Hebrew" does not originally refer to an ethnic group, but to a social group. Egyptian sources also refer, in more general terms, to "Asiatics" and the Akkadians frequently spoke of "Westerners" (*'amurru*), a name which survived in the biblical Amorites. This name was often used to designate the whole of the pre-Israelitic population of Canaan (Gen. 15:16; Amos 2:9). Sometimes it referred to one particular group within this population.

From the foregoing, then, it is possible to see Abraham as a seminomad who, as a Hebrew, came under the jurisdiction of the center of sedentary civilization in the Lower Euphrates, that was known as Ur. The Chaldaeans were the rulers of the new Babylonian empire, and the term "daughter of the Chaldaeans" (Isa. 47:1, 5), was properly applied in the Bible to the Babel of Nebuchadnezzar. In Genesis, however, the name "Ur of the Chaldees" was used, anachronistically, to refer to Ur. Ur was a great city in which the ancient "Sumerian" civilization flourished for a second time during the last centuries before 2000 B.C. This second period of prosperity was brought to an end at approximately 1950, by the great migrations of the various nations inhabiting the region, which took place at this period. This was possibly also the reason why Abraham's father migrated towards the northwest. Haran was the daughter-city of Ur and both cities maintained close and varied relations. A striking example of this is the fact that both Ur and Haran were centers of the worship of the moon-god Sin. Sin, from time immemorial, had had his earthly dwelling-place in Ur, where the "stepped tower" (*ziggurat*), the best preserved temple with a tower in the whole of Mesopotamia, was dedicated to him. The worship of Sin moved on from Ur to Haran, and the god thus became widely

known as the "Lord of Haran." This fact also emerges clearly
from the many proper names in the Bible which bear the name of
this god, for example, Sennacherib (sīn-ahê-erība = Sin has increased the number of my brothers), Sanballat (sīn-uballit = Sin
bestows life), and perhaps even Sinai. We may infer from this that
Terah emigrated to Haran and found a congenial environment
there, since the nomadic tribes who were already there belonged,
like Terah himself, to an ethnic group from which the later Aramaeans apparently originated. In the Bible, the family which Abraham left behind him in the Land of the Two Rivers was still
called the Aramaeans, and the Israelites, when they offered their
first-fruits to Yahweh, confessed: "My father (Jacob) was a wandering Aramaean" (Deut. 26:5).

According to one tradition, Abraham left Haran after the death
of his father (Acts 7:4, and the Samaritan text of Gen. 11:32, according to which Terah was 145 years old, that is, the sum of the
seventy years in 11:26 and the seventy-five in 12:4). According to
the Hebrew text (11:32), Terah continued to live for another sixty
years after Abraham's departure. According to most of the texts,
too, Abraham's call took place in Ur (Gen. 15:7; Joshua 24:3; Neh.
9:7; Judith 5:9; and especially Acts 7:2-4). On the other hand, according to the key passage, it was Terah who left Ur and went to
Haran with the intention of going on to Canaan, though he in fact
remained in Haran (11:31). There was apparently no question of
divine intervention in his case, and it was only Abraham who went
on to Canaan, an action generally attributed to his call. It has been
suggested that there was a double call, one in Ur and one in Haran.
This interpretation certainly does justice to all the various texts, but
a simpler way of looking at the question would be to accept the
existence of different lines of tradition. What the Bible aims to
establish here is that the migration from Mesopotamia to Canaan
was the outcome of a divine call and, finally, that man, in order to
follow God, had to shake off the fetters of his sheltered security. To

give an account of the way in which this migration actually took place, the dedicated writer had to refer to Israel's recollections of the past, and these were not uniform in every detail. Even before he began to write his account, it was impossible to trace the exact course of events. The dedicated writer therefore made his own interpretation of the facts as they were known to him, and vouched for this interpretation alone. What he regarded as supremely important was the distinct quality of Israel's faith, and he intended to typify this "otherness" in Abraham, the ancestor of the whole nation.

3. The God of the Patriarchs

The writer's object in Genesis was to bear witness to Israel's special situation. To achieve this aim, the "genetical" method peculiar to this book was employed—Israel's present was characterized in the point of departure of the past. The concrete nature of this past is still clearly discernible in the text, but at the same time, what is so powerfully echoed throughout the whole of Genesis is the later faith of Israel. In particular, it is the anachronistic use of the name Yahweh which gives superabundant evidence of this faith.

All that could be said of the new God of revelation was that he enjoyed a special relationship with certain individual persons, by reason of the fact that he had given a new orientation to their lives. In this respect, he was the God of Abraham. "I am Yahweh who brought thee out from Ur of the Chaldees, to give thee this land, and that thou mightest possess it" (15:7). Abraham called him the "God who brought me out of my father's house" (20:13; *see also* 24:7, 40). For Abraham's servant, he was the "God of my master" (24:12). In the only case of "theophany" which Isaac was granted, it seemed to be a legitimation: "I am the God of Abraham thy father: do not fear" (26:24). Similarly, when God first appeared to Jacob, he addressed him with the words: "I am Yahweh, the God of Abraham thy father, and the God of Isaac" (28:13; *see also* 31:42; 32:9).

Beer-sheba was closely associated with Isaac, and Jacob visited the holy place during his old age, before going to Egypt, and made an offering to the God of his father Isaac. There, God spoke to Israel (Jacob): "I am the God of thy father. Fear not . . . I will go down with thee into Egypt" (46:1–3). Finally, when Joseph blessed his sons, the new faith in God had already become a family tradition:

> God, in whose sight my fathers Abraham and Isaac have walked,
> God that has led me like a shepherd from my youth until this day,
> The angel that hath delivered me from all evils bless these boys
> (48:15–16).

If we are not to depart radically from the texts, we must be careful not to say that God appeared to the patriarchs. They were not familiar with this current idea of God. It would be better to express it in this way: that God, hitherto unknown to them, suddenly placed himself in the midst of their lives. Thus God did not correspond to their ideas, but he certainly fulfilled their deepest, human aspirations, and therefore they at once surrendered to him as the One whom they could henceforth call their "own" God. The God of the world adapted himself to man's limited powers of comprehension and allowed himself, for the first time, to be recognized and understood both as a God who was a personal protector and as the hereditary God of a human family. It has frequently been emphasized that these are well-known categories in the history of human religions. This is a perfectly reasonable claim, so long as it is not used to explain the origin of this particular religion. All that we can deduce from it is that Israel's religion was not a thoughtful, but a practical monotheism. For the Israelites, the phrase "the God of Abraham" was charged with emotional and historical significance. Their immediate response to these words was to think of Yahweh, the God of the world, who was close to them and who led them as their national God. But, at the same time, the expression "the God of

Abraham" goes back also to the original point of departure, and reminded them of the first discovery of this God by the elect, to whom he revealed himself. In this respect, Genesis was particularly successful in preserving the Israelites' historical sense. For example, it was not immediately apparent that others had anything to do with this God. Clear evidence of this is provided by the passage in which Laban, who was anxious to conclude a peace treaty, under oath, with Jacob, says: "May the god of Abraham and the God of Nahor judge between us" (31:53). This means that he and Jacob were each to swear by the god of his grandfather. This passage later gave considerable offence. In the Hebrew text, an attempt was made to reconcile it with the orthodox, monotheistic tradition, by interpolating the words "the god of their father" after the reference to the two gods. The suggestion here was that both were to swear by one and the same god. The Greek translation attempted to achieve the same end by putting the verb into the singular. The Vulgate had recourse to both means.

But what Israel heard above all, when this familiar formula was spoken, was the merciful nearness of God. This was a justifiable reaction, since it reminded them vividly of the concrete manner in which the patriarchs worshiped the true God. For the people of Israel, this God was not an abstract notion, the result of a process of intelligent reasoning, but a living Person who had made his presence felt among them in an irresistible way. The formula, "the God of Abraham," then, continued to serve the purpose in the minds of the people of keeping alive the idea of the awe-inspiring nearness of their national God. As Pascal observed, there is an enormous difference between the God of Abraham, Isaac, and Jacob and the God of the philosophers. What God makes known to man concerning the mystery of his being in terms of historical reality utterly transcends the knowledge that man can acquire of God by means of pure reason, even if man can arrive at clearer definitions in this way. In any assessment of a particular religion, it is necessary to bear in mind that a living insight is always worth more than a rational concept, however neat and tidy this may be. Furthermore, this insight into the very being of the living God may often embrace more conceptual truth than is at first sight disclosed by apparently defective formulations.

There is every reason to suppose that the totality of Israel's faith was already expressed in the account of the religious experiences of the patriarchs, and we should therefore not overlook the possibility that this archaic formula, "the God of Abraham," was consciously preserved in order to emphasize, in the sense indicated above, the personal and revelatory character of the national God of Israel. Here, as elsewhere in the biblical tradition, the dedicated writers continued to employ a familiar formula, once it had been devised, although in so doing they gave it a meaning which added to the original fact and went far beyond it. The biblical tradition is so firm that we are still able to reconstruct, at least in its main outlines, the historical course of divine revelation from the history of the patriarchs, despite all that was later set down in writing and appears in the present form of this account. We can, therefore, accept as an established fact that the true God did indeed make his first conquests, at this stage of the history of salvation, as the personal protector of certain individuals, however difficult this may be to reconcile with our contemporary trend of thought. Recent studies in the sphere of comparative religion have also provided very good evidence for the validity of this assumption. We may, then, take it that the normal course of events was for this God to become the hereditary family God, and, when this family eventually grew into a nation, to become the national God of the people of Israel.

This historical line of development is not only clearly distinguishable within the biblical account, but it is also responsible for the entire structure of this account. The extent to which this is the case becomes more convincingly apparent with the realization of the intimate connection between this historical development and the growth of the idea of the Covenant. God became the God of certain persons. He became their God by entering into particular relations with them. In Israel's theology, this relationship between God and his people was known as the "Covenant" and the whole of the history of Israel's salvation is a history of the Covenant. The idea of the Covenant is a reflection, in terms of biblical theology, of what took place, at the religious level, between Israel and Yahweh. The events which occurred at the time of Sinai marked the beginning of this historical relationship. We are bound, therefore, to conclude that it was there that the Covenant between Israel and Yahweh originated. In order to stress the fact that the national God of the people was the same as the God who entered into relations with the patriarchs, the dedicated writers characterized that relationship as a covenant between Yahweh and the patriarchs. Furthermore, when Israel's God revealed himself as the God of the world and included the whole of humanity in his dialogue with Israel, treating all men as equal partners in this relationship, then the Covenant became a new Covenant.

It is possible to gain a clear impression of the gradual growth of the Genesis account of Abraham, not only by the well-known method of detailed, literary analysis, but also by tracing this development in terms of biblical theology. In the first place, we have the simple report of the encounter between Abraham and God, as the result of which Yahweh became Abraham's God. This fact is taken up again later in Genesis. Its deeper meaning was further developed and it was given a more precise formulation in the very full description provided in another chapter of an impressive ritual in which God, in a graphic manner, appeared as the partner in a characteristically ancient, oriental covenant. Here, Genesis describes Abraham's vision of his God, in a dream, under the symbol of a burning torch, passing between the opposing rows of the sacrificial animals which Abraham had divided into two pieces (15). Finally, in a later chapter, the idea of the Covenant formed the most im-

portant topic in a detailed conversation between God and Abraham
(17). In this dialogue, the priestly author of Genesis expressed the
whole of his theological understanding of the situation. It is impossible not to feel that the dedicated writer intended this particular
episode to mark the climax of the entire story of Abraham. By this
stage in the account, the writer has thrown sufficient light on the
subject and has adequately related it to the religious situation which
prevailed in Israel at the time at which he was writing.

It is often very difficult to make a really convincing distinction
between what is ancient and what is of more recent date in the
patriarchal account. We have, of course, already referred to the concrete definition of God, as the "God of the Patriarchs," as ancient.
We have, indeed, even claimed that this was a recollection which
went back to the concrete starting point of Israel's first idea of God.
This assertion is, however, borne out by the various names given to
God, as these are without any doubt ancient in origin, and therefore serve to emphasize this particularly concrete aspect. The "God
of Isaac" is, for example, called the "feared one of Isaac" (31:42, 53),
and the "God of Jacob" is referred to as the "mighty one of Jacob"
and the "stone of Israel" (49:24; *see also* Isa. 1:24, 49:26, 60:16; Ps.
131:2, 5). The Hebrew text of the book of Ecclesiasticus which was
rediscovered towards the end of the nineteenth century contains
many interpolated invocations to God. These occur after one verse
of the final chapter (51:12), and one of these in particular, the title
"Shield" or "Protector of Abraham" dates from the post-biblical
Jewish world (*see also* Gen. 15:1). As a universal title for the "God
of the Fathers," the name *El Shaddai* occurs very frequently. Because of its archaic sound, this name was particularly favored by
the poetical writers and it occurs, for example, thirty-one times in
the book of Job alone. The early translators were unanimous in re-
producing this name as the "almighty God." This is, certainly, in
many ways a good translation. It reflects the general, emotive content of the Hebrew name and is consequently preferable to any of

the more precise, but dubious formulations, such as the "God of the high mountain," the "God of fruitfulness," or "God the destroyer" (*see* Isa. 13:6; Joel 1:15), all of which tend to portray the God of Israel as the "mighty God of nature."

The biblical names for God, then, affirm the personal character of the God of revelation and his close connection with the lives of men. This emerges most powerfully in the statement which occupies a central position in the account of the great theophany of the Covenant: "I will establish my covenant between me and thee and between thy seed after thee, from generation to generation, as a perpetual covenant: *I shall be thy God* and the God of thy seed after thee" (17:7). Everything is contained in that one sentence: I shall be thy God or, more literally, I shall be to thee as a God. That was God's side of the bargain. It meant that he vouched for the salvation of those who worshiped him and consequently would do everything that men of that time expected their gods to do. He would avert the evil that men feared and bestow upon them the good that they desired. But this God was prepared to do more than that. Those who believed in him would never cease to discover what kind of a God they had in him. They would never cease to learn in what an overwhelming sense he planned to be their God. In a word, "I shall be to thee as a God" was the all-embracing Promise.

But man had his side of the bargain to keep as well. For him there was to be no other god apart from this God. He was not to turn to "strange" gods—to the gods of other nations or peoples, however well these people seemed to fare with their gods. He was to expect salvation from no god except his own. Those who followed the one, true God were to know him. They were to lead their lives in conformity with the will of their God, and this meant, first and foremost, that they were to surrender unconditionally to him and to him alone. In a word, "I shall be to thee as a God" was the all-embracing Demand.

Promise and Demand—these form the content of the Covenant.
God vouched for his Promise and made his Demand. Man was to
believe in the Promise and obediently fulfill the Demand. God became man's possession by choosing him, but man had also to
become God's possession by surrendering completely to him in
faith and obedience. Man too had to choose his God. Thus, once
again, it becomes quite clear that Israel's faith in God and her
expectation of salvation gained concrete expression in the Covenant
and that these two phenomena had their origin in one and the
same experience of God. Both belonged together and were to grow
together until they became what we now refer to as Israel's monotheism and her messianism.

4. The Father of Faith

Israel was a people apart from other peoples. Her "otherness" was
essentially religious. It was something which developed slowly. It
was also a genuinely biblical otherness in that, after a long process
of gradual growth, it became, as it were, concentrated in one,
definite person at one, definite period of time. That person was
Abraham. The period of time was Abraham's call. It is possible to
say that Genesis 12:1–3 is a theological definition of Israel's situation as a community of faith. Abraham was more than an historical
figure. He was a biblical figure—the representative figure of the
people of God and of the believer of all times. In a word, he was
the father of faith.

With Abraham, the dialogue between God and man entered a
new phase. Throughout the whole of the cycle of Abraham, Scripture points to the beginning of this new element. It delineates this
beginning in such a manner, however, that the people of God of
both the Old and the New Testaments, already living in this new
phase, are able to understand what is implied in this beginning from
the story of Abraham itself.

God's speaking to Abraham marked the beginning of the history of his special revelation. Similarly, Abraham's actual response, in faith and obedience, marked the starting point of the tradition of faith which followed a parallel course to this special revelation. But, at the same time, the beginning of dialogue between God and Abraham was characterized as the prototype of the dialogue which has since continued between God and believing man up to the present. Abraham is thus the basis of both the Old Testament and the New, and the "father of all who believe" (Rom. 4:11f.). He is not only our model. He is also our father insofar as we are believers. By believing, we enter into a living communion with the tradition of faith which had its origin in Abraham, and was handed down from generation to generation, each generation communicating this life of faith to the next generation, which received it.

Although St. Paul knew how to make use of the Old Testament facts in the exposition of his doctrine of the Christian faith, these facts were first and foremost intended for the instruction of Israel herself in the matter of faith. This intention is reflected throughout the whole of the book of Genesis. It emerges, however, with particular clarity from two verses which form an extension of the original account, and would seem to be a direct result of this preoccupation with the need to instruct Israel how she should believe: "Abraham shall become a great and mighty nation . . . I have therefore chosen him, so that he will command his children and all his posterity to keep the way of Yahweh by doing judgment and justice" (18:18f.). Israel was thus invited, for the first time, to recognize herself in Abraham and was at the same time given an exhortation in the manner of Deuteronomy. Another striking example of this is the rather dry and repetitive account of the theophany of the Covenant (17). From the very beginning, this account stresses the generations of Israel rather than the person of Abraham: "Walk before me and be perfect. And I will make my covenant between me and thee: and I will multiply thee exceedingly" (17:1b-2).

This does not mean that Paul forced the material of the Genesis texts. His aim was to teach us how to read the Bible. If we examine the question more closely, we are bound to discover that what he was in fact aiming to impart to us was an intuition of faith in which we should share. At first sight, of course, his arguments would seem to consist of rather farfetched allusions and attempts to achieve an outward harmony between conflicting ideas, though this approach can, to some extent, be attributed to the prevailing climate and manner of argumentation of the age. His rhetorical skill cannot disguise the deep implication of his message. Abraham did not simply depict the mystery of the Crucifixion and the Resurrection in his concrete, human situation. He did not, moreover, merely join the living community of faith in the purely factual sense, for it must also be true of the father of faith, as of every human being, that no one is justified except by faith in the mystery of Christ. He must indeed have had some intimation of this mystery and have reached out, in faith, towards it. St. Paul enables us, in Abraham's faith, to perceive the specific structure and the object itself of the Christian faith. The Gospel, too, would appear to testify to this: "Abraham, your father, rejoiced that he might see my day; he saw it and was glad" (John 8:56). If the Johannine text does not affirm this, then it says very little indeed.

St. Paul's argument, then, is that Abraham is our father, the father of the Christian community, and that the promise was ultimately fulfilled when he became the father of many nations and peoples. Abraham did in fact become the father of many nations because he believed in the God *"who quickeneth the dead* and calleth those things that are not, as those that are" (Rom. 4:17). By referring to two turning points in Abraham's life, St. Paul demonstrated that Abraham's faith had the specific character of faith in the Resurrection. Paul's first instance of this aspect of Abraham's faith was Abraham's belief in God's promise of countless descendants, despite the fact that his own body was *worn out* and

Sarah's womb was *dead* (Rom. 4:19; Heb. 11:11f.). His second instance was that Abraham's faith did not weaken when he had to sacrifice Isaac, although he was told that his name would be perpetuated in Isaac, for he believed that God was able *"to raise up even from the dead"* (Heb. 11:17-19). As it is written, then, this faith was reputed to him, in God's eyes, unto justice. This was not written only for Abraham, but also for us. We shall also be justified in God's sight so long as we believe in him *"that raised up Jesus Christ from the dead"* (Rom. 4:22-24).

It is clear from the whole *corpus paulinum* that what comprises the Christian faith is an actual sharing in Christ's death and resurrection. By accepting, in faith and obedience, the crucifixion of his beloved "old man," the Christian at the same time knows that God will build up the "new man," Christ, in us from this death. This is precisely what happened in the case of Abraham, when he offered his Isaac. When Isaac was given back to Abraham, alive from the sacrifice, this was a *return from the dead*. The whole incident, of course, was enacted *in parabolam,* and it prefigured the Christian mystery, of which the entire context is full (Heb. 11:19). What happened was that Abraham did not spare his only beloved son (*unicus-unice dilectus-agapetos*). In the same way, we, as Christians, must be prepared to sacrifice our Isaac. The deepest meaning of our sacrifice and Abraham's is that God too did not spare his Isaac (Rom. 8:32; *see also* Gen. 22:12, 16), but delivered him up for our iniquities and caused him to rise again for our justification (Rom. 4:25).

It is not altogether too farfetched to assume that Abraham may well have had, in a real, though perhaps obscure way, some intimation of the Christian mystery, and perhaps even of the particular mystery which was entrusted to Paul. And thus, as a result of this insight, his act of faith may also have had a specifically New Testament character. This assumption is borne out by the extremely intense nature of his experience and by the fact that his sacrifice was one which intimately affected him as a father. It is also supported by his attitude of complete submission to a God who had the power to resurrect the dead. If this assumption is correct, we may infer that Abraham has an even stronger claim to be known as the father of faith of the "spiritual" Israel than as the father of Israel "of the flesh."

It should, however, not be forgotten that a "spiritual" Israel was always present, though perhaps concealed, within the Israel "of the flesh." It was possible for the Israelite, and for him alone, to be the child of Abraham, both in the spiritual and in the carnal sense. There is good reason to believe that every case of true faith in the Bible was at the same time faith in the resurrection. There are many situations in the Old Testament—none of them due to pure coincidence—in which a complete surrender in faith is demanded. Situations of this kind can only be compared with the sacrifice of Isaac. Furthermore, the account of this sacrifice would never have been written in this particular way if the personal experience of the author of Genesis and the collective experience of the whole of Israel had not caused it to be so written.

One example should be sufficient to support this claim. Israel, as a nation, had to make a great sacrifice, comparable to Abraham's sacrifice of Isaac, and the nation was afterwards brought back to life, as Isaac was resurrected. This national sacrifice and resurrection was Israel's downfall in exile and her return to life in that distinctive new form of existence led by the people whom we now call the remnant of Israel, the Jews. It was faith alone, faith in God's power to lead the people through death to life, which saved and preserved the remnant of Israel throughout its catastrophic history. The remnant of Israel was put to the most severe of tests, and what emerged from this tragic experience was the most profound and the most characteristically New Testament testimony of faith that the Old Testament has produced—the canticles of the suffering servant of Yahweh (Isa. 40–55). If this claim is indeed justified, we need no longer regard the Abraham cycle as isolated from the rest of the Bible. Genesis 22 no longer appears as a disconnected episode, a problem with which all exegetes are familiar but which confronts them with almost insuperable difficulties. Rather, it is an integral part of a biblical theme which is continued throughout the whole history of man's salvation. It is possible once again to recognize in the father his carnal and spiritual posterity.

5. The Promise

In the foregoing section we have reviewed the position of Abraham as the father of the faith of both Testaments. In this section, we propose to consider the Promise and its fulfillment in greater detail and to demonstrate how Abraham can be regarded, within this context too, as the basis of both the Old and the New Testaments. Certain constant themes can be recognized in the many and recurrent promises recorded in the patriarchal history. These can be basically reduced to three—the promises of blessing, land, and posterity. This threefold division is, of course, not strictly accurate, since the promise of blessing or salvation was to a very great extent fulfilled by the possession of a land flowing with milk and honey and by the material blessing of numerous descendants. Nonetheless, it is useful to distinguish these three elements in the Promise, because the promise of blessing played a very significant part in the biblical tradition, together with the promises of land and posterity. Furthermore, most exegetes recognize a messianic tendency in this promise, and this tendency towards messianism probably provides the best point of departure for our examination of the subject.

The promise of blessing occurs five times in Genesis. With slight variations, the same formula is used in each case: "In thee (or: 'in thy seed') shall all the kindred of the land (or: 'all the nations of the earth') be blessed" (Gen. 12:3, 18:18, 22:18, 26:4, 28:14). The messianic tendency is so clearly distinguishable in this blessing that

the blessing has been included among the other messianic prophecies. The fulfillment of this blessing, then, is to be found, according
to the opinion of most scholars, in the New Testament. This does
not, of course, mean that there was no fulfillment in the Old Testament. The way in which the promise is formulated is so closely
related to the expectation of its fulfillment in the Old Testament
that we are obliged to refer to the later texts of the Old Testament,
the Septuagint, and St. Paul if we are to effectively understand the
wider meaning of the promise of blessing and see how its scope
goes beyond the Old Testament.

The dedicated writer of Genesis saw this promise as already fulfilled in Israel. Uppermost in his mind was a sense of history. What
this amounts to is that Abraham and his descendants would receive
such a visible abundance of benefits from their God that they would
be a blessing. This means that they would be looked upon as the
standard type of blessed mankind. Whenever Israel's neighbors,
witnessing this blessing, wanted to wish each other well—in
Hebrew, the usual phrase was "to bless each other" and this soon
came to be understood as "to be blessed"—they were to say to each
other: may you fare as Abraham and Israel (*sec* Gen. 48:20). In
this sense, they were to express their desire to bless each other "in"
Abraham and "in" posterity. They were, in other words, to refer
to Israel's well-being as an ideal state of perfect blessedness. There
are numerous examples of texts which express this idea in a comparable form—someone or some group of people, either in Israel
or among the other nations, would be a blessing or a curse, or even
a proverb, an example, a parable, or a "shaking of the head" (*see*
Gen. 12:2b; Jer. 29:22; Zech. 8:13).

To show how the messianic implication of this promise was intimately connected with, and indeed had its origin in, the historical
content of the blessing would lead us too far from our present
theme. What we have to establish here is how this element of the
Promise was brought to its ultimate, perfect fulfillment by way of

an early fulfillment which was still incomplete, limited, and temporary. It is only by seeing the total growth of Israel's religion in its broad framework that we can properly understand how this in fact came about. In the case of the promise made to the patriarchs, we have already seen, in this way, how, in one respect at least, the Promise was the origin of both Testaments.

We cannot, however, let the matter rest here, having satisfied ourselves, for the time being at least, on this one account. The Promise forms one, single, connected whole. The promise of land and posterity was directed towards messianic salvation, and no more and no less so than the promise of an all-embracing blessing of all nations. This promise was also directly connected with that of numerous descendants. Abraham became the father of "a multitude of nations," in the fullest and most literal sense of the phrase, by becoming the father of all who believed in Yahweh. St. Paul particularly stresses this aspect of the Promise, the perfect fulfillment of which came to pass when the gentiles became the children of Abraham by sharing in his blessing. They shared in this blessing because of their faith, just as the father was blessed because of *his* faith, whether or not he was circumcised.

The purely Old Testament fulfillment of the Promise, however, is also discernible in these texts and, what is more, it occupies a most prominent place in them. It has already been established that many passages in the Bible refer back to the Genesis account and that the dedicated writers were clearly thinking first and foremost of Israel herself, who in fact became, as later texts repeatedly confirm, as the sand on the seashore and the stars of heaven, according to the Promise. Furthermore, this idea is applied in the first place to the many neighboring tribes, in some way related to Israel, of which at least forty were, in Israel's view, descended from Abraham (*see* Gen. 25 and 36). It is therefore true to say that, at this level, Abraham was the father of a multitude of peoples, indeed of an "assembly" of nations. This is, in a sense, a double fulfillment of the

Promise and illustrates how Abraham was the basis of both the Old and the New Testaments.

The promise of land is so clearly related to the Old Testament fulfillment of this promise in the conquest of Canaan, begun under Joshua and finally accomplished by David, that the New Testament implications can easily be ignored. But even in the Old Testament there are unmistakable signs that the promised land is more than a geographical area. The phrase "possession or inheritance of the land" is the formula which developed in the course of history, but it is occasionally used as a standard expression for the coming of the salvation which God set aside for his own people (Ezek. 13:9; Isa. 57:13; Prov. 2:21f.; Ps. 36:9, 11, 22, 29, 34; 24:13). The New Testament follows up this deeper implication by using land in the sense of Christian salvation (Matt. 5:5; Heb. 3; 4; 11). Abraham's posterity of the New Testament already possesses this land and looks forward to inheriting it: "Let them pass from death to life, which thou of old hast promised to Abraham and his posterity" (Mass for the Dead, Offertory).

In the New Testament, then, the terms of the ancient Promise are filled with the new salvation. The New Testament does, however, go right back to the essential meaning contained in Genesis, for the Promise had an immeasurably extended meaning even in Genesis, by reason of the inner connection between faith and justification contained in it. Saving possessions which are restricted to a particular time and place, such as those mentioned in Genesis, play a subordinate part in such a context, and may be regarded as concrete guarantees or tokens of the real saving possession which plays a decisive and essential part in both Testaments—the community of men with their God.

It is, of course, obvious that this New Testament orientation is only faintly discernible in the patriarchal history, since the Genesis account is first and foremost concerned with the provision of a direct introduction to Israel's national history, during which the Promise was only temporarily and partially fulfilled. The chosen instruments of this fulfillment were, above all, Moses and David.

The work of Moses—the law—provided the foundation, in a special sense, of the Old Testament. It consolidated and defined more precisely the religious inheritance of the patriarchs. At the same time, it was also a translation of this inheritance which narrowed it down, and a safeguard of the essential religious values of Israel which was adapted to Israel's changed circumstances and expressed in a characteristically Old Testament form; that is, it was restricted to the national experience and to the material environment.

Moses, then, laid the special foundation. On it, David raised a building which was specially suited to it. In David, the Old Testament reached a certain peak of perfection. The total collapse of the building which David had erected made the prophets aware of its temporary and limited nature, and they went back, beyond David and Moses, to the original Promise. They represent the transitory stage between the Old and the New Testaments, looking forward at the same time to the new Moses and the new David who was to lay the foundations, on the ancient piles of the Promise, of the eternal Covenant and the imperishable City of God—the permanent and complete fulfillment of the Promise.

St. Paul, in drawing a clear distinction between the Promise and the Law, showed how the New Testament believer's attitude towards Abraham was completely different from his attitude towards Moses. This was Paul's special contribution to the illumination of God's distinctive plan of salvation.

6. Religious Practices

In introducing the subject of public worship, our aim is not so much to discover the way in which the patriarchs practised their religion as to familiarize ourselves with the mentality of ancient

Israel, since this is to a very great extent reflected in what Genesis has to say concerning the patriarchs. In Genesis, we are able to see the patriarchs doing what they undoubtedly did at that time and what the Israelites most certainly did when they had established themselves in Canaan. They expressed their faith in God, worshiped their God as children of their time, and adapted themselves to the regional practices of Canaan. The holy places which existed in Canaan were taken over by the Israelites and soon became specifically holy places of Israel.

Shechem was regarded as a legitimate holy place (*maqôm*) by virtue of the fact that there Abraham experienced God and built an altar on the spot (Gen. 12:6f.). Abraham also claimed the holy places of Bethel, Hebron, and Beer-Sheba. These are the four holy places of the patriarchal account. The name of Abraham is traditionally linked to Hebron in particular, and this connection is also preserved in the literal sense; the modern Arabic name of the town refers to him (et-Khalil = the friend = Abraham, "The friend of God": Isa. 41:8; Dan. 3:35; Judith 8:22; James 2:23). Abraham lived a few miles to the north near the "oak of Mamre." Nearby the town, he bought the field with its famous burial ground, which was a place of pilgrimage for the Israelites and later for the Jews, Christians, and Arabs. Only one text gives us any indication of the special association between Beer-Sheba, with its 'Ēl 'Ôlam ("God of old" or "eternal God," Gen. 21:33), and Isaac (Gen. 26:23). Bethel, however, with its El of Bethel, is clearly associated with Jacob (Gen. 31:13, 35:7). This special association and the manner in which Jacob and Israel came to appropriate this holy place will be discussed more fully later. In the meantime, however, it is interesting to note the similarity between this and the way in which Abraham appropriated the 'Ēl 'Elyôn ("the most high God") of Jerusalem for Israel (Gen. 14:22; *see also* 14:19f.). These can certainly be taken as examples in support of the conjecture, which has already been expressed in a general way, that Genesis not only incorporates recollections of the patriarchal history, but also includes all kinds of factual data of a totally different nature. In this particular case, the facts given in Genesis concern local traditions and situations. The part played by sacred trees and stones in public worship is of special interest.

The oak of Moreh stood in Shechem (Gen. 12:6). We may surmise from the name that this was the same as the diviners' oak (Judges 9:37). It was under this tree that Jacob buried his family's idols (Gen. 35:4), that Joshua renewed the Covenant (Joshua 24:26), and that Abimelech was made king (Judges 9:6). There was also an oak tree near Bethel. This was known as the "oak of weeping" because Deborah was buried underneath it (Gen. 35:8). Saul and Jonathan were buried under the terebinth of Jabes (1 Chron. 10:12). The prophetess Deborah sat in judgment over the people of Israel under the palm tree, which was named after her, between Ramah and Bethel in Ephraim (Judges 4:5). Saul and his followers were on the borders of Gibeah, on the threshing-floor under a pomegranate tree (1 Sam. 14:2). Later on we find him on the hill in Gibeah, sitting under a terebinth with his spear in his hand and his servants gathered round him (1 Sam. 22:6). It was especially under trees that God was invoked, altars were built, votive-stones were erected, and sacrifices were made. Theophanies also occurred under trees.

It was at one time fashionable to apply the theory of evolution to religion and to use it as a means of demonstrating, for example, that the Christian idea of God was the result of a process of natural development or that there were distinct signs in the patriarchal history, despite its late editing and puritan censure, to contradict the idea of Israel's early monotheism. Those who supported the evolutionary view of the Bible claimed that men of this period had by no means reached the stage of monotheism. This did not exist in any form in the history of the patriarchs. Human religion was then still at the stage of animism or polydemonism, that is to say, of belief in the occupation or spiritualization of all natural things by spirits or higher beings. The evolutionists maintained that a monotheistic religion—or a religion which even remotely resembled monotheism—could not come about until men had first passed through the stages of polytheism and henotheism.

An animistic religion of this kind does not, however, appear to have existed, either in Canaan or in the Semitic world as a whole. There is nothing in the texts which might suggest tree-worship. It is quite clear that the tree was, in every case, merely an ingredient or an ornament in connection with the place of worship. An ancient tree, standing in isolation, or a group of trees on a hill formed a natural temple. Sacrifices were never made to the tree itself, merely under the tree. The sacred tree is thus not too difficult to bring into accord with orthodox religious practice. It was only when the danger of contamination from native paganism became too great that these native forms of worship, which had previously been taken over, were strenuously opposed. In all reverence, Abraham planted a tamarisk (Gen. 21:33)—the very fact that this is mentioned at all shows once again how ancient the facts are with which Genesis deals. But in Deuteronomy we find the clear statement: "Thou shalt plant no grove, nor any tree near the altar of the Lord thy God" (Deut. 16:21). The prophets never accused Israel of tree-worship; they did, however, take exception to what took place *under* a shady tree.

The sacred stone (Maṣṣebheh) was also no more than an ingredient of the place of worship and it has a history similar to that of the sacred tree. It was never an object of worship. In general, it was set up as a grave-stone (Gen. 35:20; 2 Sam. 18:18), or as a memorial, especially of a theophany.

The oriental mind was extremely concrete and conceived the universe as a whole. The inanimate world was, therefore, included in the world of human relationships and thought of as one with man. Any attempt to approach the biblical texts with the logic of

the western mind—and this is certainly what the evolutionists did—
is bound to result in the isolation of certain passages or statements
which strike the western ear as rather forcible. Again, following the
European practice of logical thought, conclusions are usually drawn
from these isolated statements. These may well give an impression
of correctness, but they will, in fact, be incomplete and inevitably
inaccurate. Let us take as an example what Laban said to Jacob
concerning the heap of stones: "Behold this heap and the stone
which I have set up between me and thee shall be a witness" (Gen.
31:51f.). The heap of stones and the memorial stone were to be a
testimony of their mutual agreement and their oath. The following
passage is even more graphic:

And Joshua took a great stone, and set it under the oak that was in the
sanctuary of Yahweh. And he said to all the people: Behold, this stone
shall be a testimony among us, for it has heard all the words of Yahweh,
which he hath spoken to us. It shall be a testimony unto you, lest perhaps you will deny your God. (Joshua 24:26f.).

It would be completely wrong to conclude from these texts that,
in Israel's view, sacred stones were able to hear, and thus that they
were in possession of a soul or spirit. We can, however, certainly
draw one correct conclusion—that modern man has almost entirely
lost his feeling for signs and symbols. Israel, on the other hand, was
not conscious of any gulf between the sign and what it signified and
felt no need for any explicit, logical interpretation of the symbol, as
we do now. In this instance, the sacred stone kept the idea alive in
Israel's mind that Yahweh was zealously watching over the covenant which had been concluded by him, or mutually between men,
in his sight.

The most famous sacred stone of all is, of course, Jacob's stone at
Bethel. The story of Jacob is perhaps the purest example of the
impartial Yahwistic piety which prevailed among the rural popula-

tion during the early age of the kings, especially in the ancient tribal territory of the Northern Kingdom. In this case, too, the religious practices in public worship, based on a natural bond with the deity, became Yahwistic by close association with Yahweh's historical, saving activity. It is impossible not to be aware here of the new idea of God among those within whose circle the account originated.

The *māqôm*, or place of worship, is reminiscent of the story of Abraham (Gen. 12:8; 13:3). On his flight from Beer-sheba to Haran, Jacob reached this place towards the evening of his "day of affliction" (35:3). He decided to spend the night there and, without realising it, used one of the *maṣṣebhôth* of the *māqôm* as a pillow. This caused him to dream a strange dream. In his vision of the ladder, he learned how terrible this place was, and realised that it was, in fact, the "house of God"—*bêth 'elōhîm*. The next morning, he placed this stone upright as his *maṣṣebheh,* poured oil over it and named the place Bethel. The vow which Jacob made at that time is worth quoting as an example of prayer in ancient Israel:

If God shall be with me, and shall keep me on the journey which I am making, and shall give me bread to eat, and raiment to put on, and I shall return prosperously to my father's house: then shall Yahweh be my God, and this stone, which I have set up for a title, shall be called the house of God (*bêth 'elōhîm*) and of all things that thou shalt give me, I will offer tithes to thee (Gen. 28:20–22).

God fully and literally accepted this vow. Twenty years later, when Jacob was once more in great difficulty, God appeared to him in a vision: "I am the God of Bethel!" (31:13). Having narrowly escaped the vengeance of Laban, Jacob was now living in fear of Esau's revenge. During the night before the encounter with Esau, a new Jacob prayed to God. In this prayer, we can hear the heart-felt entreaty of the oppressed people of Israel:

O God of my father Abraham and God of my father Isaac, O Yahweh
... I am not worthy of the least of thy mercies, and of the trust which
thou hast shown to thy servant. With my staff I passed over this Jordan,
and now I have become two companies. Deliver me from the hand of
my brother, from the hand of Esau, for I am greatly afraid of him;
lest perhaps he come and kill me, both the mother and the children.
Thou didst say that thou wouldst do well by me, and multiply my seed
like the sand of the sea, which cannot be numbered for multitude
(32:9–12).

God's answer came at once, in the very same night, in the mystical
wrestling-contest between God and man. We should not, of course,
presume to try to discover precisely what took place during this
encounter. The incident is very difficult to understand, but it has a
power and an extraordinary suggestiveness which cannot be mistaken. As a result of his experience during this night, Jacob was
profoundly changed. He emerged a different man, no longer Jacob,
but from that time forward Israel. In accordance with the usual
biblical practice, this change of name was the expression of an
essential, inner change, a change of being. Furthermore, this Israel
of grace was created at the expense of the old Jacob who had to go,
in order to make way for the new man, the father of faith. His
shrunken thigh was to remind him continuously, and similarly, the
ancient custom of taboo against the eating of thigh-muscle was from
that time onward to remind Israel of his and Israel's call to be a
people of Yahweh (Gen. 32:22–32).

After the favorable outcome of his encounter with Esau, Jacob
was commanded to go to Bethel and to erect an altar there to the
God who had appeared to him while he was in fear of his brother.
Jacob at once ordered his dependents to get rid of all the strange
gods in their midst, to purify themselves, and to change their
clothing. Israel was, in this way, to put a distance between herself
and the native baalism. When this had been done, the people went

to Bethel, where Jacob built an altar. He called the place 'Ēl of Bethel (35:1–7), just as he had cried out, upon the altar which he had set up in Shechem, "'Ēl is the God of Israel" (32:20). Immediately afterwards, God appeared to him in a theophany, in which his change of name was confirmed and the Promise was reestablished. Jacob-Israel then set up a *maṣṣebheh* in the place where God had spoken to him. This *maṣṣebheh* was a stone monument. Jacob poured a libation over it and anointed it with oil. The place where God had addressed him, he called Bethel (35:9–15).

Like the Abraham cycle, the story of Jacob also underwent a process of development in which several lines of tradition were interwoven. Only once do we come across the strongly worded formula: "the stone . . . shall be called a house of God" (28:22). In the same passage, however, it appears as the place called Bethel, with a note to the effect that the city was previously known as Luz. This note was certainly not made with any polemical intention, but was the outcome of erudition. It shows in the clearest possible way how animism played scarcely any part here, for the stone was never called Luz, and thus could not have been renamed Bethel. The two other traditions state explicitly that Jacob called the place Bethel because God had revealed himself to him there (35:7), and had spoken to him there (35:14f.).

The part played by the *maṣṣebheh* is graphically illustrated by the rite of the conclusion of the Covenant in Sinai. Moses built an altar at the foot of the mountain and set up twelve *maṣṣebhôth* around it, one *maṣṣebheh* for each of the twelve tribes (Exod. 24:4). The account of Sinai is well provided with material concerning sedentary practices in public worship, of the type that we find in the story of Elijah and Carmel. Elijah repaired the broken down altar of Yahweh and took twelve stones, according to the number of the tribes of the sons of Jacob, to whom the word of Yahweh had come: "Israel shall be thy name" (1 Kings 18:30–31). These texts provide the key to many archaeological finds such as an altar in a circle of stones; the altar represents the deity, and the *maṣṣebheh* represents the worshiper of the deity.

A remarkable religious ceremony merits closer attention in this connection. Abraham was to cut a cow, a goat, and a ram in two and place the pieces, together with a turtle-dove an a young pigeon, on the ground opposite to each other. "And when the sun was set and a darkness had arisen, there appeared a smoking furnace, and a lamp of fire passing between those divisions" (Gen. 15:17). In the book of Jeremiah there is an allusion to a similar rite, together with its interpretation. Yahweh said, through his oracle:

I will do to the men that have transgressed my covenant and have not performed the words of the covenant which they agreed to in my presence as I did to the calf that they cut in two and passed between the parts thereof (Jer. 34:18).

Genesis is apparently alluding here to an ancient *rite* of the Covenant which was performed until the later period of the Monarchy in the holy place ("in my presence"). The Covenant was confirmed and guaranteed (the rite also implies a sanction), by both partners passing between the pieces of the sacrificial animals. The action was probably accompanied by the repetition of a prescribed oath which briefly summed up the content of the Covenant. God, then, made it known to Abraham in a vision that he would confirm his promise to him by means of a Covenant under oath. The smoke and fire were unmistakable signs of the divine presence: we have only to think of Mount Sinai blazing and smoking (Exod. 19; Deut. 4:11), and of the pillar of cloud and fire, smoking by day and burning by night (Exod. 13:21). It is possible to see, in the rather juridical language in which the story is summarized (Gen. 15:18), the formula of the oath which would be appropriate to the religious rite. A Covenant with God is, of course, similar to a covenant or treaty concluded between men. This is why Abraham did not himself pass between the pieces of the animals. This Covenant was substantially unilateral. It was divine grace. This is clear from the language used —God *set up* the Covenant, *established, made, gave, commanded, posited* it. These are not the sort of words used in covenants made at the human level.

Data indicative of similar rites can be found both in Greek and in Roman literature—the terms *horkia temnein* and *foedus icere* were used in this connection. The Hebrew term *kārath berîth* would seem to go back to an original meaning of *cutting* a covenant. The idea of a sanction contained in the rite is powerfully reminiscent of Saul's symbolic act, when he came with his oxen from the field as soon as he heard of the Ammonites' challenge.

The spirit of the Lord came upon Saul . . . and his anger was exceedingly kindled. And taking both the oxen, he cut them in pieces, and sent them into all the coasts of Israel by messengers, saying: Whosoever shall not come forth, and follow Saul and Samuel, so shall it be done to his oxen (1 Sam. 11:6–7).

It is possible, too, that a similar threat is contained in the behavior of the levite who cut his dead concubine in twelve parts and sent one to each of Israel's tribes (Judges 19:29).

The question, however, still remains as to whether this fully explains the rite itself. It would seem that the mysterious bond which was established between the two parties by means of the sacrificial victim was of first importance. A kind of blood-communion was sought as a basis for the moral bond of the contract. A parallel case is the vital communion with the deity, sought by the blood of the animal that had already been sanctified by sacrifice (see Exod. 24:6, 8). The same desire was also at the root of the feasts after the various covenants (Gen. 26:30; 31:46; Joshua 9:14; 2 Sam. 3, 20), especially as these were at the same time sacrificial meals (Gen. 31:54; Exod. 24:11).

7. *Strange, Yet Spiritually Related*

The modern Christian is prone to a kind of religious superiority complex. A reminder of how his own spiritual ancestors expressed themselves in worship can help to remedy this attitude. He should never be ashamed of his forbears in faith, whom God himself was not ashamed to call his people. Israel was proud of her patriarchs (*see* Rom. 9:5). We find it harder to be proud of them. In religion, they expressed themselves and behaved essentially as people of the period in which they were living, and we are in every respect very far removed from this period. It is consequently difficult for us to recognize them as the fathers of our faith as well as of Israel's. We tend to stop short at the purely external image which is so amazing, and fail to penetrate to the inner core of the patriarchs' being which can reveal to us how close they in fact are to us. This inward essence is, of course, their religious attitude, an attitude which began with them, and has been continued in the Christian tradition. We are all too easily inclined to compare our *concepts* with theirs. In so doing, we tend to think of our concepts as the norm and risk judgments over their religious level. In this, we display a basic misconception of the Bible and completely reverse the relationship between the patriarchs and ourselves. The religion of the patriarchs is in fact the standard for our faith, not vice versa. This principle can indeed be held to apply to the whole of the Old Testament. Our false conception of the true position of Israel is not simply due to Israel's mental adherence to the past. It is also due to the fact that we, today, are similarly limited by our own twentieth-century way of looking at things. It is, after all, by no means certain that our religious *concepts* are better able than theirs to go to the heart of the matter.

One of the reasons why we tend to be so puzzled by the religion of Israel is that, according to the current view, religion is exclusively a matter of the soul and its salvation. These, however, are two things which are completely foreign to Israel's capacity for conceptual thought. Ancient Israel had a very clear understanding of the nature of man, but had no need of an accurately defined concept of man's soul. Since religion is not something which concerns only the soul of man, but rather affects the whole of man's being, we can learn a great deal from Israel here.

Israel, of course, rejected the heathen phantasies concerning the life after death. In Israel, the soul was never imagined to exist separately from the body (*anima separata*); the whole man was thought to lead a shadowy existence after death. Our idea of heaven and hell was quite foreign to the mind of Israel. The life hereafter is something which cannot be taken into account in any consideration of Israel's religion. For Israel, religion was concerned with this world, and the entire object of religion was to give form and meaning to man's life in this world.

In many respects, this was a thoroughly healthy view. We have only to refer to examples among the pagan religions of the Near East, and to that of Egypt in particular, to see how preoccupation with the life after death and with the kingdom of the dead always constituted a serious threat to man's religious energies. Where man's attention was taken up with the hereafter, his religious attitude towards God and his fellowmen inevitably suffered. Even if Israel's mind was not always explicitly and consciously directed towards eternal values and heavenly things, this did not necessarily prevent her from possessing, to a very high degree, that quality essential to the religious attitude which can help us today to see more clearly what is basically required of man by the Christian religion. The real value of a man's religion is not restricted exclusively to his concepts. Even less is it limited to his concepts concerning the life hereafter. Its essential worth is to be found in his faith, hope, and charity.

The true object of all religion is God. So long as man expects salvation from that God alone, and places his hope in him alone, the explicit form which this human salvation takes is really a matter of relative importance. There is, of course, no secret either about the form of salvation which Christians expect from God and his saints or about the circumstances in which religious ardor is increased. The religious attitude of Israel was characterized by the way in which the patriarchs associated with their God. In all his affairs and activities at the human level, the believer was able to perceive the presence of God. For us, this must be an example of lasting importance. Instead of feeling superior because he possesses transcendent truths of religion—truths which are all too often lamentably external to our lives—the Christian ought to look to the perfect honesty and spontaneous humanity which is the mark of the religion of the patriarchs of Israel.

There is, however, more to it than this description. Although salvation was, in the case of Israel, quite restricted to this world, it was certainly not viewed in such materialistic terms, however materialistic it may seem to us now. This is because God himself, and the community which Israel formed with him, was felt to be the all-embracing treasure of salvation, and the purely material possessions of salvation were sought and enjoyed in the service of this total treasure. Here too, the fault lies clearly with ourselves. We are only now beginning to realize that we have created, as it were, a short circuit between the religious and the purely worldly elements.

Salvation in the Old Testament is both national and terrestrial. What man expected of his God was expressed in the plainest terms in Jacob's first prayer, as quoted above (Gen. 28:20-22). This prayer even incorporates a condition. As such, it cannot be held to represent an ideal attitude on the part of the believer, though it does accurately depict the calculating aspect of the character of Jacob-Israel (*cf.* Hos. 12), and those like him. What emerges from Jacob's second prayer (Gen. 32:9-12; also quoted above), is that the seed which was always in him was already beginning to grow and that he was already showing the qualities of a future patriarch. This is the prayer of a chastened man who has already experienced the greatness of God and is conscious of his own insignificance and is therefore unable to let go of his God, whatever this God may ordain.

The salvation which Jacob prayed for and which Yahweh constantly promised to the patriarchs is recognizably of the same order as the salvation promised in the Sinaitic Covenant. In the Covenant, God as it were temporarily systematized his promise in order to adapt it to human powers of comprehension. The salvation which he promised, and which he gave in his time, was terrestrial and national. This provisional systematization of salvation is what we call the Old Testament. The Covenant of Mount Sinai is the classic expression of this saving system and, as such, forms the specific foundation of the Old Testament. The demand which Yahweh expressed in the Covenant was: "You shall serve Yahweh your God," but the promise which was made in the Covenant was not: "that your souls may be sanctified," but "that I may bless your bread and your water, and so forth" (Exod. 23:25-31). This was the salvation expected of God, and Yahweh was not ashamed to be the God and Savior of Israel in precisely this way. That is also the teaching of the Law. It was in this way that the true God succeeded in getting a hold over men and they became associated with him. They were able, in this way, to gain the necessary experience of God, with the result that they could be gradually educated towards acceptance of a higher form of salvation, by shedding the lower forms of purely material salvation as they began to realize how insufficient they were. This was not only God's way of dealing with Israel. It is still his normal way of dealing with men. He fashions Christians into true believers by this method, just as he fashioned Jacob.

If we wish to see the difference and the connection between the Old and the New Testaments in a clearer light and to follow the gradual development of salvation from the Old Testament to the New more easily, it is of the utmost importance that we should visualize these worldly, material aspects of salvation of Israel in their functional context, that is to say, as forms of experience of a universal, religious consciousness. Israel knew how to do this far better than we do today. That is why the story of the patriarchs is capable of revealing to us the full extent of the gulf which so often exists between the religious truths which we hold and our day-to-day activity as human beings among the things of this world. We have indeed to learn, in the fullest sense of the word, to pray to God to give us our daily bread.

Consciousness of religion is directed entirely towards the divine mystery, and in this respect both Testaments are homogeneous. The signs which enable the believer to approach and to experience this mystery, however, and the phenomena which enable him to see it visibly and effectively at work are always entirely dependent upon the environment in which he has grown up. If we forget this, we are bound to place too low a value on Israel's religion and fail to recognize our own religion in that of Israel. A detailed description of the promise contained in the Covenant is provided in the book of Leviticus. It is possible to savor from this account something of the unadulterated purity of the ancient endowment of salvation and, at the same time, to show how, even in this text, salvation in this world is still subordinate to something else.

If you walk in my precepts, and keep my commandments, and do them, I will give you rain in due seasons, and the ground shall bring forth its increase: and the trees shall be filled with fruit. The threshing of your harvest shall reach unto the vintage, and the vintage shall reach unto the sowing time: and you shall eat your bread to the full, and dwell in your land without fear.

I will give you peace in your land: you shall sleep, and there shall be none to make you afraid. I will take away evil beasts: and the sword

shall not pass through your land. You shall pursue your enemies: and
they shall fall before you. Five of yours shall pursue a hundred others:
and a hundred of you ten thousand, and your enemies shall fall before
you by the sword.

I will look on you, and make you increase: you shall be multiplied,
and I will establish my covenant with you. You shall eat the oldest of
the old harvest: and the new coming on, you shall cast away the old.

I will set my tabernacle in the midst of you: and I shall not cast you
off. I will live among you, and I will be to you as a God: and you
shall be to me as a people.

I, Yahweh your God, have brought you out of the land of the Egyptians, that you should not serve them: I have broken the chains of your
yoke and I have made you to go upright (Lev. 26:3–13).

In the Covenant, God adapted himself to a people who had to
lead a normal, hard, human existence and could only with difficulty
be kept on the right path. The whole of the above passage, then,
expresses what God had to say to the ordinary Israelite, so as to
appeal to him, to keep him from the worship of Baal and to bind
him to himself. Yet, despite this, this catalogue of promises reaches
its culminating point in the final verses. The faithful Israelite was
not simply to desire the fulfillment of the promises of worldly
goods, but to rejoice in Yahweh in the sign of these gifts. He could
be secure in the gracious presence of his God among his people: "I
will set my tabernacle in the midst of you." No one would be able
to mock him with the question: "Where is your God?" Here too, it
is possible to see something of the wealth of meaning and the unlimited possibilities implied in the concluding phrase: "I will be to
you as a God and you shall be to me as a people." This is indeed
not only God's first word (Gen. 17:7), but also his last (Apoc. 21:3).

This vision was borne out throughout the whole of Israel's further
development. Of all the favors which Yahweh bestowed upon
Israel, by far the greatest and most important was his living among
the people (Deut. 4:7). In chapter thirty-three of the book of

Exodus, we have a similarly ancient text which provides an even more explicit description of what the sacred writer must have felt, in terms of personal experience of the living God, when he made Moses say to Yahweh in the desert:

If thou thyself dost not go before, bring us not out of this place. For how shall it otherwise be known that I and thy people, have found grace in thy sight, unless thou walk with us, that we are set apart from all the people that dwell upon the earth?

Without Yahweh himself, all worldly saving possessions lost their power of attraction for the believing Israelite, even the inheritance of a land flowing with milk and honey (Exod. 33:15-16).

The believer, both in the Old and in the New Testament, expects *divine* salvation. The Old Testament believer saw this embodied in worldly salvation, but both God and the believer saw beyond this to something more, something further, since faith attains to God himself in and through his gifts and God wishes to give himself in his gifts. Thus worldly salvation is not something which is completely enclosed within the limits of the Old Testament horizon. It is rather a sign charged with dynamic force, a foreshadowing, in which faith implicitly strives towards what is foreshadowed and eventually reaches it. St. Paul is not simply indulging in an uncommitted, pious speculation in his epistle to the Hebrews. On the contrary, his text goes right to the heart of the matter, explicating what was for a long time implicit in the mind of the believer:

By faith Abraham, as soon as he had been called, obeyed and went out into a place which he was to receive for an inheritance; and he went out, not knowing whither he went.

By faith he abode in the land of promise, as in a strange country, dwelling in tents, like Isaac and Jacob, the co-heirs of the same promise.

For he looked for a city that hath foundations; whose builder and maker is God.

All these died according to faith, not having received the promises, but beholding them afar off, and saluting them and confessing that they are *pilgrims and strangers on the earth.*

For they that say these things do signify that they are seeking a country. And truly, if they had been mindful of that from whence they came out, they had doubtless time to return. But now they desire a better, that is to say, a heavenly country.

Therefore God is not ashamed to be called their God; for he hath prepared for them a city (Heb. 11:8–10, 13–16).

III

The God of Israel

1. God "From the Land of Egypt"

Israel's stay in Egypt formed such an essential part of the nation's ancient tradition that no study of this tradition can afford to overlook it. There must have been an historical basis for Israel's belief in an early period of time spent in Egypt. The birthplace of the patriarchal family was set in Mesopotamia and, provided that there was no irrefutable factual evidence to the contrary, this must, to some extent, have been due to the powerful influence of some prehistory on the national mind and imagination. There are also a number of minor facts scattered about in the Bible which indicate that Israel's forbears must have spent some time in Egypt in the dim and distant past.

The immortal story of Joseph forms a bridge between Canaan and Egypt, between the history of the family and that of the nation. From the religious point of view, no new facts are provided in this account. There are no new divine revelations or visible interventions. God did not even appear in the dreams which play such an important part in this account. They are merely omens. Nonetheless, the religious quality of the story of Joseph is very high indeed. It is permeated with a deep faith in God's Providence. Even though he remained in the background, the God of the Fathers was still immanent. He stayed very close to his people through this period of their history and took the lead in the complicated human affairs related in the story. The dramatic tension is maintained throughout the whole of this account, right up to the final scene, in which the principal character himself provides us with the key to the entire plot: "You thought evil against me: but God turned it into good, that he might exalt me, as at present you see, and might save many people" (Gen. 50:20). This idea, so wonderfully expressed, and indicative of such a deep understanding of the nature of faith, is to be found only rarely in the Bible, at those moments when Israel's prophetic insight reaches a culminating point. In this case, however, the ground had already been prepared for Joseph's final declaration when he first made himself known to his brethren: "Be not afraid, and let it not seem to you a hard case that you sold me into these countries: for God sent me before you into Egypt for your preservation . . . And God sent me before you, that you may be preserved upon the earth, and may have food to live. Not by your counsel was I sent hither, but by the will of God" (Gen. 45:4–8). The guilt of the brethren became instrumental in the carrying out of God's plans. It was only by Joseph's family coming to Egypt and being isolated there that it was able to grow into a nation. The suffering of one man was the origin of life for a great nation—the birth of Israel. In this respect, the story of Joseph forms the culmination of Genesis, which frequently provides illustrations of this divine law. The story of Joseph is, of course, the most striking example, and although the connection is perhaps no more than coincidental, it is bound to remind us of him who came to "minister and to give his life a redemption for many" (Matt. 20:28).

There is nothing improbable in the idea that Israel did not preserve any particular memory of her stay in Egypt, but that she did remember the very much older age of the patriarchs. It is normal that, in the oral tradition and the religious traditions of a group of tribes, the starting and turning points should remain alive in the memory, while longer, but far less eventful periods should be quite empty after a few generations. Moses was, furthermore, so very important in the entire biblical tradition as a basis of Israel's religion and history that it was felt to be quite unnecessary to detract in any way from his greatness and originality by situating another point of departure prior to him. This could only have happened if the facts had demanded it. Popular tradition is, however, generally inclined to make a complete division between the founder of the nation and its religion and the period which preceded him, so that the greatness of this one man is all the more apparent.

Yet the story of the patriarchs itself, since it is so clearly orientated towards the future, provides strong evidence that the real point of departure for Israel's national history is to be found elsewhere. According to Israel's own testimony, her deliverance from Egypt was the beginning of her independent existence as a nation. Faith in Yahweh was the creative principle of the Israelitic community— it marked the beginning and the creation of Israel as a community. Yahweh and Israel formed an indissoluble union with each other. It was in the exodus from Egypt and the journey through the desert that God and his people first found each other: "I am Yahweh thy God from the land of Egypt" (Hos. 12:9; 13:4). Yahweh was the national God of the people and the beginning of Israel's existence as a nation coincided with the fact that God revealed himself as Yahweh. Yahweh was Israel's Creator, her Father and the one who fashioned or modeled Israel, but he was this because he *redeemed* Isreal; the name Yahweh is inseparably bound up with the deliverance of Israel from Egypt. "In the day when I chose Israel and lifted up my hand (= swore an oath) for the race of the house of Jacob, and made myself known to them in the land of Egypt and lifted up my hand for them, saying: I am Yahweh thy God" (Ezek. 20:5). Hosea also alludes to Yahweh's love for Israel at this time: "When Israel was a child, I loved him: and I called my son out of Egypt" (Hos. 11:1), and "I found Israel like grapes in the desert,

I saw their fathers like the first-fruits of the fig-tree" (9:10). Jeremiah reproaches Israel for unfaithfulness, lamenting that no one ever asked: "Where is Yahweh, that made us to come up out of the land of Egypt, that led us through the desert?" (Jer. 2:6). How different it was in the beginning—"I (Yahweh) have remembered thee, pitying thy youth and the love of thy espousals, when thou followdst me into the desert." Then, observes Jeremiah, Israel was "holy to Yahweh, the first-fruits of his increase" (2:2-3). This thought is summed up by the psalmist:

> When Israel went out of Egypt
>   the house of Jacob from a barbarous people:
> Judah was made his sanctuary,
>   Israel his dominion (Ps. 113:1-2; *cf*. Deut. 32:6-12).

It is clear, then, that a completely new phase began, with the appearance of Moses, in the history of salvation. This is emphatically born out, in a biblical manner, by the fact that God, who had made himself known to the patriarchs as the almighty God ('ēl šaddai), now revealed himself for the first time as Yahweh (Exod. 6:3). How Yahweh announced this name to Moses and explained its significance is recounted in detail in the story of the burning bush (Exod. 3:13-15). These verses aim to stress the importance of the cycle of redemption. They provide no answer at all to the purely historical question of where the name Yahweh came from. Should there be any doubt on this account, it should be remembered that there was in existence another biblical tradition—equally disinterested in the purely historical aspect—according to which the origin of the name Yahweh went back to the very earliest period, when the first man to begin to "call upon the name of Yahweh" was Enos, Adam's grandson (Gen. 4:26). There is otherwise no conclusive, factual evidence from which we may be sure that the name Yahweh existed before the time of Moses.

The vexed question of the name "Yahweh" cannot be adequately dealt with in a few pages. So much has been written about the origin of the name, the place and period of its source, its original form and pronunciation, and its derivation that it would be easier to write a whole book on the subject. But, although the Bible does appear to provide some information about a few of these questions, the general opinion today is that if the real meaning of these biblical facts is to be found, we must approach them from a completely different direction. Most scholars now accept that the use of the name Yahweh expresses first and foremost Israel's consciousness or sense of God, not her linguistic knowledge. The most important consideration, then, is the theological and didactic expression of Israel's faith concerning the *nature* and *essence* of her national God, contained in the word and its usage. The philological and historical details of the *word* itself are now seen to be of secondary importance. This more recent approach to the problem has, however, given rise to a lively controversy among biblical scholars over the exact nature of Israel's view of God as expressed in Scripture by the use of this name.

2. *The Idea of Names in the Ancient Near East*

The number of names used in the Bible is so great that it is fairly easy to ascertain their nature and meaning. Whenever a name was associated in Scripture with a definite word, it was in no way necessary for the two to have any linguistic affinity. What was necessary, however, was that the sound or form of the name should remind the hearer or reader of that word. In the Bible—as in all cases of popular etymology—the apparent connection between a name and a word, enabling the two to be spontaneously associated in the mind, was always much more important than any purely etymological connection between them. The Hebrew *'ādhām* (man) is, for example, easily associated with *'adhāmāh* (ground). Similarly,

'iššāh (woman) would at first sight appear to be the feminine form
of *'iš* (man). From the linguistic point of view, however, these pairs
of words have very little or nothing at all to do with each other. Up
to and including the Middle Ages, such combinations—often highly
artificial—were very popular, and often extensively used for didactic
purposes. In the Bible, however, they were used to express something which is essentially quite different.

If we are to come to an understanding of what the Bible was
seeking to express here, we must constantly bear in mind that,
according to the ancient view, a name represented the thing or the
person itself and formed a single, natural entity with this thing or
person. The name was not simply an expression of the being. It
was charged with it. This has to do with the way in which man
thought in the ancient Near East. He approached things in their
concrete totality, and thus in their existential situation. In the first
place, he did not concentrate his attention on the thing as he perceived it, abstracting it from everything else as we do, and seeing
simply one aspect of the whole. In the second place, he saw the
thing as a dynamic point of intersection in the rhythm of life and
in the combination of dynamic forces of the entire environment.
In the ancient, oriental world, then, human thoughts and plans were
far more closely related to act and reality than they are now, with
our modern, abstract way of thinking. This applies even more to
the spoken word—the ancient, oriental formulae of curses and
blessings had something of the irrevocable in them, and contained
a power which gave shape and form to the reality.

A name, then, was a word of particular intensity. It could not be
divorced from the person or thing with which it was linked. The
person lived in his name and indeed survived in this name. The
Israelite died with the reassurance that his name would live on in
his posterity or at least in an enduring sepuchral monument.
Absalom, for example, had the stone pillar, which stands in the
King's Valley and is still known as "Absalom's monument," set up

during his lifetime for himself, for, as he said, "I have no son; and this shall be the monument of my name." That was why he called the stone by his own name (2 Sam. 18:18). The greatest calamity that could befall anyone was that his name should be wiped out or that he should remain unburied and that his corpse should serve to manure the fields and feed the birds and wild animals and that no one should drive them away (Jer. 7:33). This also implies that there would be no one to mourn him, to cut themselves for him or to break bread or to give the cup of consolation to his relatives (Jer. 16:6f.). It was said of King Jehoiachin that his corpse would be cast out into the heat of the day and the frost of the night, and that no one would mourn his death, saying: "Alas, my brother, and alas, sister!" or "Alas, lord or alas the noble one!" (Jer. 36:30; 22;18).

In the Babylonian Epic of Creation, "not to be named" and "to have no name" are similar to "not to exist." This emerges clearly from the opening lines of the poem:

> When above the heaven had not yet received a name,
> when beneath the earth had no name . . .
> when there were still no bushes or reeds,
> when none of the gods existed,
> when no name and no destiny had been established . . .

According to this view, a great deal of importance is attached to the knowledge of the name of the divinity, and indeed to the importance of knowing as many of his names as possible. The ancient world was full of the magic of names. The apotheosis of this particular poem consists of the solemn proclamation, in chorus by the assembled gods, of the fifty names of the creator-god Marduk, the god of the city of Babel. This is followed by an admonition to learn these names by heart and to impress them upon the minds of children. The invocation of the god, by pronouncing and repeating his name in a loud voice, if necessary to the point of hysteria (*see* 1 Kings 18:28f.), had as it were a compulsive effect. A knowledge of the god's name implied a power over the god himself and thus an assurance that one's prayer would be heard. The revelation of a new name opened up new possibilities. Certain divine powers could be set into motion if this new name were known. Each name gave access to a particular aspect of the divine mystery and this part of the mystery would, within the defined limits of the name, be revealed to man.

Many biblical passages can be seen in much sharper relief against this ancient, oriental background. Yahweh had this to say about the "Angel of the Exodus": "Take notice of him, and here his voice, and do not think him one to be condemned; for he will not forgive when thou hast sinned, *for my name is in him*" (Exod. 23:21). It is obvious that he intended this warning to be taken most seriously, since this "angel" appears regularly, in theophanies, throughout the cycle of the redemption and is certainly a personification of Yahweh himself. He was that aspect of Yahweh which was directed to man, Yahweh in his intervention into the sublunar world (Exod. 3:2, 4; Gen. 16:7, 48:15f. and so on). The Bible is full of statements which on the one hand reveal God's immanence and on the other hand proclaim the immeasurable distance between God and man. In addition to the "Angel of Yahweh" and the "Glory of Yahweh," the "Name of Yahweh" occurs frequently in Scripture, and this is perhaps the most important of all these expressions, especially when it is used in connection with Yahweh's dwelling in the inner sanctuary, and in Jerusalem.

The ark was called after "the Name of Yahweh of hosts . . ., who sitteth over it upon the cherubim," and this Name was invoked upon the ark (2 Sam. 6:2). His Name was also invoked, in the same way, in the temple at Jerusalem—the house of Yahweh, or "the house . . . in which the Name of Yahweh has been called upon" (*see* Jer. 7:11). The temple was built "to the Name of Yahweh" (2 Sam. 7:13). Yahweh wished "his Name . . . to dwell in it," that "his name should be there" (Deut. 12:5, 11, 21, and so on). It was felt so strongly that the Name of Yahweh was identical with Yahweh himself that the need was occasionally felt to formulate this idea in a theological definition. An example of this is to be found in the prayer of Solomon, used in the dedication of the temple:

Is it then to be thought that God should indeed dwell upon the earth? For if heaven, and the heaven of heavens, cannot contain thee, how much less this house which I have built? But have regard to the prayer of thy servant . . . that *thy eyes* may be *open upon this house* night and day; upon the house of which thou hast said: my Name shall be there . . . That thou mayest hearken to the supplication of thy servant and of thy people Israel, whatsoever they shall pray for in this place: and hear them in *heaven, in the place where thou dwellest* (1 Kings 8:27–30).

It should now be easier to understand the implication of the second commandment: "Thou shalt not take the Name of Yahweh in vain" (Exod. 20:7), and Israel's later fear of pronouncing the Name of Yahweh. In Leviticus we find the statement: "He that *blasphemeth* the Name of Yahweh, let him die." In the Greek translation (LXX, made in the third to second century B.C.), this is rendered as: "He that *pronounceth* the Name of the Lord, let him die" (Lev. 24:16). This introduces another factor into the problem.

In the postexilic period, the Jews became more conscious of God's transcendence and the name Yahweh tended to become the characteristic expression of this transcendental sense of God. This inclination to avoid the Name can be detected in the Hebrew Bible, especially in the substitution of the word *'elōhîm* (the general word for god in the Semitic languages) for the Name. This is to be found, for example, almost without exception, in the so-called Elohistic Books of the psalms (41–82). Very little, however, could be done about this, in view of the fact that the growing awe of the Name happened to coincide with the growing inviolability of the

Hebrew text of the Bible in its purely consonantal form. Yet almost every page of the Septuagint testifies to the extent of this desire to avoid the Name, which was rendered by the word *kurios* (lord). This practice was followed in the Vulgate (*dominus*) and in most later translations (*cf* our "Lord"). The fact that the Hebrew synagogues have followed the practice of the Greek Jews in this has been put forward in defence of this argument. The current view, however, that it was already customary at that time, in the synagogues, to replace the Name by the word *'adhōnāi*, the Hebrew for "lord," seems more acceptable. This is also borne out in the Greek translation.

Around the eighth century A.D., the exact pronunciation of Hebrew was established by the Massoretic system of points and strokes, indicating especially the vowels in the hitherto consonantal text. Advantage was taken of this system of vocalization to furnish certain words (which had to be read differently from the way in which they were written), with the vowels of the word to be read. In this way, it was possible to indicate where alterations or emendations ought to be made in various parts of the text. The Massoretic scholars did not, however, touch the inviolable, consonantal text (*kethîbh*), but, wherever they preferred a different reading, attached to the written consonants of the *kethibh* vowels which in many cases did not strictly belong to the word at all. They thus drew attention to the word as it was to be read. As a rule, the consonants of this emended reading (*qerê*) were placed in the margin. Now the most notorious case of *qerê-kethîbh* is that of the name Yahweh. The consonants of this name (*y-h-w-h*) were furnished with the vowels of the word *'adhonai*, lord. These vowels were *e-o-a*, since *'adhonai* begins with the guttural *'aleph*, after which the normal *šewa*, or indistinct e, is pronounced as a (*ḥaṭeph-pathaḥ*). This word, *'adhonai*, occurs some 7,000 times in the text and, for obvious reasons, the consonants do not appear once in the margin (*qerê perpetuum*).

It was during the Middle Ages that the still widely known, but completely unhistorical pronunciation *Jehovah* came into being.

3. The Biblical Etymology of the Name Yahweh

The sacred writers attached such importance to names because for them any association between names was indicative of an association between the things named—a verbal association revealed a real, objective association. The ultimate object of names was to say something about real relationships. The relationships which existed in the mind of the people between words or names were expressive of something that appealed to men of that time more than they do to us. For example, the biblical doctrine that man is by nature a material being, destined for the grave, was powerfully borne out by the striking similarity between the words *'ādhām* and *'adhāmāh*. In the same account, the teaching on the relationship between man and woman was illustrated, confirmed, and more easily memorized by the apparent connection between the words *'îš* and *'iššāh*.

The first thing that we must bear in mind concerning the biblical use of the name Yahweh is that here, too, it is not really a question of words, but of the reality itself. Inspiration is not a philological charisma, implying that the dedicated writer was bound to know the meaning of the *word* "Yahweh." It is a charisma of faith, ensuring that his sense of God was pure and that he expressed this sense of God correctly. The writer's linguistic theory was a means of helping to make clear the intrinsic worth of Yahweh himself. Since the ancient, oriental mind conceived a god to *be* what he *was called* and worth what his name was worth, the sacred writer—for this reason and for this reason alone—let it be seen that what he wanted to establish in conection with Yahweh's being was clearly expressed in Yahweh's name. It does not necessarily follow from his account that the name Yahweh is in fact connected with the more or less homonymous Hebrew verb *hāyyāh,* to be. What does, however, follow is that the real meaning of the word "to be" must, in some way or another, be attributed to the God of Israel.

In one way or another, the essential problem, however, is, in precisely what way? The exact way in which Yahweh "is" is expressed in the strange and much disputed formula: "I am who am."

The writer's aim was to show how the Name was connected with the formula. He succeeded in doing this in such an ingenious way that it is at the same time clear that this Yahweh was the same as the God of the patriarchs. The dialogue between Yahweh and Moses can be set out schematically thus:

MOSES: I shall go to the children of Israel and say to them:
      a. *The God of your fathers sends me . . .*
           then they shall ask:
      b. What is his name?
           What shall I say to them?
YAHWEH: c. I am who am.
           Thou shalt say:
      d. *I am sends me.*
           Thou shalt say:
      e. *Yahweh, the God of your fathers . . . sends me.*
      f. This is my Name for ever;
           thus shall I be named
           from generation to generation (Exod. 3:13–15).

This schematic arrangement is self-explanatory. Killing two birds with one stone, the writer shows Yahweh as identified with the God of the patriarchs and at the same time achieves the more important task of bridging the gulf between "Yahweh" (e) and the long formula (c) which contains what the writer has to say concerning Yahweh's being, by means of the short formula "I am" (c). The three sentences b, c, and f belong to each other. The intervening

sentences d and e, which are synonymous, serve as steps by which
the hearer is able to come from the complete name (c) to the customary name and at the same time serve the purpose of identifying
Yahweh with the God of the patriarchs.

There can be no doubt that the sacred writer represented the
name Yahweh (y-h-w-h) as having been derived from the verb "to
be" (h-y-h, in its archaic or dialect form, as well as in Aramaic,
h-w-h; thus *hawwah—Eve* interpreted as *ḥāyyāh*—living or giving
life). The third person singular, masculine of "to be" is, in Hebrew,
normally formed in the imperfect by the addition of the preforma-
tive (yi-, ye-, ya-), in which case the Name meant "he is" and,
according to popular etymology, the teaching was that Israel's God
"is."

The doctrinal content of the passage is, however, not fully explained even when the meaning of the word "to be" has been established in a similar, biblical context. In this case, "to be" is more
precisely defined by the whole statement, "I am who am" (*'eheyeh
'aśer 'eheyeh*) and the shortened form of this statement—"I am"
(*'eheyeh*)—is the only one which is appropriate to Yahweh as the
speaker. He could scarcely have said, referring to himself, "he is."
The third person singular, masculine of this abbreviated form is
yiheyeh (he is). The archaic form of *yiheyeh*, arrived at from the
most recent, available data, is *yaheweh*, and this is in fact the pronunciation of y-h-w-h which has been rediscovered from and confirmed by certain Greek sources. Some of the Greek Fathers mention the pronunciation *iabē*, or *iaoue*, and the artificial magic spell,
composed of all the vowels—*iaōouēe*—is preserved in certain Greek
papyri. The remaining facts concerning the pronunciation of the
Name amount to this. The Hebrew Bible has the short form *yāh*,
which occurs especially in the invocation *hallelûyāh*, "praise Yahweh," and many proper names, alluding to Yahweh, either begin
with *yehō-* or *yô-* or end in *-yahû* or *-yah*. Furthermore, Yahweh is

always called Yahû or Yahô (y-h-w) in the Elephantine papyri. Finally, there is the causative explanation which many supported in the past—"he causes to be," hence he gives life, he creates, and so on. This explanation is generally regarded nowadays as untenable, and can be disregarded.

The sacred writer thus conceived the name Yahweh to be an evocation of the longer formula, with the result that his dogmatic aim was completely dependent upon the meaning of this formula. There is no unanimity of opinion concerning the meaning of this formula, but there are only two opinions, or rather tendencies, which can really be of any help in the question of its interpretation, though the leading protagonists on each side have maneuvered themselves into a position from which their views now seem to be mutually exclusive. So much that is valid is contained in each of these two interpretations, and so much of both fits in admirably with many sets of biblical data, that to take sides in this dispute must inevitably result in an impoverishment of the full scope of the texts in question and in a certain one-sidedness. This is hardly to be wondered at, in the case of a complex subject such as this, with its long history and many ramifications, even within the Bible itself. The wisest and safest course would seem to be not to tie oneself down too soon to any one of these opinions, but to adhere firmly to the solid facts adduced by each side, and to stop short at the point where they part company with each other. In this way, one may learn from both sides and at the same time remain open to the possibility of a synthesis of the two.

4. Not an Exclusive Sense of God's Distance

If we follow the first of these two opinions to its ultimate conclusion, then it is of no importance to go into the biblical meaning of the divine "being." The Name ought to imply exclusively that the name and thus the being and essence of Israel's God was completely inaccessible to mortals. This undoubtedly constitutes one element of Israel's sense of God, but it does not by any means express this sense fully. It is true that the passage from Exodus which we have been considering does not necessarily say everything that there is to say on this subject, but it would be too risky to limit what it has to say simply to this. All the related biblical texts to which one can refer here demand a wider interpretation, and those scholars who favor the second opinion have brought forward other texts as evidence that Israel was positively bound to hear from the Name that Yahweh "is."

The arguments on both sides are well worth considering, since they are capable of giving us a better insight into the nature of Israel's sense of God. This was certainly marked by a lively feeling for the unbridgeable distance existing between the divine and the sublunar world of man. This feeling was in fact so strong that it is unlikely that Yahweh would have conveyed the nature of his essence to Israel simply and solely in his name. Again and again we come up against the idea that man cannot behold Yahweh or even hear his voice. It is impossible for man to stand firm in Yahweh's presence. He cannot survive the experience of Yahweh. Yahweh is too powerful for him—he is as a consuming fire. When Gideon realized who it was with whom he had been speaking, he said: "Alas, my Lord Yahweh; for I have seen the angel of Yahweh face to face!" Yahweh's answer was: "Peace be with thee. Fear not, thou shalt not die." The altar which Gideon built there for Yahweh he called "Yahweh (is) Peace" (Judges 6:22–24).

The standard term in Scripture for this specifically divine quality of Yahweh's is "holiness." Any encounter with Yahweh's holiness at once made man conscious of his own frailty and sinfulness. He was at once aware of the fact that he was a creature, and indeed an unclean creature. The vision of Isaiah is the outstanding example of this:

In the year that King Uzziah died, I saw the Lord sitting upon a throne high and elevated: and the hems of his garment filled the temple.

Above him stood the seraphim: one had six wings, and the other had six wings: with two they covered his face, and with two they covered his feet, and with two they flew. And they cried to one another, and said:

> Holy, holy, holy
> is Yahweh of hosts,
> all the earth is full of his glory.
> And the lintels of the doors were moved
> at the voice of him that cried:
> and the house was filled with smoke.

and I said:

> Woe to me, because I,
> a man of unclean lips, dwelling in the midst
> of a people with unclean lips,
> I have seen with my own eyes the King,
> Yahweh of hosts (Isa. 6:1–5).

No attempt to describe Yahweh is ever made in the Bible. His presence is indicated indirectly, though quite unmistakably, by his environment. In this case, we are told of his throne, surrounded by seraphs—this throne, or ark, of the temple is, of course, the heavenly throne—and the hem of his garment or train, which always played a special part in the Bible and elsewhere as a personal cachet.

Moses was permitted to approach Yahweh, but the seventy ancients of Israel who had come up with him were obliged to remain at a distance:

And they saw the God of Israel: and it was as if under his feet lay a work of sapphire stone, as the heaven when clear. Neither did he lay his hand upon those of the children of Israel that retired afar off. And they saw God, and they did eat and drink (Exod. 24:10; *see also* Ezek. 1:22, 26–28; 10:1).

Moses and Elijah were both favored with remarkably similar theophanies, and it is from these that we gain a clear insight into Israel's feeling for God:

He (Elijah) came to a cave (on Horeb, the mountain of God), where he spent the night. And behold, the word of Yahweh came unto him, and he said to him: What dost thou here, Elijah? And he answered: With zeal have I been zealous for Yahweh, the God of hosts . . . And he (Yahweh) said to him: Go forth, and stand upon the mount before the face of Yahweh. And behold, when Yahweh was to pass, a great and strong wind came before Yahweh, overthrowing the mountains and breaking the rocks in pieces. Yahweh was not in the wind. And after the wind an earthquake. Yahweh was not in the earthquake. And after the earthquake a fire. Yahweh was not in the fire. And after the fire a whistling of a gentle air. And when Elijah heard this, he covered his face with his mantle, and coming forth stood in the entrance of the cave. And behold, a voice came unto him, saying: What dost thou here, Elijah? And he answered: With zeal have I been zealous for Yahweh, the God of hosts (1 Kings 19:9–14).

It may be noted, in passing, that the "afternoon breeze" mentioned in the paradise story might possibly have the object of making known to the first two human beings the presence of Yahweh *'elōhîm* (*see also* 2 Sam. 5:24).

An even more graphic illustration is provided by Yahweh's appearance to Moses, as a preparation for the revelation of the decalogue on worship (Exod. 34:14–26), and the comparable encounter between Yahweh and Moses which led to the revelation of the "ethical" decalogue (Exod. 20:1–17; Deut. 5:6–21). So close is the parallel between these two theophanies—both accounts allude to the same realities (compare Exod. 34:27f. with 24:7f.)—that the following quotation should be sufficient in itself to show how inadequate the first opinion in fact is.

(Moses said:) Shew me thy glory. He (Yahweh) answered: I will make my splendour to pass before thee, and I will *proclaim the name Yahweh before thee:* and I will have mercy on whom I will, and I will be merciful to whom it shall please me. And again he said: Thou canst not see my face: for no man shall see me and live. And again he said: Behold, there is a place with me, and thou shalt stand upon the rock. And when my glory shall pass, I will set thee in a hole of the rock, and protect thee with my hand, till I pass. And I will take away my hand, and thou shalt see my back parts, but my face thou shalt not see.

And Yahweh came down in a cloud, stood by him and *proclaimed the name Yahweh.* Yahweh passed before him and called out:

> Yahweh, Yahweh, God merciful and gracious,
> patient and of much compassion and true,
> who keepest mercy unto thousands,
> who takest away iniquity, wickedness and sin,
> but who leaves nothing unpunished,
> and visits the iniquity of the fathers
> upon the children and the grandchildren,
> unto the third and fourth generation.

And Moses making haste, bowed down prostrate unto the earth, and said: If I have found grace in thy sight, Yahweh, then go thou Yahweh with us . . . and possess us. Yahweh answered: Behold, I will make a covenant . . . the whole people will see the work of Yahweh (Exod. 33:18–23; 34:5–10).

The revelation of the Name Yahweh and the theophany are one and the same in this case. The revelation of the Name, however, defines the content of the theophany and, since this is the theophany of the Covenant, it also defines the meaning of the Covenant for Israel and shows why the God of the patriarchs made himself known to Israel as Yahweh.

5. A Full Consciousness Also of God's Nearness

A strong sense of God's distance from man emerges from these texts. This is, of course, why those who support the first view quote them extensively. But there is, at the same time, great emphasis upon Yahweh's nearness to man, and it is precisely the connection between God's transcendence and his immanence which constitutes the dynamic force of these passages: there is a limitless distance between God and man, but it is bridged. No mortal is permitted to approach Yahweh. Yet Isaiah, Elijah, and Moses come close to him and they do so in the most stupendous way. This is exactly what the sacred writers frequently attempted to do. By stressing the great distance between Yahweh and man, they wished to reveal the full extent and deep implication of his immanence and, at the same time, to make known the exceptional privilege enjoyed by these three great figures in Israel's history. Yahweh had to tone down the full splendor of his being, but he did not in any way withdraw himself from these men. On the contrary, they were granted something which was always hidden from ordinary mortals.

This is reflected very clearly in the passage from Exodus quoted above. Yahweh promised to *proclaim the Name Yahweh* before Moses. What we have here is a special dispensation of grace, in which Yahweh promised to reveal his Name, in the recognized biblical sense of the word. The revelation did in fact occur. It took place literally and explicitly. Yahweh uttered his Name twice and then listed the familiar series of divine attributes (Exod. 20:5f.; Num. 14:18; Deut. 5:9f., 7:9f.). These attributes express above all Yahweh's immanence—both in the avenging and the beneficent sense—and at the same time they constitute the concrete meaning and content of Yahweh's Name and being, that is, they show *what Yahweh in fact is for his people* and *what he wishes to be* for them.

It should not be assumed that the formula "I am who am" does not express in one way or another the kind of God that Israel had in Yahweh, as the God of the Covenant. It is generally agreed that for Israel the name Yahweh was charged with the idea of the Covenant. Again and again this Name set, as it were, the seal both on Yahweh's promises and on his demands. Indissolubly bound up with Israel's redemption, the Name opened for Israel unlimited opportunities of salvation, and at the same time reminded Israel of the God of Sinai, the zealous guardian of the Covenant. In the stereotyped catalog of attributes quoted above, both aspects of God's immanence are prominent and are emphasized in a striking context. This faith in Yahweh is also bound to be noticeably reflected in the only passage which avowedly attempts to formulate the quintessence of this faith in such a way that the *word* yahweh was automatically reminiscent of this faith.

Israel's consciousness of God was based on the conviction that Yahweh was as a consuming fire, but a fire which burnt in the midst of the people. It would seem that the reason why the sacred writers of the Bible placed so much stress on Yahweh's unapproachable holiness is because they wished to bring out the full significance of the fact that he was deeply concerned with Israel. His holiness was well known. It was the experience of his immanence which caused amazement.

Behold, Yahweh our God hath shown us his majesty and his greatness: we have heard his voice out of the midst of the fire, and have seen this day that God speaketh with a man, and that man hath lived.

Why shall we die therefore? For this exceeding great fire shall consume us: for if we hear the voice of Yahweh our God any more, we shall die. What mortal is there, that he should hear the voice of the living God, who speaketh out of the midst of the fire, as we have heard, and be able to live? (Deut. 5:24–26; *see also* Exod. 20:19).

This text tells us of the terrifying nearness of the transcendental holiness. Elsewhere in the Bible this holiness is the source of Israel's courage and national confidence: "Neither is there any other nation so great, that hath gods *so near* to them, as our God, Yahweh, is present to all our petitions" (Deut. 4:7). Or, more fully elaborated:

Ask of the days of old, that have been before thy time from the day that God created man upon the earth: ask from one end of heaven to the other end thereof, if ever there was done the like thing, or it hath been known at any time.

Hath ever a people heard the voice of God speaking out of the midst of fire, as thou hast heard, and lived?

Hath ever a god done so as to go, and take to himself a nation out of the midst of nations . . . as Yahweh your God did for you in Egypt, before thy eyes?

Thou hast seen these things, that thou mightest know that Yahweh is the one God: and there is no other besides him.

From heaven he made thee to hear his voice, that he might teach thee. And upon earth he shewed thee his exceeding great fire: and thou didst hear his words out of the midst of the fire.

Because he loved thy fathers, and chose their seed after them, he brought thee out of Egypt, going before thee with his great power . . .

Know therefore this day, and think in thy heart that Yahweh is the one God in heaven above and in the earth beneath, and there is no other (Deut. 4:32–39).

It is again and again evident that it was the early experiences of Israel as a nation which formed this consciousness of God's immanence. This emerges too from David's prayer of thanksgiving:

Therefore thou art magnified, Lord Yahweh, because there is none like to thee: neither is there any God besides thee, in all the things we have heard with our ears.

And what nation is there upon earth, as thy people Israel, whom God went to redeem for a people to himself, and to make him a name . . . before the face of thy people, whom thou redeemest to thyself out of Egypt, from the nations and their gods?

For thou hast confirmed to thyself thy people Israel to be an everlasting people: and thou, Yahweh, art become to them as a God (2 Sam. 7:22–24).

The passage in which Yahweh reveals his name to Israel, seen in the context of Israel's national redemption, clearly needs to be given an interpretation which corresponds with Israel's sense of God, as based upon Yahweh's great acts. The whole cycle of Israel's redemption certainly provides an account of these acts, and the intention is to keep this sense of God alive in the minds of later generations.

6. *"Why Dost Thou Ask My Name"?*

The many texts quoted do little more than provide the general framework into which the declaration by Yahweh of his name has to fit. There are, however, two texts which offer a much closer comparison, in that both deal with theophanies and in each case the man to whom the theophany is granted asks the name of the supernatural being whose presence he experiences. In both texts there is a refusal to go more deeply into this question, and for this reason it is tempting to see, in Yahweh's declaration of his name—again an answer to a question, asking his name—a similar refusal.

The first text is that which tells us of Jacob's struggle with the mysterious stranger. Unable to overcome him, he eventually asked Jacob to let him go, for day was breaking. Jacob, however, answered: "I will not let thee go except thou bless me." The stranger then asked Jacob: "What is thy name"? When Jacob replied that he was called Jacob, the stranger answered that he would henceforth be known, not as Jacob, but as Israel, having struggled with God and with men and having gained a victory over them. Now it was Jacob's turn to ask what the stranger's name was. The reply that he received was: "Why dost thou ask my name"? This must almost certainly mean: "How canst thou—how darest thou—ask such a question"? The stranger gave Jacob his blessing, and the passage continues with the information that Jacob called the place Penuel ("the face of God"), for he had seen God face to face and was still alive (Gen. 32:23–32).

In the second text, Samuel's father Manoah received exactly the same answer. His wife had told him that a man of God had come to her, in appearance like an angel, full of glory. She had not dared, however, to ask him where he had come from or what his name was. When this man of God appeared for a second time to Manoah's wife, Manoah took advantage of the opportunity to ask him bluntly: "What is thy name"? The answer was: "Why dost thou ask my name, which is wonderful"? (By "wonderful" is meant, clearly, beyond human comprehension.) Then Manoah offered a sacrifice to Yahweh "who doth wonderful things," and, as the flame went up to heaven from the altar, the angel of Yahweh ascended in it. Manoah understood then that the visitor had been Yahweh's angel and said to his wife: "We shall certainly die, because we have seen God" (Judges 13).

The theophanies of Jacob, Manoah, and Moses have this basic similarity: in all three there is a question regarding the name of the visitor. In the first two cases, the answer takes the form of a refusal, expressed in more or less the same words. This explicit refusal is not present in the case of the third theophany. Instead we have the reply: "I am who am." Is this also a refusal? The formula is not entirely clear and it has, of course, been the subject of much controversy and thus an unfavorable point of departure for an interpretation of the whole passage. A safer and more methodical approach would be to begin the other way round, that is, first of all to ask what the object and meaning of the passage really is, and then to try to understand the formula from that perspective.

At first sight it would seem as if a positive answer is given, in the passage as a whole, to the question "What is thy name"? The reply is, after all, "Yahweh." But this is a *new* name, here, introduced for the first time, into the story. This would appear to condemn in advance any exegesis which does not proceed from the evidence that what we are dealing with here is an original account, authentically biblical and thus significant, of the fact that Israel's God was called Yahweh. Irrespective of the means employed, the fact remains that the account *had* to communicate this new name. The problem, then, is whether a possible refusal to answer the question contained in the formula can be reconciled with this fact. It does not seem to be completely unfeasible, though as yet no one has attempted to approach the difficulty from this viewpoint. What the passage aims to say, then, is both yes and no at the same time. This is, after all, not an altogether absurd situation in a case where men are talking about the nature of God. If the answer is possibly "no," then some kind of "yes" must be contained in the formula, in view of the fact that the formula is a definition of the new name. Let us, however, leave the possibility of a refusal, and go a little more deeply into the established fact that a new name was revealed to Moses.

Whatever was refused to Moses was clearly different from what was refused to Jacob and Manoah. This much is obvious, since, although all three phrased their question in the same words, they did not by any means imply the same question. Both Jacob and Manoah had an intimation as to who it was with whom they were concerned, but neither knew for certain. Their question: "What is thy name"? amounted in fact to "Who art thou really"? Here, a refusal to answer was strictly in place. God shows his grace to whom he will. Man's part is to wait for this grace. God may show himself with astonishing and compelling certainty. He may, on the other hand, show himself only through signs which merely suggest his presence, signs which are enough to give those to whom they are revealed a basis for their faith in the future (*see, for example,* Luke 24: the disciples on the road to Emmaus). In cases such as this, it is only later that those who are given these signs become conscious of what has really happened. This, of course, is vividly illustrated in the account of the theophany revealed to Moses—we are told how Moses saw Yahweh only from behind, when he had passed before him (Exod. 33:23). In many cases, the spell would have been broken if God had revealed himself too fully. Both Jacob and Manoah were not aware until afterwards who it was with whom they had spoken, and then they were extremely disturbed by the realization. In both cases, there was tension in the dialogue because the partner was unknown. It was the identity of this partner which was the vital issue at stake. A final and unambiguous sign was given, in each case, at the end of the encounter.

Moses could not, nor did he need to ask the same question as Jacob and Manoah. God told him more or less at once who he was —"I am the God of thy fathers." At this, Moses hid his face, not daring to look at God (*see* Exod. 3:6). In other words, this theophany begins at the precise point at which the other two end. This essential difference is bound to change the whole content of the question "What is thy name"? In this case, the question formed part of a dialogue, the object of which, on Moses' side, was not to ascertain the identity of the one with whom he was conversing, but to find out for certain the task that the other was giving him and the redemption that he was promising.

A few years later, when Moses' courage was waning, he was favored with a special theophany, in which Yahweh's name and being were unmistakably revealed. Elijah, whose representation as a second Moses was not accidental, had a similar encounter with Yahweh at a time when he was completely disheartened. This theophany aimed to strengthen Moses in his task and to give him a guarantee of authenticity for the incredible news he was to bring to his people.

If Moses had said: "The God of your fathers sends me," the people would have been expected to ask: "What is his name"? The sacred writer could not have implied in this question: "Who is he"? for the people knew that he was the already familiar God of the patriarchs. There was no doubt as to the identity of this God. What the people would have doubted was his power and readiness to fulfill his incredible promises. They needed a special guarantee and this could, in the ancient view, be provided by a new name. (There can be no doubt at all that the sacred writer was conscious of the guarantee contained in the new name.) A new name, then, and the guarantee which it contained, could make a totally new appeal to the divine possible. On a basis of a new name, new things could be expected of God. The usual name, God of the fathers, was simply not enough. As El Shaddai, this God had certainly guided and helped the patriarchs (*see* Exod. 6:3), but he had apparently left the descendants of the patriarchs in Egypt for four centuries without help. Something quite new was needed to stimulate the people in a situation of this kind, which had continued unchanged for as long as men could recall.

If we regard the formula as a pure refusal to answer the question, then "I am who am" does not fit into the situation, in two ways. In the first place, it would be an evasive answer to a question which had not been asked, that is, "Who art thou"? In the second place, it is difficult to see how an evasive answer such as this could have satisfactorily strengthened the people's trust in the God of the patriarchs, for that was, in the purport of the account, the result of the revelation of the new name.

A further difficulty, already alluded to in passing, is that the passage, whatever is done to turn it, still does in fact provide a new name. It can, however, be a good method, when there is considerable disagreement over a given text, to look at the whole passage in which this particular text occurs, from a certain distance, and try to see it in a more universal context. This passage from Exodus has the object of conveying, within the entire account of Israel's history, first, how the name of Yahweh originated and second, what the name really signified.

At the time when the account was written down, Yahweh had become the familiar name of Israel's God and the property of the nation. The use of this name must therefore have originated elsewhere and at another time. What the author tells us is how this name became the name of Israel's God: it was a name revealed to Moses himself, a name directly associated with the nation's deliverance from Egypt. The name Yahweh originated at the same time as Israel's national life began to emerge. According to the account, God in fact revealed a new name. A pure refusal thus seems to be fundamentally contradictory to the general purport of the story. What emerges from the passage is precisely this name, whose origin the writer intended to convey. The conclusion of the account is also: "This is my Name for ever; thus shall I be named from generation to generation" (Exod. 3:15).

At the same time, it was also the writer's aim to explain what this new name meant. It is generally agreed that this meaning was expressed in the formula "I am who am." What we may not do in this case is to interpret the formula in such a way as to make it appear that the fact of the new name was denied, since that fact is contained in the formula. What we may, on the other hand, expect of the formula, and what we ought to look for in it, is that the meaning given to the new name by this formula was of such a kind that it was possible for the Israelites to accept the name as a guarantee that the God of their fathers would carry out all that he had promised to them.

7. The Meaning of Divine "Being" in the Bible

We must now turn to the second of the two opinions on the subject of the name Yahweh and divine "being" in the Bible. The great advantage that it has over the first opinion is that it certainly coincides with the expectations aroused by the context in which the formula stands. If it is true that the formula in one way or another positively asserts that Yahweh "is," then it amounts to an assurance that he can be relied upon. Those who favor the first opinion see the verb "to be" in the formula as a copula, a verb linking subject with predicate (to be this or that, to be such and such). This is not a very plausible view, as a glance at any reputable dictionary will prove at once, and, even assuming that it is correct, it must mean that the whole passage revolves around the question of Yahweh's identity—"Who art thou"?—and that the answer can only be understood as an evasive tautology—"Yahweh is what he is." According to the second opinion, "to be" is an independent verb, with the meaning of "there is." Seen in this way, the crucial point is not the inaccessible mystery, *who* Yahweh is, but the unshakable certainty *that* he is there. There can be no doubt at all that the most accurate definition that can be given of Yahweh, on a strictly biblical basis and, even more particularly, on a basis of Old Testament prophetism, is that he is a God who really is—he was there in so real a sense that both his promises and his threats had to be taken seriously. This is not only the outstanding characteristic of Israel's God. It is also the feeling expressed by his Name.

This real "being" of Yahweh is not the "being" of the philosopher. The Old Testament was not concerned with philosophical concepts, but with spontaneous thoughts and ideas. These can certainly form a basis and a point of departure for philosophical speculation, but they are not in themselves a philosophical attempt to comprehend reality. The Bible does contain implicit philosophical concepts, but it is up to the philosopher to discover these for himself. Israel's belief that Yahweh "is" only appears to coincide with the philosophical definition of God as the one who exists independently in and through himself (*aseitas*) and who is the fullness of "being" (*actus purus*). There is certainly a connection between the two; there is also, even within the framework of the Bible itself, a development from the spontaneous to the reflective. The Bible provides a starting point for theology, a point from which theological speculation is able to proceed quite harmoniously, and it is possible to detect, in the last stages of Israel's religion, under the influence of Greek thought, a certain philosophical element. This is something that the Christian philosopher was able eagerly to seize. A well-known example of this is the Greek translation of the Exodus formula—"I am the Being" (*Egō eimi ho ōn*). This translation reflects the speculative faith of the Greek translator more than it does the original evidence of Exodus.

Yahweh's "being" in the Bible naturally presupposes his existence, but Yahweh's "existence" is not the real object of the evidence given so often and with such emphasis in Scripture. The dedicated writers were not aiming their words at unbelievers, but at those who were heedless of God and his commandments, and at those who turned for safety to other gods.

> The sinner with his nose in the air (thinks):
>> He will not call me to account;
> All his thoughts are:
>> There is no God (Ps. 10:4).

The meaning of the second half of this verse is clear from the first half: that God does not exist implies that he does not concern himself with men. The sinner feels that he is able to oppress the righteous without fear of punishment:

> For he hath said in his heart: God hath forgotten;
> he hath turned away his face, not to see it in the end
>> (Ps. 10:11; *see also* 13:1; 52:1f.).

In confessing that Yahweh "is," the Israelite was confessing his faith in Yahweh's immanence. Yahweh's "being" was an active and effective state of being present, a presence known by his actual intervention in the affairs of men—by his salvation of the good and his punishment of the evil men.

Elisha struck the waters of the Jordan with Elijah's mantle, but the river was not divided until he cried out: "Where is Yahweh now, the God of Elijah"? (2 Kings 2:14). The question was never whether a god existed, but what he could or wished to do. A failure to intervene on Yahweh's part was always a severe test of Israel's faith, an experience made even worse by the scorn of her enemies: "Where is thy God"? (Pss. 41:4, 78:10, 113:2; see also Mic. 7:10; Joel 2:17; Judith 7:21). That is why Israel's adversity was a profanation" of Yahweh's Name among the nations (Ezek. 36; see also Exod. 32:12; Num. 14:16; Deut. 9:28). It was by helping Israel and punishing her enemies that Yahweh showed her that he "is," that is, that he was there and that he was Yahweh. There are repeated examples from Exodus 7:5 onwards.

The gods whose cities were conquered by the Assyrian king had apparently been powerless to defend their subjects. The conqueror mocked them with the words: "Where are they now"? and was firmly convinced that he would soon be able to mock Yahweh too, in the same way. In contrast, Israel's faith in her God was expressed thus in the prayer of Ezechiah, who

went up to the house of Yahweh and spread it (i.e. Sennacherib's mocking letter) out before Yahweh, and prayed in his sight, saying:

Yahweh, God of Israel, who sitteth upon the cherubim, thou alone art the God of all the kingdoms of the earth. Thou madest heaven and earth.

Incline thy ear, and hear: open, Yahweh, thy eyes, and see: and hear all the words of Sennacherib sent to upbraid the living God.

Of a truth, Yahweh, the kings of the Assyrians have destroyed na-

tions and the lands of them all, and they have cast their gods into the
fire. For they were not gods, but the work of man's hands of wood and
stone: and they destroyed them.

Now therefore, Yahweh, our God, save us from his hand, that all the
kingdoms of the earth may know that thou, Yahweh, art the only God
(2 Kings 19:14–19; *see also* 18:30–35; Isa. 10:5ff.).

Unfaithful Israel was also reproached, in her turn, by her own
prophets mocking the gods in whom she had sought salvation
(Deut. 32:37; Jer. 2:28). Yahweh "is" alone in the sense that he
alone was a God who could save. The "not being" of the other gods
was above all to be found in their complete impotence and useless-
ness (1 Sam. 12:21). This contrast plays an extremely important
part in the Old Testament's feeling for God and is especially
evident in the prophets, who were constantly engaged in polemics
against polytheism. Yahweh is simply *the* God, the only God (*hû'
hā-'elōhîm:* Deut. 7:9; 2 Sam. 7:28; 1 Kings 8:60; Isa. 45:18, and so
forth). There is no other god besides him (Deut. 4:35, 39; Isa. 46:6,
8, 45:5, 6, 14, and so forth). There is no god who can be compared
to him (Exod. 15:11; Mic. 7:18; 2 Sam. 7:22; Ps. 17:32, and so
forth). He is the God of gods (Deut. 10:17; Ps. 135:2; Dan. 11:36).
He is the great God (Deut. 10:17; Neh. 8:6), the holy God (1 Sam.
6:20; Isa. 5:16), the faithful God (Deut. 7:9; 32:4; Isa. 65:16) and,
in a word, the true God (Jer. 10:10; Ps. 30:6).

These are not vain titles. Yahweh gained them one by one for
himself by his deeds. Paramount among these were his creation,
and his redemption or deliverance of Israel. Constant reference is
made to this in the Bible. He is the saving God (*see* the psalms)
and indeed the only one who can save (Hos. 13:4; Isa. 43:11, 45:15,
and so forth). He is, in the fullest sense of the word, the living God
(1 Sam. 17:26, 36; Hos. 1:10; Jer. 10:10, 23:36; Isa. 37:4. 17; Deut.
5:26; Pss. 41:3, 83:3). "By this"—by Yahweh's miraculous deeds—

"you shall know that the living God is in the midst of you" (Joshua 3:10; *see also* Num. 16:22, 27:16).

8. *Israel's Feeling for God's "Being" Expressed in the Name*

Many of these texts would suggest that it is the name Yahweh which expresses this feeling for God. When Israel's fortunes took a miraculous turn for the better, she was to know that "I am in the midst of Israel: and that I, Yahweh, am your God, and there is none other besides" (Joel 2:27). "I am Yahweh, thy God, from the land of Egypt, and thou shalt know no God but me, and there is no Redeemer beside me" (Hos. 13:4). It was by the judgment passed on Israel's enemies that it became known that Yahweh was the name of Israel's God—"thou alone art most high over all the earth" (Ps. 82:19). Yahweh's glory and his praise were intimately connected with his Name. It is for this reason that Isaiah was able to express so vividly the emotive force of the name Yahweh in this polemical passage:

> I am Yahweh: this is my name.
> I will not give my glory to another,
> nor my praise to graven images (42:8).

Chapters forty to forty-five of the book of Isaiah are, indeed, a kind of running commentary on the name Yahweh. The following passage, taken from these chapters, is illustrative of the emphatic way in which Yahweh claims this name for himself alone:

> You are my witnesses . . . and I have chosen you,
> that you may know and believe in me and understand
> that I am it (*'anī nû'*)

Before me there was no god "formed":
and after me there shall be none (*lō yih 'yeh*)
I, I am Yahweh,
and there is no savior besides me (43:10f.).

The sentence "and after me there shall be none" certainly appears
to be an allusion to the name Yahweh. It is possible to see it as
meaning: "after me, no Yahweh," for Yahweh was *one* (Deut. 6:4).
A similar play on words may also be present in Hosea. Hosea was
told to call his son "Not my people" (*lō 'ammî*) so that Israel's rejection would be exemplified in him: "for you are not my people,
and *I shall not be for you*" (*lō 'eheyeh lākhem*). What this sentence
amounts to, both literally and factually, is that he would not be
Yahweh any more for Israel. But everything was to change for the
better and, instead of saying "You are not my people" to Israel, "it
shall be said to them: you are the sons of the living God" (Hos.
1:9f.). Israel's recovery and new prosperity would be a visible and
palpable sign that Yahweh once again "is," that he was "living,"
and that he was "with them." The promise "I shall be with you,"
which occurs repeatedly from Exodus 3:12 onwards, provides the
most succinct and the clearest definition of what the Bible understood by the "being" of a god.

If it is possible to detect, in the disputed Exodus passage, the
implication that Yahweh wished *now* to be Israel's God *just as* he
had *formerly* been the God of Israel's patriarchs, then the idea of an
everlasting, unchangeable, and loyal Yahweh is clearly emphasized
in the sixteen celebrated chapters of Isaiah (40:55). Yahweh was
an everlasting God of old (Isa. 40:28); the false gods, on the other
hand, were newcomers (*see* Deut. 32:17). We have already quoted
Isaiah as saying: "Before me there was no god 'formed' and after
me there shall be none" (43:10). The standard formula in Isaiah,
however, is: "I am the First and the Last" (41:4; 44:6; 48:12). It
is clear from the context how this should be understood. In the past

—in the beginning—Yahweh performed his work of creation and accomplished Israel's redemption. These were the first, the former things (41:22; 43:9, 18; 46:9; 48:3) that he did and in which he showed himself as Yahweh. In the same way he will accomplish the last and the new things (42:9; 48:6), for he has the future as well as the past in his hands. He was always the same Yahweh. His "being" was unchangeable and eternal and it was essentially a being concerned with man.

In these chapters, Isaiah looks forward to a more speculative concept of God and prepares the way for the Greek translation of the formula "I am the being" and for St. John's "I am Alpha and Omega, the beginning and the end; he who is and who was and who is to come, the Almighty, the First and the Last" (Apoc. 1:8, 17; 22:13). St. John's formulation is fully in accordance with the spirit of Isaiah and with the whole of the Old Testament and is clearly connected with the emotive force of the name Yahweh.

Chapters 43–46 of Isaiah should, of course, be read here in their entirety. A few quotations must suffice for the purpose of this book:

Thus saith Yahweh, the king of Israel and his Redeemer, Yahweh of hosts: I am the First and I am the Last: and besides me there is no God. Who is like to me? . . . You are my witnesses. Is there a God besides me? There is no other Rock. I know no other (44:6–8).

I am Yahweh, and there is none else: there is no God besides me. I girded thee (Cyrus): and thou hast not known me: that they may know who are from the rising of the sun, and they who are from the west, that there is none besides me. I am Yahweh: and there is none else. I "form" the light and create darkness. I bring about salvation and create evil. I am Yahweh, that do all these things (45:5–7).

Finally, a passage follows which illustrates clearly how Yahweh's reality was judged according to tangible results. The people of Africa were to fall at Israel's feet with these words of supplication:

Only in thee is God; and there is no God besides thee
... the God of Israel, the Saviour.
They are all confounded and ashamed:
the forgers of errors are gone together into confusion.
But Israel is saved by Yahweh with an eternal salvation:
you shall not be confounded and ashamed for ever and ever.
For thus saith Yahweh that created the heavens,
God himself that formed the earth and made it,
he did not create it in vain,
but formed it to be inhabited.
I am Yahweh; and there is no other (45:14–18).

Confronted with Yahweh and his reality, the idols, the false gods, the "strange" gods, the national gods—all are reduced, literally, to nothing. The prophets made use of extremely colorful language to impress upon Israel the insignificance of these gods and the folly of trusting in them. They described them as abhorrent filth and ordure (Deut. 7:26, 29:17; Isa. 66:3; Jer. 4:1, 16:18; Ezek. 5:11, 7:20, and so on), lies and deceits (Amos 2:4; Jer. 16:19; Ps. 39:5), vapor (Deut. 32:21; Jer. 2:5, 10:3, 15; 1 Kings 16:13, 26; and so on), vanity (Jer. 18:15; Jonah 2:9; Ps. 30:7), unprofitable absurdities (1 Sam. 12:21; Isa. 41:29; 44:9; and so on), nothings (Lev. 19:4; 26:1; Isa. 2:8, 18, 20; and so forth), inventions (Ps. 95:5), carcasses (Jer. 16:18f.), or simply as no gods (Deut. 32:21; Jer 2:11, 16:20; 2 Kings 19:18). They were dumb, lifeless, and without movement (Hab. 2:18f.). They lacked senses and were unable to walk, speak, or help themselves in any way (Ps. 114:4–7; 134:15–17). Again and again, throughout the Bible, these false gods were mocked and derided (1 Kings 18:20ff.; Jer. 10:1–16; Isa. 40:18–20; 44:10–20, 46:5–7; Baruch 6; Wis. 13).

But one outstanding example can say much more than a great number of references. The verses which follow show clearly how Israel's contempt for false gods and idols was basically the antithesis to her deep consciousness of Yahweh's ineffable reality. The contrast is indicated no less than four times in this single passage from Jeremiah.

(1) What the heathens fear is vain:
for the work of the hand of the workman
hath cut a tree out of the forest with an axe.
He hath decked it with silver and gold:
he hath put it together with nails and hammers,
that it may not fall asunder.
They are like to scarecrows in the field
and cannot speak:
they must be carried to be removed,
because they cannot go.
Therefore fear them not,
for they can neither do evil nor good.

Yahweh, there is none like to thee,
thou alone art great,
great and mighty is thy Name.
Who shall not fear thee, O king of nations,
for thine is the glory.
Among all the wise men of the nations
and in all their kingdoms
there is none like unto thee.

(2) They shall be all proved together
to be senseless and foolish:
the doctrine of their vanity is wood.
Silver spread into plates is brought from Tharsis,
and gold from Ophaz:
the work of the artificer
and of the hand of the coppersmith:
violet and purple is their clothing:
all these things are the work of artificers.

But Yahweh is the true God:
he is the living God and the everlasting King.
At his wrath the earth shall tremble,
and the nations shall not be able to abide his threatening.

(3) Thus then shall you say to them:
the gods that have not made heaven and earth,
let them perish from the earth
and from among those places that are under heaven.
But Yahweh hath made the earth by his power;
he hath established the world by his wisdom
and stretched out the heavens by his knowledge.
At the sound of his thunder,
he giveth a multitude of waters in the heaven,
and lifteth up the clouds from the ends of the earth.
He maketh the lightnings for rain
and bringeth forth the wind out of his treasures.
Every man is become a fool for knowledge,
every artist is confounded in his graven idol.

(4) For what he hath cast is false,
and there is no spirit in them.
They are vain things and a ridiculous work:
in the time of their visitation they shall perish.
The portion of Jacob is not like these:
for it is he who formed all things
and Israel is his tribe and his inheritance.
Yahweh of hosts is his Name (Jer. 10:3–16).

Does this in any way affect the interpretation of Yahweh's name, given by Exodus? In the author's opinion, the following does not seem to be too farfetched. It is an established fact on the one hand that the sacred writer associated the verb "to be" with the Name Yahweh and that "to be" and the Name were associated in the Hebrew mind. It is, on the other hand, also a fact that it was crucial to Israel's sense of God that Yahweh alone was capable of being regarded as a God who "is." It would be unreasonable to regard these two facts as accidental, parallel phenomena. They must be taken in combination. There are so many texts which indicate that this sense of God is expressed in the Name, and that it is this feeling for God which constitutes the special emotive force of the Name, that we are compelled to relate them. There is every reason for interpreting this disputed formula, in the only passage in which this relationship is explicit, in a manner which is in accordance with this broader, and in no way uncertain, context.

9. *"I Am Who Am"*

The few passages containing reference to the name, which those who support the other opinion cite as evidence, cannot outweigh the facts given in the foregoing paragraph. What is more, as we have already shown, they are not such close parallels as they would at first sight appear to be. The appeal which the exponents of this opinion make to the wider contest of the whole of the Old Testament, that is, to the idea of God's transcendence, carries, of course, much greater weight. This broader context is, however, in the first place too general for the quite particular conclusion (that Yahweh declined to answer the question concerning his Name), to be drawn from it. In the second place, full justice is done to the idea of God's transcendence, though not in the one-sided and exclusive sense, in the opinion put forward here. It should be possible for this idea of God's transcendence to be expressed in the singular way, determined by the Hebrew idiom, in which "being" was attributed to Yahweh. Yahweh did not say "I am," but "I am who am." However difficult it may be for the westerner to completely understand this distinctly oriental, linguistic turn of phrase, one thing is, however, quite certain. Hebraists have established, on a basis of some fifty closely related, but not absolutely identical, linguistic constructions, that what we have to deal with here is the normal, Hebrew manner of vague, indefinite expression. Several well-known examples of this are provided in reasonably close context.

After trying in vain to escape from his difficult mission, Moses eventually said openly to Yahweh: Send someone else (Exod. 4:13). What he said literally was: "Send whom thou wilt send" (or: whom thou sendest). He did not wish to be more precise about whom Yahweh should send, and said therefore: let him send whom he will; it is of no importance whom he sends, so long as he leaves me alone.

On another occasion, Moses said to Yahweh: "Show me thy glory." But what he was asking here was too much. It was entirely up to God, in his sovereign goodness, to decide to whom he should show such an unprecedented favor. Human initiative was completely misplaced in such an instance. Moses was not, after all, the first comer, and Yahweh was prepared to show him this absolutely *unmerited* grace, "for I will have mercy on whom I will, and I will be merciful to whom it shall please me" (Exod. 33:19; *see also* Rom. 9:15). This turn of phrase also expresses vagueness and in this way served to correct what Moses was attempting to do. Man has no right to be too precise in this matter; "I will be merciful to whom it shall please me."

This lack of precision is also expressed by a repetition of the same verb, the two forms of which are connected to each other by a relative particle. "Bake what thou wilt, and cook what thou wilt" means: thou mayest do what thou wilt with the manna" (Exod. 16:23).

What frequently occurred was that the action expressed by the verb "in any case" either did take place, or was to take place, or had to take place in the future. The writer or speaker either could not or did not wish to define the exact circumstances of the action more precisely, as irrelevant to the purpose. Elisha said to the Sunamite woman: there will be a famine in the land. See to it, then, that you get away from here and go and live *somewhere* in a foreign land. You must in any case go away; it does not matter where you go, so long as you go away. In Hebrew, this was expressed as: settle down (in a foreign land) where you will settle down (in a foreign land), that is, where you want to or where you can (*see* 2 Kings 8:1). Similarly, David, fleeing from Absalom, said: "I go where I am going," by which he meant that, whatever happened, he had to go away, but he had not the slightest idea where he would end up. He did not, however, wish to involve the faithful Ittai who, since his banishment from the city of his birth, had found rest in Jerusalem, in this fate (2 Sam. 15:20; *see also* 1 Sam. 23:13; "they wandered up and down uncertain," or, they wandered where they were wandering).

Assuming that the Exodus formula is also an example of this construction, it follows that the verb "to be" is used here, both times, with the same meaning. In the case of the Greek translation, "I am the Being" and the many derivative translations, such as the Canisius Bible ("I am 'I am'"), the version "I am the one who is," and so on, the first "to be" was assumed to be a linking verb whereas the second was taken to be an independent verb. There is no doubt that the result was to make the formula sound reasonably meaningful in western ears, but it did scant justice to the original Hebrew construction, which consisted of a simple repetition.

To avoid giving a misleading impression, the translation must be framed in such a way as to render the first "to be" as an independent verb, not as a verb which links subject and predicate. The latter, however, is inevitable so long as the particle in Hebrew is translated by a relative pronoun. There are, however, other possibilities. The Hebrew particle is always used as a linking word and requires further definition. According to how it is defined, it may acquire the meaning of a relative particle, or it may be given a meaning similar to that of a conjunction. Frequently, however, the Hebrew omits any further definition of the relationship, especially in poetical constructions and lapidary inscriptions, and in such cases this can only be supplied by the context. As such, the Hebrew particle has no direct equivalent in English. Confining our attention solely to those cases which actually occur in the Old Testament, and disregarding the cases where the particle, used on its own, may be translated by "the one who," which is good Hebrew but which presupposes a linking verb, the isolated particle can be translated by "that," "so that," or "because," and even, in certain instances, by "in case," "as," "such as," or "where." The following suggested translations may help to give a better understanding of the construction. It should be noted, however, that they are intended merely as a working hypothesis, and not to provide a final choice of translations:

> I am there inasmuch as I am there.
> I shall be there as I shall be there.
> I am where I am.

It is thus possible to give quite an acceptable meaning to this construction, parallel to the examples quoted, on a basis of those parallels. On the one hand, the assurance that Yahweh "is" is fully implied in the formula. On the other hand, however, there is an explicit exclusion—or even a refusal on Yahweh's part—as to how, what, and when he "is."

If we wish to form a really clear idea of the importance of this possible refusal, then it should be possible to say that Yahweh's being cannot be defined by one special name, because this name would normally be a more precise formulation and thereby a limitation of the divine, within certain clearly defined categories taken from human relationships. The Name which Yahweh revealed must have been a name which expressed his unnamable essence. It must have been as if he had said: I am called the Unnamable One (*see also* Judges 13:18; Prov. 30:4; Apoc. 19:12, 16). This, or something like it, would certainly seem to be the case here. Yahweh revealed his Name to Israel, but what the Name at the same time expressed was that Israel would have to be content with the assurance that Yahweh "is with Israel," that he "is" there, whatever might happen, in every conceivable situation, and in every eventuality.

To express the same idea in a different way, a person's name is the definition of that person's essence. In this way, the true God can never be comprehended by man. He would thus never deliver his Name to man. Although he revealed his Name, this was entirely at the existential level—He is there! Man is bound to ask speculative and theoretical questions about the essence of things. Israel, however, asked a practical question, and Yahweh's answer was one which was perfectly satisfactory at the practical level and which, at the same time, rebuffed the human desire for knowledge.

Viewed in this way, Yahweh's answer nonetheless included both a yes and a no. In this way, the formula gives expression to an extremely pure consciousness of God, so pure in fact that the passage in which the formula occurs may justifiably be seen to be in complete accordance with all that has been said or thought at the deepest level about the nature of God throughout the course of human history. Even the ideas of divine aseity and *esse purum,* in the philosophical and theological sense, can be seen as legitimate translations and as genuine extensions, though in a completely different environment of thought, of what the Bible meant but expressed in an ancient, oriental, and therefore concrete manner. In the first place, however, this interpretation of the formula is strikingly in accordance with Israel's faith in God, insofar as this is known to us from the factual evidence provided in the rest of the Bible.

We may say, then, that Israel looked on the name Yahweh as the proper name of her national God, the God of the Covenant, and thus as the name which distinguished him from all other national gods. Furthermore, the essential difference between Yahweh and the other gods—a difference which was stressed again and again in the Bible—was that Yahweh was the authentic, divine Reality, whereas the others were false gods. These pseudogods, insofar as they were really false, were human inventions and, as such, were the projection into the divine sphere of certain human needs, worldly situations, and natural phenomena. As a general rule, the names given to these gods were an expression of these needs, situations, and phenomena. This is clearly the case with those names which were derived from the forces of nature. It is less strikingly evident, but equally applicable to those names which ascribe a definite character or a specific spiritual attribute to the deity.

But the true God did not permit himself to be defined in this way. The very construction of the formula "I am who am" precluded any such definition and the name Yahweh was, therefore, in itself the brief resume of Israel's sense of Yahweh's complete transcendence, though not of his exclusive transcendence. The fact that Yahweh is not and cannot be defined serves to accentuate, all the more strongly, the one thing that can be said positively about Yahweh—the fact that he "is." And, in the Bible, Yahweh's "being" is nothing more or less than his all-embracing and all-permeating immanence. Yahweh was a God far off and a God at hand (*see* Jer. 23:23). Israel's faith in God was, so to speak, suspended between the opposite poles of divine transcendence and divine immanence. Unless we are very much mistaken, this polarity is also the mystery of the *tetragrammaton ineffabile,* the inexpressible Name in four letters: Y-H-W-H.

IV
The Worship of Israel

THE SACRED WRITER aimed to impart faith to Israel by means of his account of the origin of the name Yahweh. The generation which came out of Egypt did not, however, come to this faith through theoretical arguments, but by experiencing Yahweh's great deeds in the whole cycle of redemption spanning the Exodus, the journey through the desert, and the entry into the promised land. A number of crucial facts are recorded in the biblical account. Although all kinds of incidents crystallized around these facts, these incidents, judged according to their period and setting, probably do not belong at all to the facts themselves, but elsewhere. It was these crucial facts, however, which made the first impact on the various groups which were, at that time, still only loosely associated. As these groups began to merge and form one racial community, so their story became more coherent, until it, in turn, became an important factor in the formation of the community. It was more or less in this way that the decisive facts of redemption became the articles of Israel's creed and thus remained the formative principle binding the religious federation of the tribes together—for this is all that Israel was at this period—and either assimilating heterogeneous elements or rejecting them. Israel's redemption, then, was a series of events which together made Israel what she eventually became. This was the starting point of Israel's existence as a nation and at the same time the immediate point of departure of her religion. Through this redemption, or deliverance, Yahweh called Israel into existence. It was this which gave him his special claim to Israel and made him Israel's God from the land of Egypt.

The central fact was the making of the Covenant at the foot of Mount Sinai. This "feast of Yahweh" (*see* Exod. 5:1), was the positive aspect of Israel's redemption. The deliverance from Egypt was more or less the negative side—a special obligation to Yahweh after having been taken out of a pagan environment. Israel had to separate clean beasts from unclean beasts, because Yahweh made this distinction between peoples (Lev. 20:24f.), separating Israel from the others to make her a holy people, that is, a people dedicated to his service. This separation was the necessary outcome of Israel's election. It was to remain an insistent demand throughout the whole of Israel's history, constantly stressed in the Bible. Reading or hearing these accounts, the Israelite or Jew was able to know where he was. He could see Abraham's call as a separation, even as a redemption (Isa. 29:22). But the classical redemption, the prototype of all later redemption, was the redemption from Egypt. Miraculously and in triumph, Yahweh, like a king (Exod. 15:18; Num. 23:21), led the lowly Israelites away, through the midst of and out of a mighty people, into his "rest" (Ps. 94:11; Deut. 12:9; Hebr. 4:3), the holy and hereditary land of Yahweh, the land flowing with milk and honey.

1. The Character of the Biblical Data

The biblical account of the events on Sinai was designed to make the eternal Covenant between God and Israel as clear to the people as it had been when Yahweh, in the midst of his people, took possession for ever of the temple of Jerusalem and made it his lasting dwelling place, in order to safeguard the nation's well-being there, as a source of holiness and salvation. In Israel, an extensive theology of the nation, as the people of the Covenant, crystallized around very diverse memories, which might have come to Israel along various channels. Faith provided an interpretation of and a standard for the life of Israel here, as it was lived during her existence as a nation in Canaan.

Even though it is possible to reconstruct the historical course of events from this extremely theological writing of history, we shall confine our attention in this chapter to the image of Israel's religion provided by the Pentateuch. This image must, of course, be built up from the detailed biblical facts on the subject of public worship. What the desert generation thought, and how this generation acted in this respect, is of less interest, and it is in any case difficult to go beyond generalizations here. What fundamentally concerns us are the religious ideas and institutions which determined the image of Israel's religion for centuries and eventually led to the agglomeration of laws and treatises on liturgy which are so difficult for the modern reader of the Bible to fathom. We propose to extract a few points from this collection of laws, points which either summarize the biblical datum or arrange it according to its historical development, wherever this seems to be sufficiently clear. There is, in this field, an inordinate number of complicated problems which have not yet, by any means, been unravelled. An example of just such a problem is given in the third section of this chapter.

It is obvious that Israel's worship was subject to a long process of development and that the biblical descriptions of this worship, to a very great extent, reflect the final stage in this development. It is also clear that, in public worship, Israel's practices and institutions were in the first place based on ancient, oriental patterns. Even though the letter of the Bible says so continually, God did not reveal that cattle had to be slaughtered in his honor. But it was the custom in the Ancient Near East to express reverence for God in the form of blood-sacrifices. That is why Israel too made blood-sacrifices, in honor of Yahweh. Whenever this is the case, we have simply to put up with a wide margin of uncertainty. Yet in two totally different ways, attempts have been made to force certainty.

In the first of these two cases, it is assumed that worship at the time of Moses and David was organized exactly as it is described in the Bible. Those who accept this view do so because the Bible itself attributes worship to these two founders of the state and the people. In the first place, this view is based only on a certain group of biblical data, such as the giving of the Law and the idealized biographies of David and Solomon. All kinds of less striking and less tendentious evidence in other accounts and in the prophetic books are, however, overlooked. Secondly, and consequently, these facts are used without a true understanding of the literary genre of the biblical descriptions, in which worship is ascribed to Moses and David. In these passages, insofar as they do not merely provide a classic and conventional, juridical formula, the attribution of worship to Moses and David has an appreciative and qualitative, rather than a strictly historical implication.

In the second of the two instances, an ideal construction is seen only in the biblical image of Israel's worship, something which originated in the minds of certain postexilic priests and was given body by the ritual of the second temple.

The truth lies somewhere between the two. The ritual of the second temple certainly plays an important part in the descriptions of Mosaic and Davidic worship provided in the Bible (a valid, liturgical code of law is not a historical study), but this ritual, naturally conservative, included very many, extremely ancient elements. It was, moreover, the final stage and the extension of a worship which, as far as its essential structure is concerned, had remained consistent and which can, and indeed must, go back, in its essential features, to Moses and David. Anyone who is inclined to doubt this has only to look at the evidence of Egypt and Mesopotamia—and especially Canaan itself—long before and at the same time as Israel's oldest period. There were, of course, many differences. But the evidence also shows many analogous examples in the arrangement of the sanctuaries, the hierarchy of the temples, the diversity of the sacrifices, the wealth of feasts, processions, and so on. There is, therefore, no need to wait until after the Exile for Israel to have a more detailed ritual. The postexilic ritual must have been quite different, since the Jews would certainly have chosen to take another path. They had only to draw on their national past. The ancient Israelites, however, did not simply take over a given ritual from others. Rather, a specifically Israelitic tradition was gradually formed out of the general pattern of worship in the ancient Near East. In the beginning at least, Canaanite customs must have played a special part in this process. This is not guesswork. It is clear from the data, including the new data resulting from the finds at Ugarit (Ras Shamra), in the nineteen-thirties.

2. *The Sanctuary and Its Arrangement*

It would be quite unreasonable to doubt that the nomadic Hebrews had a sanctuary. What the Bible describes is a typical nomad sanctuary. It is perhaps a little too accurately classified and arranged in comparison with the later, sedentary sanctuary, the temple of Solomon, but there was an obvious similarity, in that the sacred tabernacle was a portable temple (*templum ambulatorium;* Augustine, De Civ. Dei, 15. 20. 4: PL 41. 465). The people had no fixed dwelling place, and their God had consequently none. He too dwelt in a tent, called the "dwelling" (*mišekǎn*), or the "tent," or "tabernacle" (*'ōhel*). It was frequently known as the "tabernacle of testimony," a term which referred first and foremost to God's testimony (*'ēdhôth*) of the ten commandments, as a revelation of his will, as did the expression "(stone) tablets of testimony" (Exod. 31:18, and so forth). More common, and even more significant, was the name "tabernacle of meeting" (*'ōhel mô'ēd*), by which is meant the tent of "assembly" or of "coming together." This was the place, the "pre-arranged spot," where the people came together in assembly or meeting (Num. 10:3), and even more particularly where God and the people were able to meet or encounter by coming together. The daily sacrifice had to be made "at the entrance of the tabernacle of meeting, where I will come together with thee (Moses) and speak to thee. I will come together there with the Israelites, and they will be sanctified there by my holiness" (Exod. 29:42f.; *see also* 30:36). The actual meeting, however, took place between Yahweh and Moses: "Thou shalt place the propitiatory above the ark and into the ark thou shalt put the testimony that I will give thee. And I will come together with thee there and will speak to thee over the propitiatory, and from the midst of the two cherubim upon the ark of the testimony, about all things which I will command the Israelites" (Exod. 25:21f.; *see also* 30:6; Num. 17:4). The term "tabernacle of the covenant" is not biblical. It is due to an inaccurate translation in the Vulgate (*tabernaculum foederis:* Exod. 33:7, and so forth).

A space around the tabernacle was set apart for those of the people who were clean. This area is well known to us in the Arabic name *haram*, a word meaning "separation" ("entry forbidden"). It can be compared with *herem*, meaning anathema or excommunication, and *harem*, meaning women's quarters—*Hermon* was apparently a sacred mountain! Many fine examples of such sacred areas have been preserved, such as Herod's haram of the temple of Jerusalem and of the sanctuary of Abraham on Hebron. In the middle of this area, on an elevation and directly in front of the entrance to the tabernacle, stood the altar for the fire offerings. The altar was sometimes hollowed out inside and filled with earth. The four corners, projecting upwards, formed the "horns" which are familiar from many finds and illustrations. These horns were the most sacred part of the altar. The sprinkling and smearing of these horns with the blood of the sacrificial animals formed an important part of the rite (Exod. 29:12; Lev. 4:25, 30, 34), and their especial holiness is the point of the following text, and of similar passages:

> When I shall begin to visit the transgressions of Israel,
> I will visit upon him and upon the altars of Bethel:
> and the horns of the altar shall be cut off
> and shall fall to the ground (Amos 3:14).

Closer to the tabernacle stood a basin, for ritual ablutions. The priests had to perform these ablutions before they approached the altar or entered the tabernacle. They alone were permitted to enter the tabernacle. The foremost part of the tabernacle, which was also the largest, and corresponded to the royal hall (*hēkhāl*) of Solomon's temple, was called the "Holy" (in Heb. 9:6, the "first tabernacle"). In the middle stood the altar for the incense offerings. On the left burnt the lamp, which developed later into the well-known candelabrum with seven branches. On the right was the table with the "shewbreads" (*panes propositionis*), literally "breads of the pile." There were twelve loaves in two piles of six each, with incense on top of them (Lev. 24:5-9; 1 Sam. 21:6). The name "breads of the face" perhaps reflected the ancient origin of this custom—the placing of food before (the face of) the image of a god as nourishment for the deity (*see* Dan. 14:26; Deut. 32:38; Jer. 7:18, 44:17-19). But even if this had ever been the intention in Israel, there is no trace of it in any text. The weekly renewal of the twelve loaves was a weekly renewal of the memory of the Covenant of the twelve tribes with Yahweh. The incense was burnt then as a "commemorative sacrifice (?) of the bread." The incense clearly represented Yahweh's share, since the loaves were eaten by the priests. In this way, the shewbreads had the character of an offering of food, continuously made as a confession of lasting loyalty to the Covenant.

There is nothing which has been mentioned so far that does not go back to the ideas and customs common to the Semitic world. In

Israel, however, it was all related to Yahweh, and that gave a new spirit and sometimes, in the case of the shewbreads, a new meaning to the ritual. This new content and meaning had, in the long run, to express itself in the form of the worship. By analogy with or in polemical reaction to existing forms, and thus never departing from the basic pattern of the Ancient Near East, Yahwism created its own forms and recreated existing forms by assimilating them and applying them to its experience of its own; and so different sense of God. An example of this is, of course, the ark in the "Holy of Holies."

This "rear," that is to say, inner space in the sanctuary—the "second tabernacle" of Hebrews 9:7, and the *debhir,* or "rear chamber" of Solomon's temple—corresponded to the *cella* of ancient, oriental sanctuary. Only the high priest was permitted to enter this dark space: "Yahweh hath set the sun in the heaven, but said that he would dwell in darkness" (1 Kings 8:12, improved translation). In the cella, there was always an image of the deity. In the Holy of Holies, however, was the ark, as the visible sign of the divine presence. This precious chest, measuring 125 by 75 by 75 cm., contained the stone tablets of the ten commandments. These tablets were known as the tablets of testimony (Exod. 31:18), or the tablets of the Covenant (Deut. 9:9). The ark was consequently called the ark of testimony (Exod. 25:22), or the ark of the Covenant (Num. 10:33). In the oldest accounts, it was referred to with forceful simplicity as the ark of Yahweh (1 Sam. 4:6), the ark of God (1 Sam. 3:3), or the ark of the God of Israel (1 Sam. 5:7). The people needed a concrete and central object for their worship. An image of Yahweh was not tolerated in Israel, and for this reason the ark was chosen. It was possible for the ark to appeal directly to the people, since sacred chests were carried in procession both in Mesopotamia and in Egypt. There is perhaps some connection between these chests and the ark.

Whether this is so or not, the ark had a special significance in

Israel. Without in any way lessening Yahweh's transcendence, it powerfully suggested his awe-inspiring immanence. In the ark, Yahweh dwelt in the midst of his people. The cherubs especially suggested this divine immanence, for they were the guard of the palace and the throne of the King and God. The ark was Yahweh's throne (1 Sam. 4:4; *see also* Ps. 17:11; 79:2; 98:1). It was his footstool, the place where his feet rested (Ps. 98:5; 131:7; *see also* 109:1; Lam. 2:1; 1 Chron. 28:2). Between the two cherubs, on the precious covering of the ark, the cloud which shrouded Yahweh's "glory" appeared. It was from this cloud that Yahweh addressed Moses. For this reason, the sanctuary around the ark was known as the tabernacle of meeting—the point of contact between Yahweh and the people. In the sanctuary, therefore, the Israelite was "before the face of Yahweh" (1 Sam. 1:12, 15, 19, 22; 2 Kings 19:14f.). He went up to the sanctuary to "see the face of Yahweh," that is to say, to visit Yahweh or to enter the temple (Deut. 16:16; Isa. 1:12; Ps. 41:3).

The ark was also a portable throne, a representation of the heavenly throne carried by the cherubs (Ezek. 1:10; 43). When the ark was lifted up, Moses said:

> Arise, Yahweh,
> and let thine enemies be scattered,
> and let them that hate thee flee from before thy face.

Whenever it was set down, he said:

> Return, Yahweh,
> to the ten thousands of the thousands of Israel (Num. 10:35f.).

That is why the Name of Yahweh Sabaoth—the God of Israel's hosts—was invoked over the ark (2 Sam. 6:2), and why it was brought into the thick of the battle as a safeguard (1 Sam. 4:3ff.; *see also* 17:45). It is also why, in liturgical processions, it aroused valid memories of the exodus of the redeemed people from Egypt into the Promised Land, under the guidance of Yahweh (Pss. 67; 23; *see also* Exod. 7:4).

At the same time, the ark served as a "chest." Elsewhere in the ancient Near East, important documents were placed at the foot of the image of the deity, by which tolerance between men gained a divine sanction. In the same way, the tablets of the Law were placed in the ark (Exod. 25:16, 21), and the book of the Law was placed beside them "before the face of Yahweh" (Deut. 31:26; 1 Sam. 10:25), as a testimony which was untouchable and guarded by Yahweh. In this way, Yahweh zealously watched over the Covenant.

3. Priests and Levites

Wherever there were sanctuaries, there were of necessity priests, dedicated entirely to the service of public worship. It is inconceivable that Moses should have left such an important matter as this purely to chance. It is extremely likely that he made his brother Aaron responsible for public worship.

(a) Levites and the Sons of Levi

Aaron was also known as "the levite" (Exod. 4:14), a name which gives the impression, both here and in other texts, of being more of a vocational name than a family name. There is indeed reason to wonder whether the "levites," the vocational priests of Israel, can simply be identified with the descendants of Levi, who were naturally known as "levites." It would probably be safest to disregard the offspring of Levi, particularly since this detracts very little from the question under consideration here. The levites were in any case a complex, historical phenomenon, which the Bible, in accordance with its usual practice, has tried to classify under one, single genealogy, that of Levi. The complication has arisen because the levites in later texts were ministers of the sanctuary, but as such frequently distinct from the priests proper. Among the personnel of the temple, the levites were the non-priests, whereas the "levite" Aaron was the type of the Old Testament priest. A considerable change must have taken place in the use of words in the Bible, a change reflecting as great an alteration in the institute itself.

The position of the vocational levite is vividly illustrated in an ancient story in the Bible which sums up the first phase of Israel's religion so well that it is worthy of inclusion here. A certain Micah had stolen eleven hundred pieces of silver from his mother. But she pronounced such a powerful curse on the thief that Micah gave the money back to her. In order to cancel out her curse, she gave two hundred pieces of silver to a silversmith, so that he could make a molten image of them for her son. This image was taken to Micah's house. In this way, Micah came to possess a household shrine. He made an ephod (a box with oracular stones), and theraphim (household gods, similar to the penates), and dedicated one of his sons as a priest. There was also a young man from Bethlehem in Judah who, being a levite, lived there simply as a guest. This young levite left the city of Bethlehem and went off to try to find somewhere to live in another place. In the course of his journey, he reached Mount Ephraim and came to Micah's house. Micah asked him where he had come from, and the levite answered: I have come from Bethlehem in Judah and I have been looking for somewhere else to live. Micah said: Stay with me and be a father and a priest for me. I will give you ten pieces of silver every year, in addition to your clothes and keep. The levite decided to stay with the man, who treated him as one of his sons. Micah appointed him priest, and the young man became his priest and stayed in his house. And Micah said: Now I know that Yahweh is favorably inclined towards me, for I have a levite as priest (Judges 17:1-13).

The kind of resistance that Yahwism had to overcome is quite clearly illustrated in this story. The new faith claimed the allegiance of the primitive society, but did not force allegiance. It took time for customs which had hitherto been applicable only to heathen society to be purified or eliminated. Anyone who finds these pagan elements scandalizing has clearly misunderstood the nature of revelation and the way in which revelation took place.

It should be noted, in connection with our problem, that even at the time of the Judges it was considered valuable to have a levite as a priest. Strictly speaking, a priest was, even here, not the same as a levite. What is more, the social position of the levite was not high. Possessing no tribal territory of their own—we are told in the story that the young man, because he was a levite, lived in Bethlehem, the city of his birth, simply as a guest—they often had no firm basis to their lives. This particular levite seized the opportunity that was offered to him in both hands, even though the sanctuary was private and by no means attractive. Deuteronomy provides many insights into social motivation in Israel and, referring to the "levite that dwelleth in your cities," recommends him to Israel's generosity (12:12, 18f.), naming him in the same breath as the stranger, the orphan, and the widow (14:27-29; 16:11, 14; 26:11-13). The judgment pronounced on the house of Eli undoubtedly called to mind a very real image from everyday life: Yahweh said that he would appoint a faithful priest in Eli's place and "whosoever shall remain in thy house shall come that he may be prayed for; and shall offer a piece of silver and a roll of bread; and shall say: Put me, I beseech thee, to somewhat of the priestly office, that I may eat a morsel of bread" (1 Sam. 2:36).

If we compare these facts with the oldest text which refers to the *tribe* of Levi, we find nothing in it, strangely enough, which tells us about the function of the priest. On the contrary, this text assumes precisely the same, miserable, social position and attempts to give an explanation of it. Levi's descendants are scattered about Israel, without any tribal territory of their own, but the old oracle does not attribute this scattered existence to a particular election, as current, biblical theology seeks to do, but to a curse hereditarily laid upon the tribe by the appearance of Simeon and Levi in Shechem (Gen. 34:25):

> Cursed be their fury, because it was stubborn,
> and their wrath, because it was cruel.
> I will divide them in Jacob,
> and will scatter them in Israel (Gen. 49:7).

It is not possible to ascertain from the available facts whether there were originally two distinct kinds of levites, levites by calling and levites by family. If this was in fact the case, then certain social and religious relationships must have existed between them—not necessarily blood-relationships—on a basis of which the Bible was able to classify them under the same genealogical heading.

(b) The Levitical Priest

It is only with difficulty that this connection, as expressed above in terms of genealogical relationship, can be based upon a later construction, since another, equally ancient, series of oracles—the "blessing of Moses"—provides, in contrast to the "prophecy of Jacob," an entirely priestly image of the tribe of Levi:

> Give thy Thummim to Levi
> and thy Urim to thy favored one . . .
> They teach Jacob thy precepts
> and thy Law to Israel.
> They put incense in thy nose
> and holocausts upon thy altar (Deut. 33:8, 10).

If this text is taken at its full value, it is clear that the priest's duties included very much more than simply his ministration at the altar. There is a greater emphasis, in many texts, on instruction in the

Law (this was of considerable importance later on for the rise of the scribes and their exposition of the Law), and on the cases which were heard in the sanctuary. The way in which the oracle—Urim and Thummim—was used in these cases is clear from the "lawsuit" between Saul and Israel. The priests stood ready with the ephod, the container in which the oracular stones were kept. On one side stood Saul and Jonathan, on the other the people. Then Saul prayed: "Yahweh, God of Israel, if the fault be in me or in my son Jonathan, give Urim; if the fault be in thy people Israel, give Thummim." Jonathan and Saul were found guilty and the people acquitted. Then Saul commanded them to cast lots between him and his son, and Jonathan was taken (1 Sam. 14:40–42; *see also* 10:20–24; Acts 1:23–26).

Generally speaking, the older texts give the impression that the whole tribe of Levi was priestly (Exod. 32:29). The name "levite" would appear to mean "priest" (Exod. 4:14; Deut. 17:9, 18; 21:5). The name Levi (*lēwî*) was probably an abbreviation of *lēwî'ēl* which might have meant "the one who is attached to God." Lea was alluding to this meaning when she said: "Now my husband will be *joined* to me . . . therefore she called his (her new born son's) name Levi" (Gen. 29:34). *Lēwî* also occurs in a related dialect of Southern Arabia as a generic name, with the meaning of "priest."

According to more recent texts, it is only the "sons of Aaron" who were priests, and these are clearly distinguished from the other sons of Levi, who were "only" levites. A recent explanation of the name Levi suggests that the levites were so called because they were "associated" with the priests and helped them (Num. 18:2, 4).

On the one hand, it would be wrong to consider the difference between levites and priests separately from Moses, since it is quite obvious that Moses himself designated a special family for worship and that Aaron must have occupied a special place in or beside this family. On the other hand, the later hierarchy can only have been the result of a long process of development, which cannot be traced in its entirety, but of which at least some factors are visible.

(c) The Levite as a Non-priest

One factor is to be found in the fact that public worship became so complicated and all-embracing, especially since the establishment of the temple, that the "tribe of Levi" could not attend to it unaided. As a result, a hierarchy came into being. There is mention of the high priest, called the "great priest" (*sacerdos magnus*) in Leviticus 21:10, the "chief priest" (2 Kings 25:18), the "anointed priest" (Lev. 4:3) or preeminently "the priest" (Exod. 29:30). This high priest had a regular deputy, the "second priest" (2 Kings 25:18). Once only we hear of the "ancients of the priests" (2 Kings 19:2), which presupposes a large group of priests. Finally, there were all kinds of subordinate functions and offices; those who occupied the lowest of these were not even levites and one category was not even comprised of Israelites. Joshuah gave the Gibeonites, a Horitic enclave within the population of Canaan, the task of "hewing wood and drawing water for all the people and for the altar of Yahweh in the place which he hath chosen, *until the present time*" (Joshua 9:27; *see also* Deut. 29:11). These later had a juridical place as servants or slaves of the temple (*nethûnîm,* or those who are given), beside the "servants of Solomon" (Ezra 2:43, 55).

Another factor may have been that by no means all the levites were associated with the sanctuary. This must, in the long run, have resulted in a clear distinction in social position and esteem, and finally in rank and authority. It is not difficult to imagine how certain family groups of levites, having once been ministers in one of the many local sanctuaries, and having secured a hereditary monopoly, managed to establish a tradition and develop a professional technique. On the other hand, other families of levites, living simply among the people, must gradually have begun to feel that they were outside the privileged circle, especially since they had no hereditary possessions and were without the regular income derived from a sanctuary. This difference in status between the levites is perhaps related as well to the original distinction—if it ever existed—between the vocational levites and the descendants of Levi. Although, according to the genealogical system of the Bible, all levites were classified under the tribe of Levi, not every levite was a levite by vocation. It is possible that the vocational levite had a better chance of being appointed to a sanctuary. In any case, it must always have been possible, if the situation existed within the group, by that time known as the sons of Levi, to find an opportunity of maintaining or introducing a distinction between priests and non-priests.

The most important factor, however, was probably the difference in status between the various sanctuaries. Some were very popular and flourished, others declined in importance and even ceased to exist. All were, however, overshadowed by the royal sanctuary, the first local sanctuary of the royal residence and, as such, indisputably the first among equals, but at the same time the national sanctuary and, as such, occupying an unrivaled position. With the passage of time, the other places of worship came to be regarded as inferior to Jerusalem and eventually—and not always without good reason—as unorthodox. The priestly caste of Jerusalem, the family of Zadok, or the Zadokites (the later Sadducees boasted that they were descended from Zadok), certainly claimed to be the only true priests, and the Bible gives evidence of the beginning of the tendency to refer to the priests of the "high places" with the word *ḳemārîm*, which, until this time, had been reserved for the priests who sacrificed to idols and false gods (2 Kings 23:5; Hos. 10:5; Zeph. 1:4).

In any case, there were definite occasions when a certain amount of sifting took place. An example of this is Josiah's reformation: "He gathered together all the priests out of the cities of Judah, and he defiled the high places, where the priests offered sacrifice, from Gibeah to Beer-sheba (i.e. from the most northerly to the southern-most point of the Southern Kingdom) . . . The priests of the high places were not permitted to come up to the altar of Yahweh in Jerusalem, but only to eat of the unleavened bread among their brethren" (2 Kings 23:8f.). A passage in Deuteronomy (18:6–8), may or may not allude to the same situation. If it does, it would contradict Josiah's rule and, in the opinion of many, would not have been put into practice because of the action of the priests of Jerusalem.

Clear, factual evidence is given by Ezekiel who, in his program of worship in the rebuilt temple of his prophecy, had the following to say concerning the priests of the sanctuaries in high places:

The levites that went away far from me when the children of Israel went astray and have wandered from me after their idols, they will bear their iniquity.

They shall do service in my sanctuary as doorkeepers of the gates of the house and as ministers to the house: they shall slay the holocausts and the victims for the people: and they shall stand in their sight, to minister to them . . .

And they shall not come near to me to do the office of priest to me, neither shall they come near to any of my holy things, to the holiest of holy things: but they shall bear their shame and their wickednesses which they have committed.

And I will make them ministers of the house, for all the service thereof and for all that shall be done therein.

But the levitical priests, the sons of Zadok, who kept the service of my sanctuary when the children of Israel went astray from me, they shall come near to me to minister to me: and they shall stand before me, to offer me the fat and the blood, saith Yahweh, the Lord. They shall enter into my sanctuary and they shall come near to my table, to minister to me and to keep my service (44:10–16).

In this way, and along similar paths, the classic division upon which the legislation in the Pentateuch concerning public worship was chiefly based was ultimately reached. Those who were descended through Aaron from Levi were the priests proper and at the service of Yahweh. The rest of Levi's descendants were levites in the narrower sense of the word and were at the service of the priests, of the people, and of the sanctuary. The "sons of Aaron" therefore were responsible for the priestly ministry. They carried out all the blood rites, "approached" the altar and placed the offerings upon it, went in behind the screen, taught the people the Law, and made all kinds of decisions. They alone were permitted to pronounce a blessing over the people, since Yahweh had told Moses:

> Say to Aaron and his sons:
> Thus shall you bless the children of Israel:
> Yahweh bless thee and keep thee;
> Yahweh show his face to thee and have mercy on thee;
> Yahweh turn his countenance to thee and give thee peace.
> And they shall invoke my Name upon the children of Israel,
> and I will bless them (Num. 6:23-27).

(d) Explanatory Accounts

In certain biblical accounts there is a tendency to justify the situation outlined above. In the book of Exodus, for example, the sacred character of the tribe of Levi is attributed to one, definite incident. When Moses came down from Sinai, and saw that the people had become unfaithful, he stood at the entrance to the camp and called out: "If any man be on Yahweh's side, let him join with me." All the sons of Levi gathered around him. Then he ordered them to draw their swords and go through the camp, killing brothers, friends and neighbors, that is to say, avenging the sin of apostasy without regard to persons. Afterwards, Moses said: "You have consecrated yourselves today to Yahweh: every man at the price of his son and his brother, that a blessing may be given to you" (Exod. 32:25–29). This is the so-called "blessing of Moses," and the same incident is narrated, in a poetical form, in Deuteronomy, where Moses says of Levi:

> Who hath said of his father and of his mother: I do not see them.
> And of his brethren: I know you not;
> and his children he has not known.
> These have kept thy word,
> and observed thy covenant (Deut. 33:9).

Deuteronomy goes on to relate, in general terms, without making any distinction between priests and levites: "At that time Yahweh separated the tribe of Levi: to carry the ark of the covenant of Yahweh, to stand before the face of Yahweh in the ministry and to bless in his Name until this present day. Wherefore Levi hath no part nor possession with his brethren, because Yahweh himself is his possession, as Yahweh, thy God, promised him" (10:8f.; *see also* Jer. 33:18–24).

There is, however, more emphasis in the account of Aaron's election, and especially in the story of the uprising of Korah and his adherents. Korah, who was himself of the tribe of Levi, maintained that the entire community was holy and that Yahweh was among them all. Why, he asked, do you lift yourself up above Yahweh's people? In his reply, Moses sharply defined each man's territory: "Hear ye sons of Levi! Is it a small thing unto you, that the God of Israel hath separated you from the people, and joined you to himself, that you should serve him in the service of the tabernacle of Yahweh and should stand before the congregation of the people and should minister to them? Did he therefore make thee and all the sons of Levi, thy brethren, to approach unto him, that you should demand the priesthood also? And that all thy company should stand against Yahweh? For what is Aaron that you murmur against him?" (Num. 16:8-11). This is followed by the divine judgment, which was confirmed by the blossoming of Aaron's rod (Num. 17).

Two passages, both of which stress that the levites were at the service of "Aaron and his sons," provide a theological explanation of the place of the levites. Yahweh claimed the levites in the place of Israel's firstborn, to whom, since his slaying of the firstborn of Egypt, he had a right (Num. 8:16-19). In another account, this took place in the following, graphic manner. After the levites had been numbered, Moses had to number all the male firstborn. There seemed to be 273 too many, or rather, there were 273 levites too few. From that time onward, the levites belonged to Yahweh and the 273 firstborn who were not covered by a levite had to be redeemed by the whole community, by five sicles per head (Num. 3:11-51).

Finally, the prominent place of the Zadokites is justified historically in the account of the appearance of Phinehas, when Yahweh addressed Moses: "Behold, I make my covenant with him (Phinehas), and the covenant of the priesthood for ever shall be both to him and his seed, because he hath been zealous for his God and hath made atonement for the Israelites" (Num. 25:6-13; Ps. 105:30f.; Ecclus. 45:28-30; 1 Macc. 2:54; 1 Sam. 2:35). The Jerusalem priesthood thus owed its monopoly in the first instant to the figure of Zadok, the influential priest who was closely related to David (2 Sam. 8:17), and who became, under Solomon, the most important priest in Jerusalem (1 Kings 2:26, 35). This man, Zadok, was consequently regarded as a direct descendant of Phinehas, Aaron's grandson (1 Chron. 6:3b-8).

4. The Sacrificial Service and Its Conditions

Israel must have offered all kinds of sacrifices, even in the very earliest period. It is neither possible, nor very rewarding, to distinguish, in the classifications provided in the Law, between those elements which are of earlier date and those which belong to a later period. A brief survey should be sufficient to establish the data from which a concrete image of the way in which Israel experienced and expressed her unity with Yahweh can be formed.

(a) Readiness to Sacrifice

Religious man realizes that his God, as the one who possesses both the land and the people, has a right to the whole of his person and to everything that he possesses. The Nazaritic oath made personal dedication possible in Israel both for men and for women. Certain external obligations were, as a sign of this personal dedication, taken on, among them, abstention from wine and the practice of allowing one's hair to grow. It was usual to take this vow only for a short time, but it was possible, as in the case of Samson and Samuel, for it to be binding for life.

We have already seen how the separation of the levites was regarded as a kind of sacrifice of the firstborn, which the people of Israel made as a whole and by which Yahweh waived his claim to the firstborn. All the same, each firstborn had to be "redeemed." Among the nations, Israel was Yahweh's firstborn and, as such, a holy people dedicated to Yahweh and to his service. The Pharaoh was commanded, under the threat of punishment, namely the death of his own firstborn, to let the firstborn son of Israel go (Exod. 4:22f). By killing the firstborn of Egypt, both the firstborn of men and those of animals, and by sparing those of Israel, Yahweh established a new right. As a result of this, every male animal which opened the womb had to be sacrificed to Yahweh, and every firstborn son had to be redeemed (Exod. 13:11–16). In this way—an authentically Yahwistic manner—the ancient, oriental practice of sacrificing the firstborn was rooted in Yahweh's historical acts, within his plan of salvation. It was in his sacrifice of the firstborn that the faithful Israelite confessed his faith in his nation's redemption and acquired a share in this redemption. We should also not overlook this aspect of Abraham's sacrifice (Gen. 22). The fact that Isaac was replaced by a ram, and in such an emphatic way, stamps the entire episode as the original account of Israel's first sacrifice of the firstborn, giving meaning and justification to all subsequent sacrifices.

This story at the same time gives a clear indication of the way Israel's religious feeling should follow and protects Israel against the unfortunate error of sacrificing children. The story undoubtedly contains an echo of the protest, so often heard in the Bible, against human sacrifice. In the ancient Near East, man was clearly prepared to kill his firstborn son for his god in the last extremity (2 Kings 3:27; *see also* Judges 11:30ff.; 1 Kings 16:34). The sacrifice of one's own children and of human beings in general was not uncommon in Israel's environment. Human sacrifice was in complete accordance with the pagan outlook of those times and the belief that the deity could be forced in this way into hearing and granting a petition. When the king of Moab offered his eldest son, the crown prince, publicly as a victim on the wall of his capital in full view of the army of the Israelites, the siege was at once raised and the Israelites went away, fearful of the effects of such a sacrifice (2 Kings 3:27). Once she had been contaminated by the pagan environment surrounding her, Israel too was obstinately inclined towards this kind of sacrifice. This is clear from the sharp reaction against this type of offering on the part of the Law (Lev. 18:21; 20:1-5), the prophets (Jer. 32:35; Ezek. 16:20f., 20:26, 23:37; Isa. 57:5), and the historical books (2 Kings 16:3, 17:17). Israel allowed her sons and daughters to "pass through the fire" even in honor of Yahweh (Mic. 6:7; Deut. 12:31, 18:9f.), but especially in honor of Moloch, the Baal of the Ammonites (1 Kings 11:7). In the valley of Hinnom or Gehenna, which bounded the two hills of the city of Jerusalem on the south, was Topheth, the notorious place where this Baal devoured his victims (2 Kings 23:10; Jer. 7:31f., 19:5f., 11-14).

Personal possessions were also offered at the sanctuary, either as a kind of tax or as a consecrated gift (Exod. 25:1–8; Num. 7). These especially included valuables, such as gold, silver, ornaments, precious stones, and all kinds of fabrics, but useful objects were also brought as offerings. The assurance that even the money received in taxes would be a "memorial of them (the Israelites) before the face of Yahweh, as an atonement for their lives" (Exod. 30:11–16) is clear evidence of the fact that the idea of sacrifice was very much alive here. Even the "buckles, bracelets, signet-rings, earrings and necklaces," brought to the sanctuary and given spontaneously in addition to Yahweh's prescribed share in the booty of war, were called "gifts to Yahweh, in atonement before the face of Yahweh." These gifts were taken by the priests into the tabernacle "for a memorial of the children of Israel before Yahweh" (Num. 31:48–54).

David gave Goliath's sword to the sanctuary at Nob, where it stood, wrapped in a cloak, behind the ephod (1 Sam. 21:9), just as the Philistines put Saul's armor in the temple of Ashtoreth at Beth-shan (1 Sam. 31:10), and as they had previously put the ark of the Covenant, which they had taken as a trophy in war, in the temple at Ashdod, near the statue of their god Dagon (1 Sam. 5:2).

The idea of sacrifice or offering is, however, most clearly reflected in the prayer of thanksgiving attributed by a late writer to David, after the collection which was made for the building of the temple. The almost synagogal character of this prayer should be noted. In his thanksgiving, David praised Yahweh in front of the entire assembly and said:

Blessed art thou, Yahweh, the God of our father Israel, from eternity to eternity.

Thine, O Yahweh, is magnificence, and power, and glory, and victory: and to thee is praise. For all that is in heaven, and in earth, is thine. Thine is the kingdom, O Yahweh, and thou art above all princes.

Thine are riches, and thine is glory: thou hast dominion over all. In thy hand is power and might: in thy hand greatness, and the empire of all things.

Now therefore, our God, we give thanks to thee: and we praise thy glorious Name. Who am I, and what is my people, that we should be able to give thee all these things? All things are thine: and we have given thee what we received of thy hand.

For we are sojourners before thee, and strangers, as all our fathers. Our days upon the earth are as a shadow, without hope. Yahweh, our God, all this wealth that we have prepared to build thee a house for thy holy Name is from thy hand: and all things are thine.

I know, my God, that thou provest hearts, and lovest simplicity. Wherefore I also in the simplicity of my heart have joyfully given all these things: and I have seen with great joy thy people, which are here present, give thee these gifts.

Yahweh, God of Abraham, and of Isaac, and of Israel, our fathers, keep for ever this will in the heart of thy people, and let this mind remain always for the worship of thee (1 Chron. 29:10–18).

(b) Types of Offering

The usual material offered for sacrifice included everything that was eaten or drunk by man for his own nourishment—the fruits of his field or of his livestock. Animals had, of course, to be slaughtered before the sacrifice, and this led to the original, and very general division between victims of blood offerings and bloodless offerings. The latter were in the main offerings of food and drink, and these were seldom offered on their own, but accompanied blood offerings. Both kinds could be offerings of the first fruits. When the whole of a slaughtered domestic animal was offered, this was known as a burnt offering or holocaust. In contrast to this whole offering, there was a partial offering. In this type of sacrifice, the most appetizing parts of the beast, or those parts in which its life was believed to be situated, were given to Yahweh. The priest received his share and the rest, especially in the case of a peace offering, was eaten by the one who had brought the animal and his family, in a communal meal.

Even in the case of normal slaughter, with no sacrifice in view, the animal's blood had to be allowed to pour on the ground and then was covered with earth, since uncovered blood cried to heaven (Isa. 26:21; Ezek. 24:7f.; Job. 16:18). When an animal was killed in connection with public worship, however, all kinds of blood rites accompanied the slaughter. The altar formed the object of these rites. Its sides were sprinkled with blood and the horns smeared with it. Blood was poured out over the foot of the altar. The sign of blood marked the whole of the Day of Atonement. Indeed, the general impression that one has is that "almost all things, according to the Law, are cleansed with blood; and without the shedding of blood there is no remission (of sins)" (Heb. 9:22). Here too, Israel shares the view common to the ancient world: "Because the life of the flesh is in the blood: and I have given it to you, that you may make atonement with it (exclusively) on the altar for your souls, for the blood achieves atonement by means of the soul" (Lev. 17:10–16; Deut. 12:23–27; Gen. 9:4).

Partly according to the rite and partly according to the material used, a distinction was made between various types of offering. The principal types were the burnt offerings, fire offerings, incense offerings, drink offerings, and the offerings incorporating movements of the hands.

In the case of the last named, the priest placed the part of the animal intended for him in the hands of the believer. Putting his own hands underneath, he made a stretching movement, first forward in the direction of the sanctuary and then back. Closely connected to this stretching sacrifice was the lifting sacrifice, so called because of the upward movement of the hands which the priest made. Both types of movement—the horizontal and the vertical—signified that the sacrifice was offered to Yahweh and given back by him.

Peace offerings were made, according to motive, as offerings giving thanks, votive offerings, or voluntary offerings. The offering of expiation took, according to the nature of the sin committed, the form of a sin offering or of a guilt offering. The names morning and evening sacrifice—sometimes known as constant offerings—and offering of the first fruits are self explanatory.

The offering of food consisted of vegetable matter—meal with oil and incense, flour baked in oil or corn which was grilled or roasted with incense. It was partially burnt. Some of the offering was kept for the priest, who was permitted to eat it only in the sanctuary (Lev. 2). The shewbreads can be included among this type of offering.

In drink offerings or libations, oil (Mic. 6:7) was poured out, and even more commonly wine (Hos. 9:4; 1 Sam. 1:24). In exceptional circumstances, water was used. Three of David's heroes broke into the Philistines' camp in Bethlehem, drew water there, and brought it back to their thirsty king. David, however, would not drink the water, but offered it to Yahweh, saying: "Shall I drink the blood of the men that went at the peril of their lives?" (2 Sam. 23:16f.). The prescribed pouring out of the blood of sacrificial animals was never called a drink offering. In Psalm 15, we read that libations of blood were a pagan abomination (*see also* Jer. 7:18, 19:13).

In accordance with the ancient custom common to the Near East, Israel also made offerings of all kinds of perfumes and scented incense "compounded by the work of the perfumer," that is to say, mixed according to the rules of the art (Exod. 30:34–38). The altar of incense stood behind the screen in the sanctuary, but it was also possible to make incense offerings outside the sanctuary by using the censer (Num. 16:46–48). This was a pan with a short handle. Fire was taken from the altar and placed in this pan. The perfumed incense was placed on top of the fire (Lev. 10:1, 16:12).

Man sought communion with his God by means of his offering.

By accepting the gift, God entered into a close relationship with the giver, who was represented in his gift and whose independence from and surrender to his God were expressed in this gift. The purest expression of this communion is to be found in the peace offering. Here, a part of the gift, which was sanctified by the offering and the altar, was burnt. This was Yahweh's part. After the priest's share had been set aside, the rest was consumed in a sacrificial meal, "joyfully before the face of Yahweh" (Deut. 12:12, 14:26). The same idea was also expressed in the rites of laying on of hands and sprinkling of blood.

The offering of expiation was, however, more directly aimed at removing the obstacles standing in the way of this communion with God. By it, God's anger, aroused by man's sin, was assuaged, and human sin and uncleanness were removed. On the Day of Atonement, this was vividly illustrated by the sending of the scapegoat into the desert, and in the case of leprosy, by the releasing of a bird in the open country outside the city (Lev. 14:7, 52).

As has already been observed in connection with the shewbreads, a very human idea of the deity may well have been reflected in the pre-Israelitic origin of such rituals. Traces of this are to be found in several biblical passages. Yahweh's share in the peace offering was, for example, referred to as food of the fire offering for Yahweh (Lev. 3:11, 16). Again, the priests had to be holy, "for they offer the fire offerings of Yahweh, the food of their God" (Lev. 21:6, 8, 17; 22; 25). It was the priests' duty to offer "My sacrificial gifts, my food, the fire-offerings of most sweet odour, in their due seasons" (Num. 28:2). Even the technical term "offerings of sweet odor" (*in odorem suavitatis*), for that matter, betrays, a least in some passages, its primitive origin. An example of this is Genesis 8:21. The translation, "Yahweh smelt the pacifying, or assuaging odor" would be preferable here (*see also* Lev. 26, 31; 1 Sam. 26:19; "stench" in Ezek. 8:17).

(c) Clean and Unclean

What was unclean could not be offered up, and could not even be used as food. What is more, even among clean animals, only domestic animals could be considered for the purpose of sacrifice. The dietary laws formed simply one part of a very extensive and complex system of regulations concerning cleanness, which were originally based, with the exception of hygienic considerations, on magic and animistic ideas (taboo). These ideas permeated the whole of society in the ancient Near East and frequently demanded the best of man's religious energy, to the detriment of essential religious values. The pious pagan had to be constantly on his guard. Always on the defensive, he had to be ready to take steps to neutralize the effects resulting from his inevitable contacts with objects capable of exercising a harmful influence. By taking on a definite historical and national form in such an environment, the new religion had also to find a concrete form for itself in a set of laws on cleanness. This is an example of how revelation monopolized the whole of ancient, oriental man, and placed his forms of expression at the disposal of true religiosity, by giving them a new content and meaning and by gradually purifying them.

Israel made a distinction between clean and unclean because Yahweh had distinguished between the nations: "You shall be holy unto me, because I, Yahweh, am holy: and I have separated you from other people, that you should be mine" (Lev. 20:25f.). In this way, the laws pertaining to cleanness acquired a pure religious character and became an important means of binding the Israelite in his daily life to his God: "For I am Yahweh, your God. Be holy, because I am holy. Defile not yourselves . . . For I am Yahweh, who brought you out of the land of Egypt, that I might be your God. You shall be holy, because I am holy" (Lev. 11:44f.).

Holiness and cleanness were closely related concepts. Israel kept the laws of cleanness because the Holy One of Israel was in her midst. At the same time, however, these laws were also a very effective means of preserving Israel from all that was preeminently unholy—false gods and that which was connected with the worship of idols. Since these false gods were unclean, the lands and people belonging to them were also unclean. In order to stress Israel's duty to be clean and holy, the Bible went so far as to express her election in the following way. Yahweh had appointed the heavenly bodies to be the share of "all the nations, that are under heaven" (for their worship), "but Yahweh hath taken you and brought you out of the iron furnace of Egypt, to make you his people of inheritance" (Deut. 4:19f.). Israel, however, believing in Yahweh, had chosen the better part (*see* Ps. 15).

The laws of cleanness thus became a practical experience of Israel's exclusive bond with Yahweh and a means by which she was always able to resist all forms of paganism. As soon as Israel, however, threatened to lose the new content and meaning of these forms and to degenerate into the external formalism that was characteristic of the pagan way of life, the prophet, conscious of the relation between the form and the content, began to emphasize the importance of inward religious attitude. The sages and teachers of wisdom stressed Yahweh's moral demands almost to the exclusion of the laws of cleanness. The distinctive character which the customs and practices relating to cleanness throughout the ancient Near East acquired in Israel is clearly discernible in this development.

Both animals and vegetable foods were divided into clean and unclean. Detailed lists have been preserved of the unclean animals (Lev. 11; Deut. 14). The fruits of the earth were clean, but the products of foreign lands were regarded as unclean (Amos 7:17; Hos. 9:3; Dan. 1:8). The fruit of trees was considered unclean during the first three years of the tree's life. The fourth year's crop was reserved for Yahweh, and thereafter the Israelites were allowed to eat the fruit (Lev. 19:23–25). They were permitted to eat new corn only after they had offered the first fruits, that is to say, the first sheaf of the new harvest, to Yahweh (Lev. 23:14). They were also not allowed to harvest the entire crop of the field, the orchard and the vineyard. The last of the harvest had to be left for the poor to glean: "Remember that thou also wast a bondman in Egypt: and therefore I command thee to do this thing" (Lev. 19:9f., 23:22; Deut. 24:19–22).

The faithful Israelite was thus made aware, in these and similar laws, of the essence of his religion, namely that his entire person and all that he possessed belonged absolutely to Yahweh. These laws also enabled Israel, as a faithful community, to experience her redemption once again, the redemption which had made her Yahweh's people in a pagan environment. The following quotation illustrates the spirit which underlay and sustained the apparatus of worship in Israel:

And when thou art come into the land which Yahweh, thy God, will give thee to possess, and hast conquered it, and dwellest in it: thou shalt take the first of all thy fruits, and put them in a basket, and shalt go to the place which Yahweh, thy God, shall choose, that his Name may be invocated there. And thou shalt go to the priest that shall be in those days, and say to him:

I profess this day before Yahweh, thy God, that I am come into the land, for which he swore to our fathers, that he would give it us.

And the priest, taking the basket at thy hand, shall set it before the altar of Yahweh, thy God. And thou shalt speak thus in the sight of Yahweh, thy God:

My father was a wandering Aramaean, who went down into Egypt with a very small number of men, and sojourned there as a stranger, and grew into a nation great and strong and of an infinite multitude.

When the Egyptians afflicted us, and persecuted us, laying on us most grievous burdens, we cried to Yahweh, the God of our fathers: who heard us, and looked down upon our affliction, and labour, and distress.

And Yahweh brought us out of Egypt, with a strong hand, and a stretched-out arm, with great terror, with signs and wonders, and brought us into this place, and gave us this land, a land flowing with milk and honey.

And therefore now I bring the first-fruits of the land which thou, Yahweh, hast given me.

And thou shalt leave them in the sight of Yahweh, thy God: thou shalt bow down before Yahweh, thy God: and thou shalt rejoice in all the good things which Yahweh, thy God, hath given thee and thy house: thou and the levite, and the stranger that is with thee (Deut. 26:1–11).

5. *Israel's Calendar of Feasts*

The fact that the purely religious element was of first importance in Israel's worship is particularly clear in the nation's calendar of feasts. Although this was composed of very ancient elements, for the most part traceable, these elements acquired in Israel a significance which linked them directly to Yahweh's historical acts of salvation. This applies too to the three great annual feasts, when the whole nation—probably acting in accordance with a purely theoretical ideal (1 Sam. 1:3; Luke 2:41)—made a pilgrimage to the sanctuary (Exod. 23:14–17, 34:23f.; Lev. 23; Deut. 16).

(a) The Great Feasts

Passover gives the impression of having been originally two feasts of the first fruits which, in the course of time, merged into one, single feast. In the Bible, two such feasts are clearly distinguished. The ritual of the paschal lamb must have had its origin in the pastoral way of life. The feast of the unleavened loaves, on the other hand, undoubtedly goes back to the practices of an agrarian population. This feast was celebrated when the sickle was used for the first time to cut the standing corn (Deut. 16:9). The offering of the first fruits of the harvest—the first sheaves of barley—played a part in the rite (Lev. 23:10), and the conditions under which the harvesters had to work undoubtedly resulted in their making do with unleavened bread and grilled corn of the new crop (Joshua 5:11; Ruth 2:14). This happened in all cases of haste (Gen. 18:6, 19:3; Exod. 12:33f.).

Although the association with the cycle of peasant life was never broken in these rites, the recollection of past history became more and more important in their celebration. The word pāsaḥ, meaning to leap or to pass over was connected in the minds of the people with the word *pesah,* "Pasch" or "Passover," and the ancient blood rite used to ward off disaster, since the angel of destruction had passed over the houses of the Hebrews in Egypt which had been signed with blood. Similarly, the unleavened loaves reminded the people of the haste in which they had departed from Egypt, under pressure from the Egyptians themselves: "The people took dough before it was leavened: and tying it in their cloaks, put it on their shoulders . . . And they baked the meal, which a little before they had brought out of Egypt, in dough. And they made unleavened loaves, for they had no leavened dough, the Egyptians pressing them to depart and not leaving them time to prepare food for the journey" (Exod. 12:34, 39; Deut. 16:3).

The agrarian nature of the second great feast is expressed in the name by which it is reported in the Bible. This feast was called variously the "feast of the harvest" (Exod. 23: 16), the "feast of the first-fruits of the wheat" (Exod. 34:22), or the "feast of the weeks." This last name was the most common and is explained by the fact that the feast occurred seven weeks after the celebration of Passover, thus on the fiftieth day (Lev. 23:16). The Greek word for "fiftieth," *pentēkostē,* has provided us with the name of the Christian feast of Pentecost, or Whitsun (*see* Tobias 2:1; 2 Macc. 12:31f.). The agrarian origin of this cycle of seven weeks or fifty days is clearly discernible from the way in which it was calculated—the cycle includes the entire corn harvest from the beginning of the barley harvest to the end of the wheat harvest. Pentecost, then, was the great feast of the corn harvest (Deut. 16:9–12). The offering of the first fruits of two leavened loaves (Lev. 22:17), is evidence of the fact that the harvest time, which had begun with the eating of unleavened bread, was at an end and that life was about to resume its normal course.

The liturgical prayer from the book of Deuteronomy, quoted at the end of the preceding section, provides clear proof of Israel's powerful memory of her deliverance from Egypt and of her gratitude for this redemption within the framework of an agrarian feast (*see also* Deut. 16:12). This grateful memory and its historical significance within the plan of salvation became more and more important when, in the Jewish period, the feast had lost most of its close associations with the cycle of agricultural life. It is clear that the many pilgrims who witnessed the miracle of Pentecost at Jerusalem (Acts 2:5), had not come to the city to celebrate a feast of the harvest. Why, then, had they come to Jerusalem? An explicit reason is given in sources dating back to the second century A.D. The feast of the weeks was a memorial of the giving of the Law to Moses on Mount Sinai, the revelation of the Torah.

At least in certain circles, however, the feast had this special significance much earlier than the second century A.D. The book of Jubilees (6:17), says that the feast of the weeks was celebrated each year as an annual renewal of the Covenant. This is confirmed by the finds made since 1947 near the Dead Sea. The Qumran sect called itself the "community of the New Covenant," and the feast of the weeks was the titular feast of the community because it was the annual renewal of the Covenant.

The dating given in Exodus 19:1: "In the third month after the departure of Israel out of the land of Egypt, . . . they came into the wilderness of Sinai" may perhaps explain this. It was halfway through the first month (the fourteenth day of Abib or Nisan, Lev. 23:5; Exod. 23:15; Esther 3:7), that the Israelites left Egypt.

Seven weeks after this brings us into the third month. In the light of this, there is something to be said for the claim that the great renewal of the Covenant at the time of king Asa took place (according to 2 Chron. 15:10), in the third month!

The year ended with the celebration of the feast of the fruit and wine harvest. This was the most popular and the most joyous feast of all, and was known as the "feast of the gathering in" (Exod. 23:16, 34:22), the "feast of Yahweh" (Lev. 23:39), or simply *"the feast"* (1 Kings 8:2, 65: *see also* John 7:10, 37). The tabernacles—huts or cabins covered with foliage—were erected in the orchards and vineyards so that the vine dressers could guard their crops (Isa. 1:8; Job 27:18; Ps. 78:1). It is probable that many vine dressers camped out with their families in the vineyards at harvest time.

In the opinion of some scholars, the ancient Canaanite form of this feast is to be found in an incidental reference to the citizens of Shechem: "They went out into the fields to harvest and to tread down the grapes and to celebrate a feast. And they went into the temple of their god and ate and drank" (Judges 9:27). Similarly, the Israelitic form of the feast is possibly that of the "annual feast of Yahweh at Shiloh," when the Benjamites, in order to take the maidens of Shiloh captive while they were dancing, chose the vineyards as a hiding-place (Judges 21:19–21).

The feast increased in importance because of Solomon's decision to dedicate the temple on this day. This was the religious coronation of the capital and of the dynasty, and thus a feast of the royal enthronement. "Solomon made a solemn feast, and all Israel with him: a great multitude, from the entrance of Hamath (that is, from the extreme north) to the river of Egypt (the extreme south), before Yahweh, our God, for seven days. And on the eighth day he sent away the people. And they took leave of the king, and went to their dwellings rejoicing and glad in heart for all the good things that Yahweh had done for David, his servant, and for Israel, his people" (1 Kings 8:65f.). The Northern Kingdom initiated its own tradition in the celebration of this feast, keeping it a month later than Judah. Just as Solomon had made offerings at the time of the dedication of the temple, Jeroboam went up at this time each year to the altar of Bethel (1 Kings 12:26–33).

The Israelites were ritually bound to live in tabernacles at the time of this feast, and this practice characterizes the feast to such an extent that the name "Feast of Tabernacles" became general in the later books of the Bible, from Deuteronomy 16:13 onwards. The feast's association with the harvest was never lost sight of, but the practice of living in tabernacles during the feast was enriched by Israel's living memory of her redemption and, less explicitly, of the culmination of this redemption in the Davidic monarchy: "When you shall have gathered in all the fruits of your land, . . . you shall take the fruits of the fairest tree, and branches of palm trees, and boughs of thick trees, and willows of the brook: and you shall re-joice before Yahweh, your God, seven days . . . And you shall dwell in bowers seven days. Every one that is of the race of Israel shall dwell in tabernacles: that your posterity may know, that I made the children of Israel to dwell in tabernacles (tents), when I brought them out of the land of Egypt" (Lev. 23: 39–43).

It was the Feast of Tabernacles when Ezra read the Law before the great assembly of the whole people, who had come together as one man on the square in front of the Water Gate. The account of this gathering, in Nehemiah 8, can give us a good impression of Jewish practices at the time of this feast, as it was clearly compiled with the purpose of legitimizing these practices and of giving them a deeper meaning. What this account does is to standardize a program for the feast in narrative form.

The inhabitants of the city had to go up to the Mount to fetch foliage from the olive-trees and branches of myrtle and palm. With this foliage they made tabernacles on the roofs of their own houses, in their own courts, in the forecourts of the temple, and on the squares in front of the Water Gate and the Ephraim Gate. During the feast, the entire community lived in tabernacles and a spirit of great joy prevailed. The Law was read on every day of the feast, from the first day to the seventh and last. The last day of the feast was marked by special festivity. This was henceforth the prescribed pattern of the Feast of Tabernacles.

The Christian counterpart to this is to be found in the popular festivities which are loosely connected with the liturgical season, but which take place outside the Church—carnivals, fairs, the popular celebration of Christmas, and so on. But this popular celebration of the Feast of Tabernacles was definitely encouraged in Israel. When, for example, the people were moved to tears by the words of the Law, Ezra told them: "This is a holy day to Yahweh, your God: do not mourn or weep . . . Go, eat fat meats, and drink sweet wine, and send portions to them that have not prepared for themselves; because it is the holy day of our Lord, and be not sad. For the joy of Yahweh is your strength" (8:9f.). The people at once went off to eat and drink and to distribute gifts in a joyful mood. The writer of this account, who knew from his own experience that such words would not fall on deaf ears, adds that the people had understood what Ezra had told them!

The ritual practice of waving willow branches and the *lûlab*, a bunch of leafy branches, mentioned in post biblical sources, can already be discerned in this passage from Ezra. Another undoubtedly ancient rite, performed for the purpose of obtaining rain, is also mentioned in later documents. Every morning during the week of the feast, priests drew water from the pool of Siloam, and carried it in procession in a golden vessel to the temple, where it was poured out on the southwest side—the rainy side—of the altar for the burnt offerings (*see also* John 7:37f.). This rite was also a historical recollection of the water from the rock, and at the same time a foreshadowing of the messianic salvation (Isa. 12:3).

This third great annual feast was preceded by a day of general fasting and penance, the Day of Atonement. The most significant rite which took place on this day was that of the two goats. These were brought to stand "before the face of Yahweh." Lots were cast over them, one for Yahweh and one for the demon of the desert, Azazel. The goat whose lot fell to Yahweh was sacrificed as a sin offering. The high priest took some of its blood behind the screen and sprinkled it on the propitiatory of the ark and seven times in front of the propitiatory. The same rite was also performed outside at the altar. This was followed by the confession of sins, during which the high priest kept both his hands on the head of the living goat. Finally, this goat was sent off into the desert, where it became a sacrifice to the wilderness, that is, to Azazel. In this way, Israel's sin was removed from human society, far from the sight of Yahweh and his people (Lev. 16).

As has already been pointed out at the beginning of the third section of this chapter, blood, as the seat of life, had a very special function in the levitical ritual. The essential part of the sacrifice was not the slaughtering of the sacrificial animal. The priests themselves did not perform this action, and it never took place on the altar. The actual offering came about when the blood came into contact with the altar, and this rite was reserved for the priest. In the whole of the sacrificial act, it was the blood which signified the people's living communion with Yahweh. Above all, the blood referred to the restoration of this communion. This accounts for the special significance of the blood rite in the sin offering. The Day of Atonement was, above all, the solemn and detailed accomplishment of a sin offering for the priests and the people. The blood rite described above must, therefore, be regarded as the essential and crucial part of the ceremony. Its deep significance was brought vividly to the minds of the people by the ancient and popular rite of the scapegoat, which also served to expand the ceremony.

(b) The New Moon and the Sabbath

In normal life, the day of the new moon and the seventh day of the week—often referred to in the same context (Hos. 2:11; Amos 8:5; Isa. 1:13, 66:23)—occupied a special place, which was closely connected with the overriding importance of the moon in chronology. A new month was begun as soon as the crescent moon appeared, and an intercalary month was inserted in the spring whenever it was clear, from the state of the corn, that Passover and the feast of the weeks, considered in connection with the prescribed offerings of the first fruits, would fall too early in the year. It was also possible that the paschal lamb had to have been born during the current year—a "son of the year" (Exod. 12:5). This meaning is acceptable, so long as one is bold enough to challenge the view that the phrase must necessarily mean one year old.

On the day of the new moon, it was the custom to rest from work (Amos 8:5), and to make pilgrimages to a man of God (2 Kings 4:23). Widely scattered families would come together for a solemn, sacrificial meal in the place of their birth, and at the court a festive meal was held, only those who were clean being permitted to take their place at table (1 Sam. 20). Special offerings were made in the temple, as on all days of particular importance (Num. 28f.).

The remarkable thing about the sabbath is that it was dissociated from the four phases of the moon with which the week was originally connected. In Israel, the weeks were counted one after the other, independent of the moon's phases. It may well be possible that this was done in counteraction to the very widespread and popular moon cult. Even in the oldest texts there is mention of the day of rest (Exod. 20:8-11, 16, 34:21, 35:3; Num. 15:32), but it would seem that this was, in practice, very slackly observed (Jer. 17:21-27; Ezek. 20:13, 16, 21:24, 22:8, 26; Neh. 13:15-22). After the Exile, however, the sabbath was kept more strictly than ever, as it became one of the important means by which the Jews were able to preserve themselves in their pagan environment (1 Macc. 1:41–45, 2:32–41; 2 Macc. 5:25f., 6:6–11; *see also* Isa. 56:2–6, 58:13f.).

Whatever may have been the origin and point of departure for Israel's sabbath in the ancient Near East, the fact remains that it developed into a distinctively Israelitic observance, something through which Israel was able to experience and express her faith in practice. Keeping the sabbath, the Israelite was regularly confronted with Yahweh as his Creator and the Redeemer of his people. Not only was it possible for the Israelite to be recognized by his keeping of the sabbath, but the sabbath also reminded him constantly of his own vocation. The sabbath was the sign of the Covenant (Exod. 31:13, 17). The "sign between me and them: that they might know that I am Yahweh that sanctify them," in other words, a sign that Yahweh was Israel's God (Ezek. 20:12, 20). The seventh day was a "day for Yahweh." It belonged to him as a kind of consecrated gift. This law was contained in the nature of the proportions which the Creator had established, once and for all time. In order to impress this upon men's minds, the Genesis story of creation spread God's work over six days, with the result that he rested on the seventh day and sanctified it (Exod. 20:11; 31:17; *see also* Gen. 2:3).

Apart from its religious significance, the day of rest also had a social basis, which was particularly reminiscent of Israel's redemption: "that thy ox and thy ass may rest, and the son of thy handmaid and the stranger may be refreshed" (Exod. 23:12). "Remember that thou also didst serve in Egypt, and Yahweh, thy God, brought thee out from thence with a strong hand, and a stretched-out arm. Therefore hath Yahweh, thy God, commanded thee that thou shouldst observe the sabbath day" (Deut. 5:15).

What is true of the whole of Israel's calendar of feasts and the whole of her worship is, therefore, also true of the sabbath. Together with all the other aspects of Israel's worship, the sabbath did not draw the faithful Israelite's attention away from his essential religious and social duties. Its aim was, on the contrary, to enable him to experience a communion with Yahweh. The psalms, which were inspired by worship, give ample evidence that this was no mere theory. It is also possible to hear the voice of personal experience in a prophetical text such as this:

> If thou dost not violate the sabbath,
> dost not seek thy own will on my holy day:
> but call the sabbath delightful,
> the holy day of Yahweh glorious;
> while thou dost not thy own ways
> and thy own will is not found:
> then shalt thou be delighted in Yahweh,
> and I will lift thee up above the high places of the earth,
> and will feed thee with the inheritance of Jacob, thy father,
> For the mouth of Yahweh hath spoken it (Isa. 58:13f.).

6. Israel as a Worshiping Community

In the previous chapter, in our discussion of the name Yahweh, we gave a concise description of Israel's sense of God. What has emerged from this discussion of Israel's worship is how this sense of God was expressed in Israel and the demands that it made upon Israel as a community. It should be possible, then, to form an idea of how the phenomenon Israel originated and how it could continue to exist. Just as the temple later on formed the focal point of the state, so did the tabernacle in the earlier stages form the central point of the camp. By forming a holy and priestly community of worship around the sanctuary, the tribes grew together and became one, close, national community, capable of preserving itself. The difference between Israel and the other nations is to be found in Israel's faith in Yahweh—a pure understanding of what was authentically divine, that is without precedent. It is this which made Israel a holy people in the midst of unclean nations—unclean as the result of the worship of false gods, the source of all uncleanness, as Yahweh was the source of all holiness.

(a) The Priestly People

Because of this, Israel was a priestly people. The priest is set apart in society so that he is free to devote himself to those things which are directly related to God and religion, whereas the layman's attention is, in the main, claimed by secular matters. In this way, Israel existed in the midst of other nations as a priestly people, a "kingdom of priests" (Exod. 19:6), since the service of false gods was preeminently profane, that is, unclean, whereas only Israel was Yahweh's people (Deut. 4:19f.).

Israel, therefore, was called priestly, neither because the whole people was called to the priestly ministry, nor because she had a class of vocational priests—what national group did not have such a class?—but because she was the only people in her environment to have found her God in an entirely new way. Thus it was that the psalmist saw the theocratic son of David of the messianic future, in contrast to the unfaithful kings of the house of David. To the psalmist, the future Messiah seemed so devoted to Yahweh that he called him a priest of the order of Melchizedek, the priest-king of Jerusalem during the earliest period of Israel's existence (Ps. 109:4). The prophet Isaiah similarly depicted the messianic people as a nation of priests, in contrast to unfaithful Israel. Others would do all the secular work:

Strangers shall stand and shall feed your flocks:
and strangers shall be your husbandmen and the dressers of your vines.
But you shall be called the priests of Yahweh;
to you it shall be said: Ye ministers of our God (Isa. 61:5f.).

In calling Israel holy and priestly (the two terms are in fact synonymous), the Bible was expressing, in one way, Israel's exceptional position among the other nations of the world. If it had simply been a question of one national god among others, this description might have sufficed. But the sacred writers of Scripture were conscious of the fact that they were dealing with the God of the World who had concerned himself with one nation in particular. This inevitably led to a tentative and diverse terminology. Israel was consequently called Yahweh's "firstborn" among the nations, a word implying all the privileges attached to the firstborn son of the family. The same idea of privilege was implied in Yahweh's choosing Israel from among the other peoples, in his having separated Israel, or set her apart, and above all in his having redeemed her. (By redemption is meant, of course, buying off or ransom, the support given by a close relative to someone unable to stand up for himself.) The Bible also speaks of Yahweh having "acquired" Israel as his strictly "personal possession" and as his "inheritance," or everlasting possession. Almost all these terms are to be found in the following text:

Thou art a *holy* people to Yahweh, thy God.
Yahweh, thy God, hath chosen thee to be his *peculiar* (*own*) people of all the peoples that are upon the earth.
Not because you surpass all nations in number is Yahweh *joined* unto you, and hath *chosen* you: for you are the fewest of any people.
But because Yahweh hath *loved* you, and hath kept his oath, which he swore to your fathers, hath Yahweh . . . *redeemed* you . . . and thou shalt know that Yahweh, thy God, is the only God, the faithful God, keeping his covenant and mercy to them that love him . . . unto a thousand generations (Deut. 7:6–9).

Although most of these terms are sufficiently clear in themselves, the emotive force contained in the word "own" (Israel as Yahweh's own people among the nations), is often overlooked.

(b) The People of Yahweh's Possession

Because they were created by him, all the nations were Yahweh's possession, but only Israel was chosen from among them all to be the particular people of his possession (*'am seghullāh, laos periousios, populus peculiaris—populus peculii*). Seghullāh can be defined as a possession that has been acquired as a result of one's own labors and special effort, and thus a strictly personal, precious, and well-loved possession.

It was that part of a man's property which he treasured above everything else, and which he kept apart from all the rest as a precious jewel. The Talmud, for example, refers to the laboriously acquired savings (see the Latin translation) or precious stones which were always carried in a bundle, close to the heart. The emotive force of the word can be felt strongly in the passage in which David urged the people to contribute to the building of the temple. First of all he enumerated all the things which he had personally contributed—gold, silver, bronze, iron, and wood; onyx stones, carbuncles, jasper, and chrysolite, and an abundance of other precious stones and marbles. Then he went on to say: "Now over and above the things which I have offered into the house of my God I give, of my own proper goods (*seghullāh* = my own personal possession), gold and silver for the house of my God, beside what things I have prepared for the sanctuary." *Seghullāh* here was clearly the family property of a royal house, possibly the estate of the Crown, and royal possessions in a different sense from the rest of the land. It must have been David's personal possessions, and indeed his precious possessions, since *seghullāh* implies above all valuable and rare pieces, the pride of the eastern monarch (*see* Eccles. 2:8). David, then, made available all gold and silver that he had in his treasury. This came to three thousand talents of gold from Ophir and seven thousand talents of silver. Inspired and encouraged by his royal example, the heads of Israel's tribes and families voluntarily offered their gifts; parting with their personal property of precious stones ("all that they had"), for the treasure of the house of Yahweh, rejoicing in their voluntary gift, "because they offered them to Yahweh with all their heart; and David the king rejoiced also with a great joy" (1 Chron. 29:1–9).

Thus it is that Israel was Yahweh's special possession; the people belonged to Yahweh in the same special way that a royal estate or a private collection of precious stones and jewels belonged to the nation's king. This emerges with great clarity from the classic text (Exod. 19:5); the entire earth belonged to Yahweh and the peoples of the earth were his possession, but, among them, only Israel was his *seghullāh,* and therefore a kingdom of priests and a holy people (*see also* Deut. 7:6; 14:2; 26:18; Mal. 3:17; Ps. 134:4). The New Testament too refers back to this concept which is so rich in meaning. Christ ransomed and purified us, and thereby acquired us as the people of his possession (Eph. 1:14; Titus 2:14; 1 Pet. 2:9).

(c) The People of the Covenant

In the last resort, it was always the same, basic reality that the Bible was seeking to define by these many formulations. The fact that there is, however, such an abundance of them also reveals just how rich in implicit, religious content the relationship of the Covenant was. This relationship was not confined merely to the ritual level. It had an impact on the whole life of the people. It was the driving force behind Israel's organization as a nation. This was clearly expressed by the rites employed in Israel's worship. Israel's beginning as the "community of Yahweh" (*qāhēl yaheweh*), led to her eventual formation as a national community. The people were summoned by Yahweh to come together in his service. Yahweh called them together (*ekklēsia*). Israel's service of Yahweh extended to every sphere of life (the Covenant), but it was expressed in, and nourished by her worship, with the result that the community of

Yahweh was not only the people of the Covenant, but also, and preeminently, a community of worship (*see* Leviticus).

As long as Israel remained sound, the ritual and the moral elements were inseparably linked. The moral decalogue (Exod. 20:2–17; *see also* Deut. 5:6–21), and the ritual decalogue (Exod. 34:14–26) are both found among the oldest elements of the Pentateuch, and the Covenant came about on a basis of both (Exod. 24:8 and 34:27).

It was not without good reason that the tablets of the Law were kept in the ark. The ten commandments summed up the natural law and, in their moral insight, were quite without parallel in the whole of the ancient Near East. Together with the book of the Covenant (Exod. 20:22–23:19), which was, to a very great extent, a Yahwistic, that is to say, an Israelitic formulation of the common law practised throughout the entire eastern world, the commandments express the ethical nature of Israel's feeling for God. The rite of the making of the Covenant on Mount Sinai emphasized this even more strongly. After having sprinkled one half of the blood of the victims over the altar, Moses read the book of the Covenant aloud in the hearing of the people, who said: "All the things that Yahweh hath spoken we will do. We will be obedient." Then Moses took the remaining half of the blood and sprinkled it over the people, pronouncing the words which are so important for the proper understanding of the Christian mystery: "This is the blood of the covenant which Yahweh hath made with you: it is based upon all these commands" (Exod. 24:4–8; *see also* 1 Cor. 11:25; Luke 22:20; Matt. 26:28; Mark 14:24).

This blood rite, which was, according to the ancient, oriental view, effective in bringing about a blood relationship in the literal sense between a people and their god, who was represented by the altar, was a vivid and bold portrayal of the intimate sense of community brought about between Yahweh and Israel by the Covenant. This, however, was counterbalanced by the great stress laid on the conditions of the Covenant. In spite of the blood rite, the Covenant was not based on a natural bond which had been brought about automatically and whose inner core of meaning could be sensed by pure, religious instinct. It was, on the contrary, based on mutual free choice, a choice expressed in the very word "covenant." It was not by chance, then, that the word "covenant" occupied such an all-important place in the theology of Israel, in which it was used to characterize the relationship between God and people. Man had to make a free, religious decision, a personal choice, of necessity involving his entire life and conduct, to surrender to Yahweh. For his part, Yahweh was free to choose and to show his grace and favor to whom he wished. The mutual nature and the freedom of this allegiance between Yahweh and Israel is emphasized in the following passage:

Thou hast chosen Yahweh this day to be thy God; and Yahweh hath chosen thee this day, to be his peculiar people (= the people of his possession), as he hath spoken to thee.

Thou shalt walk in his ways and keep his commandments, and listen to his voice.

And he shall make thee higher than all nations which he hath created in praise, in name, and in glory,

that thou mayest be a holy people, sanctified to Yahweh, thy God, as he hath spoken (Deut. 26:17–19).

The obligation, which Israel voluntarily undertook in the Covenant, is expressed thus in the book of Deuteronomy:

And now, Israel, what doth Yahweh, thy God, require of thee: but that thou fear Yahweh, thy God, and walk in his ways, and love him, and serve Yahweh, thy God, with all thy heart and with all thy soul: and keep the commandments of Yahweh . . . that it may be well with thee (Deut. 10:12f.).

This was the necessary human response. The question, on God's part, was no less than the offer of his Covenant to the people of his choice:

Behold, the heaven is Yahweh's, thy God, and the heaven of heaven, the earth and all things that are therein. And yet Yahweh hath been closely joined to thy fathers, and loved them, and chose their seed after them: that is to say, you, out of all nations, as this day it is proved (Deut. 10:14f.).

So long as Israel remained faithful to this Covenant, her salvation was assured: "I shall bless your bread and your waters: and shall take away sickness from the midst of thee. There shall not be one fruitless or barren (woman) in thy land. I will fill the number of thy days" (Exod. 23:25f.: Lev. 26). An adequate exposition has been made about these saving possessions in the final section of the chapter on the Patriarchs of Israel. Without obscuring their essentially worldly character, they must, nevertheless, be seen in their functional connection with Israel's sense of God. In this context, Israel's worldly, saving possessions—so closely tied to the immediate human needs of the time—give shape and form to the purely religious values in an authentic human and living reality. Through them, Yahweh demonstrated that he was indeed Yahweh. In them, he revealed his saving will, and in her faithful expectation and her appreciation of these possessions Israel was able, for the first time, to give tentative, but concrete expression to her longing for divine salvation.

In this chapter, we have attempted to provide an insight into the religious system of Israel, insofar as this is reflected in the Bible. Israel's vague concept of God and her scarcely defined expectations of her oldest period, firmly rooted in the same sense of God, gradually developed to the point where they eventually crystallized into permanent forms. From then onwards, these forms were stereotyped. These fixed and unchanging forms were, for the centuries which followed, to be the religion of Israel as an ancient, oriental people. The name Yahweh was a summary of the truth that Yahwism was Israel's religion.

V

The King of Israel

IN THIS CHAPTER, special attention will be devoted to the historical framework within which Israel's religion acquired the shape and form described, in the preceding two chapters, as a finished whole rather than as a historical process. This framework will, at the same time, supply the background to the chapter which follows. The last time that Israel's social and geographical situation was discussed in this book was at the beginning of the second chapter, in connection with the name "Hebrew." The survey which follows should be read with this in mind.

1. The Nature of the Biblical Data

As Israel proclaimed her greatness in history in well-defined terms, this self-definition must have begun to develop during the Hebrew period (about 1800–1200). Is it at all possible to trace the process of this development? The biblical data can only with difficulty be applied to such a task, because the detailed account of this period is overwhelmingly theological in purport. The Bible did not, after all, confine itself to pure history, aiming as it did to tell the history of salvation. In this, Israel made use of her historical memory—that most important source for the biblical historiographer—of the Hebrew period. Scripture, then, narrated past history because of the message which Scripture had for the present. The material as-similated into the Pentateuch was situated entirely in the Hebrew period, and it is undoubtedly in that period that we must look for its origin. Nonetheless, the Pentateuch provided a religious inter-pretation of the phenomenon of Israel and even of the phenomenon of the Jewish world, just as each of these phenomena in turn mani-fested themselves in, for example, the ninth and the fifth centuries. Or, to express this in another way, the account of Israel's origin was filled in with empirical data relating to Israel during the age of the kings and even to the postexilic Jewish society, and these facts were kept constantly in mind during the writing of the account. The bib-lical authors thus tended to schematize and to simplify their histori-cal material. This has led to frequent misunderstandings on the part of biblical scholars in the past.

The most important of these simplifications is that mature Israel, as a whole, can be found in the Hebrew period of her infancy. Simi-larly, the whole of Israel was oppressed in Egypt, journeyed through the desert, and conquered Canaan. The Jewish historiographers, who exerted a powerful influence on the Pentateuch, extended this thought still further, and the belief that the society of the Jews was the community of Yahweh impressed itself on the pentateuchal ac-count. The ancient, biblical histories frequently provide a recon-struction of the Israelitic camp in the desert—the twelve tribes, each within its strictly defined area, assembled around the tent of the sanctuary. It will always be difficult to understand exactly what this corresponds to in the past. Nonetheless, no doubt can be cast on the essential value of these chapters (Num. 1-4), since they aimed to give a vivid picture, based, after all, on all kinds of historical facts, of the religious situation of the people of God as such. The Jewish world, gathered round the restored temple of Jerusalem, was literally giving, in this desert image, a picture of itself and of its own situa-tion.

Aaron set up a golden calf at the foot of Mount Sinai. Several cen-

turies later, king Jeroboam did the same in the royal sanctuaries of
Bethel and Dan (Exod. 32; 1 Kings 12:26ff.). It is not pure coincidence that both accounts should contain so many points of agreement, and that both should have their climax in the sentence: "O
Israel, behold the God that hath brought thee out of the land of
Egypt." Once again, it may well be very difficult to understand
exactly what Aaron did, in view of the fact that the Exodus text
was first and foremost intended as a condemnation of and a warning against the worship of the calf to which Israel was so inclined in
Canaan. It should not, however, be overlooked that it was the
normal course of events in the Bible for a warning of this kind to
occur in close connection with a recollection of an incident in the
desert. It would, nevertheless, be a great pity if, in our assiduous
search for and exclusive appreciation of established historical fact,
we should fail to perceive that what we have here is an account of
national, original sin. The story of the golden calf is significant and
original in that it reveals the most conspicuous national sin which
beset Israel during her sedentary period and the most important
cause of her national disaster.

These two examples are illustrative of the way in which Scripture
related past history so as to pass on a message applicable to the
present. The Bible, then, preaches by telling a story. This preaching
is never vague, because it is always crystallized around facts. That is
why it is always possible to learn from Scripture how events occurred in broad outline.

2. *The Rise of the Hebrew "Amphictyony"*

It is possible to distinguish several different stages in the gradual
formation of certain Hebrew clans into a separate, national community. There were three stages during Moses' life. By making the
heterogeneous group which came out of Egypt into a people of God,
Moses marked this group out as a separate people. The full year

spent in the vicinity of Sinai was no more than a not too successful beginning, an attempt to create order out of chaos. The stories of the manna in the desert (Exod. 16), and of Jethro's visit (Exod. 18), are indicative of memories of measures concerning the provision of food and the administration of justice. The fact that such an extensive complex of laws could be linked with Sinai is a clear indication that Sinai was the point of departure.

The long period spent around the desert sanctuary of Kadesh was undoubtedly of far greater importance in the process of national development (Num. 20:1; Deut. 1:46). It was there that the unmanageable Egyptian generation literally died out (Num. 14:21–35), so that it was possible for something new to be built up from the ground. A social, and even a liturgical legislation could acquire a fixed form in this ordered and stable society. Kadesh, fifty miles south of Beer-sheba, was an extensive complex of oases, and clearly the ideal environment for the religious federation of tribes which must have had its beginning here.

The Bible has made us very familiar with the twelve tribes of Israel. It goes without saying that this system, which would seem to lay itself open to the charge of artificiality by being based on the number twelve, was held in great suspicion by scholars of the nineteenth century. One such view was that it was a later theoretical construction, originating in the priestly circles of the postexilic society. Now, however, the tendency is to accept the existence of twelve tribes. Modern exegesis accepts the biblical statement of Nahor's twelve sons (Gen. 22:20–24), first and foremost as an indication that sedentary Israel recognized twelve Aramaean tribes. Leaving the question undecided as to whether Nahor did in fact have twelve sons, we may say with certainty that this passage does, in the form of a genealogical list, reflect a definite ethnographical, social, or religious situation. From the list given in Gen. 25:13–16, too, it is possible to conclude that there were twelve Arab tribes known to Israel. In the same way, Gen. 36:10–14 establishes the historical existence of twelve Edomite clans. There can be no question here of priestly invention. What we are up against here is clearly a form of organization common to the nomadic society of that period. This social organization must therefore have existed prior to Israel's sedentary period and certainly before her organization into a state. Israel's twelve tribes, then, have once again been accepted, and the system is regarded as a historical fact relating to the early stages of Israel's development.

Since the appearance, in 1930, of Martin Noth's now standard work on the twelve tribes, it has become common practice to refer to the twelve tribes as an "amphictyony," thus using, as a point of comparison, a phenomenon well known to us from the Greek world (*amphiktiones* = dwellers around). Such leagues of six or twelve tribes, sharing a common sanctuary or temple, were well known in the ancient, Greek world. The Greek city-states were also organized in a similar way into amphictyonies. The most famous was, of course, the Delphic Amphictyony. Similar tribal organizations occurred also in Asia Minor and in Italy. The amphictyonies of Greece have, however, become the best known to history because the amphictyony never developed, in Greece, into a unified state.

The "amphictyonic" organization of the people of God is most clearly illustrated in the diet of Shechem (Joshua 24). This gives a good picture of the amphictyony in operation (*see also* Joshua 8:30–35; Deut. 11:29–32; Deut. 27!). Moses was therefore the founder of Israel's national existence, in that he welded the Hebrews together into a close national community around the sanctuary of Yahweh. The outcome of his work was the religious federation of the Hebrew tribes. The number of these tribes was eventually twelve. It is reasonable to assume that there was a prehistory to this religious federation of tribes, or at least certain ramifications in the past. This supposition is based on the biblical account of the origin of the tribes of Lea (Gen. 29:31–30:20), a group of six, standing out among the twelve sons of Jacob and gradually achieving a close, geographical connection. The organization of the people of God into a state under David and Solomon resulted in this tribal organization being forced more and more out of public life. Nonetheless, the tribal amphictyony remained sufficiently important in local affairs for it to achieve a new prominence after the collapse of the state. It was also strongly emphasized in the theology of the Jews.

This federation of tribes was consolidated in the third and last stage of Moses' work, which was enacted on the plains of Moab (Num. 22:1). Israel's memory of this stage is reflected in the setting of the book of Deuteronomy.

3. The Sedentary State Community

The people of God, once established by Moses, went through two radical processes of development, of which the second was the result and the completion of the first. The people of God, after having been nomadic, adopted a settled way of life, at the same time developing from a nation into a state. Once it had adopted a settled way of life, the nation came to be known as Israel. Provisionally, however, it was the Hebrew, tribal federation which became a settled group. The process, of which only the most prominent stages are in any way discernible, was long and slow. It was preceded and accompanied by conquest. It should hardly be necessary to observe that the Bible, in its account of this long process, so to speak concentrated on one definite period of time and on certain definite incidents—one year the people were nomads, and the next they had a fixed abode; one day they were still a federation of tribes, and the next day they had become a kingdom. This historical simplification gave the sacred writer an opportunity of bringing his religious vision of the entire course of the history he was dealing with vividly to life. He was able, in this way, to write a passage such as this:

And Yahweh gave to Israel all the land that he had sworn to give to their fathers: and they possessed it and dwelt in it. And Yahweh gave them rest round about . . .

Not so much as one word, which he had promised to perform unto them, was made void: but all came to pass (Joshua 21:41–43; *see also* 23:14).

But even here it is possible to discover the course of events from the schematic account of the Bible. After the conquest of the Transjordan (Num. 21:21–35), Reuben, Gad, and half of the tribe of Manasseh became sedentary (Num. 32). By conquest what is undoubtedly meant here is that the Hebrew invaders put so much fear into the hearts of the settled population by their raids that they were, in the long run, able to settle themselves in the thinly populated, mountainous country, and maintain their position there. The same must have happened in the conquest of the Cisjordan. Joshua established a bridgehead over the Jordan (Gilgal), and made expeditions from that point. He made, for example, a successful onslaught against a coalition of southern kings, which would have made it possible for certain tribes, the chief among which being Judah, to settle in the south or to lead a wandering life there with their cattle —the Negeb was in the nomadic zone (Joshua 10). In another expedition, Joshua defeated a coalition of northern kings—this was connected with the settlement of the Hebrew tribes in the mountains of Galilee (Joshua 11). The most important concentration of the Hebrew tribes was, however, to be found around Shechem, with a close link with the bridgehead. The account given in Genesis 34 shows that the close relationships with the native population in the past had not been forgotten. What is more, according to the biblical plan it is clearly possible that the sedentary way of life was only partially adopted, or adopted only by certain groups. For this reason, it is quite likely that the house of Joseph was able to settle in the mountainous region without any striking feats of arms being preserved in the memory of the people.

What has been said here about conquest is logically connected with the later situation. This situation is known to us from the books of Judges and Samuel. The biblical facts have also been confirmed and augmented by archaeological research. Round about the year 1200, the national group which was shortly to become known as Israel was beginning to settle permanently and, when the situation had eventually quietened down, four Israelitic concentrations emerged, which formed separate enclaves within the native population. These enclaves were isolated from each other by natural frontiers and by native, fortified cities (Judges 1). This was to be substantially the situation until the time of David. Until that time, life in this central enclave was authentically Israelitic, with the result that this enclave was simply known as Israel, long before the existence of the Northern Kingdom of Israel proper. "Israel and Judah" are frequently referred to in the books of Samuel; taken together, these names designated the people as a whole at that period.

This state of being divided into various enclaves, a situation which moreover compelled the people of God to assimilate a totally new social pattern, constituted a grave threat to Israel's separate existence, in the form in which this had developed within the federation of Hebrew tribes. The fact that Israel surmounted this danger and continued to produce leaders who were constantly aware of the real source of Israel's distinction and national strength argues convincingly for the authentic inspiration of the pre patriarchal religion. National and religious consciousness went hand in hand, and both were eventually embodied in the striking figure of Samuel, who was half a judge and half a prophet. It was Samuel, too, who made it possible for Saul to emerge as a biblical figure—Saul, the first and still very primitive king, who was above all a commander in battle and, as such, half a judge and half a king who, in between his royal activities, ploughed his fields. Apart from many local skirmishes, he waged one, major, national war, summoning all the military forces at his disposal for this purpose. His life's work was the union of the three northern enclaves, which together were to form the kingdom of Israel. The Philistines were anxious to prevent this by driving a wedge between the central enclave and that of Galilee, and Saul finally lost his life in battle against the Philistines.

It would appear that Saul never had very much to do with the south. Judah, which was at this time still partially nomadic and assimilating other groups (Judges 1:9–20), continued to lead her own life. David was the first man to emerge from Judah and assume a position of importance. When Saul died, it was David who was summoned by the Judeans in their center, Hebron, to be king. The outcome of this was the development of the tribal federation into two kingdoms which, as a whole, can be termed Israel. The Northern Kingdom, ruled by Saul's son Ishbosheth, came more and more to be known especially as Israel. The Southern Kingdom, under David, was *de-facto* Judah. The North had very few connections with the Southern Kingdom. Isolated from each other since the time of the Judges, their relations had been characterized by a spirit of opposition and rivalry. Nonetheless, the North called upon David to be king of the Northern Kingdom. Henceforth, David made it his task to make this personal union into a national union. His most masterly move in this task of unification was his choice of Jerusalem as the royal residence.

Jerusalem was situated exactly halfway between the central points of the Northern and the Southern Kingdoms and, although it was theoretically on the southern boundary of Benjamin, it belonged to neither kingdom. Even after the conquest, the city was not transferred to Israel. Belonging neither to Israel nor to Judah, it became the personal possession of the king. It was not tribal territory, but literally David's city (2 Sam. 5:6–9), and soon became populated by a very mixed group of citizens—those who had previously lived in the city were joined by many from outside. The transference of the ark to the city of David must have confirmed David's choice and made his city into a national and religious center.

The conquest of Jerusalem fitted in perfectly with David's plan to round off his kingdom geographically. By the conquest and incorporation of those native enclaves which still remained, namely the powerful cities and the fertile plains, the theoretical tribal territory became real property, and the historical Israel known to us from the age of the kings began, from this time forward, to take on a permanent, ethnical structure. The wars which David waged outside the tribal territory were entirely his own, personal affair, and not tribal undertakings (*see* 2 Sam. 12:26-31). They were not undertaken in order to extend Israel's territory, but in order to safeguard the tribal territory, by making the neighboring tribes pay tribute as vassals. This was also, of course, beneficial to the royal treasury.

The outcome of David's work was a curiously constructed political pattern, consisting of two kingdoms and a capital city in the form of a state within the state, surrounded by a number of vassal states. The monarchy of David and Solomon was of sufficiently long duration for something quite new to be able to develop. In the first place, the Israelitic people became a distinct and separate nation with a permanent, ethnical composition. Secondly, the South also developed in conjunction with David's generation and consequently with his dynasty, with the result that when the split occurred between North and South, Jerusalem, together with the tribal territory of Benjamin, went over to the new, Southern Kingdom. Finally, an authentic, state system, with a developing official machinery and a more and more centralized and bureaucratic form of government, began to emerge (2 Sam. 8:15-18, 20:35-26). This development meant, of course, the end of the old federation of tribes and the patriarchal democracy which was based on this federation. The clearest example of this final development is Solomon's division of the whole country into twelve districts. The boundaries of these new districts cut right across the old tribal frontiers. They were made for the purpose of collecting taxes and recruiting labor for the king's great undertakings (1 Kings 4:7-19). In view of the fact that it was the Southern Kingdom which profited most, it is true to say that Solomon's autocratic rule was a prominent factor in the complex of factors leading to the national division. The dynasty of David became unacceptable to the Northern Kingdom, and Jeroboam was acclaimed king at another democratic diet of Shechem (1 Kings 12:1, 20). Succession to the throne of the Northern Kingdom frequently came about in a charismatic manner. It is only in the case of Omri, the founder of Samaria, and of Jehu that the beginning of a dynasty can be discerned. Altogether, the royal family changed nine times. The house of David was, by contrast, miraculously stable.

4. The New Pattern of Civilization

The foregoing survey may help to give an idea of the social and political framework within which Israel's religious system, as this has been outlined in the preceding chapters, attained its classic form. At the same time, it may also give some impression of the society in which the prophets appeared. Before passing on to a discussion of the prophets, however, we must try to understand the consequences of the development outlined above. Here was a totally new pattern of society, and Israel had to learn how to express her religion and her distinctive quality within this new civilization. The people of God, whose social structure had, up to that point, been based on a nomadic way of life under the patriarchs, had to realize that its way of life was now based on a settled existence as a state. Israel was obliged to assimilate this pattern of life and to use it to express her own distinctive and original character. This was vitally necessary if Israel was to remain Israel. Success came only after great difficulty, and it was short-lived. Eventually it became apparent that the only way of rescuing the people of God was to dissociate this pattern of life by violence from this sedentary situation. Thus Israel's settled period, taken in the context of the whole of the nation's history, was in the nature of an episode and almost of an experiment, especially as the Jews themselves referred back, beyond the settled period, to the nomadic community of Yahweh with which they felt such close ties and in which they rediscovered their own essential being.

The risk involved in the settled way of life, which culminated in the risk of the monarchy, was, in the last resort, the risk involved when the human element became the embodiment of the divine. In this case, however, the risk was particularly great because the Canaanite pattern of civilization taken over by Israel was in fact a social pattern which was, from the religious point of view, degenerate. The native population of Canaan had a religion which was adapted to a settled way of life, a religion which had grown together with peasant life. Canaan's gods, Baal and Ashtoreth, had grown together with the blood and the soil of Canaan. But this married couple had been folded and cut to human measure, according to local requirements, to such an extent that every settlement and even particular fields, trees, springs, and hills rejoiced in their own Baal and their own Ashtoreth. Their worship gave rise to the sacrifice of children and to sacred prostitution on a scale not found elsewhere in the ancient Near East. From all that we have learnt about Canaan's mythology in recent years, it is quite possible that it was only a cause of disintegration, even among the native population, as it might have been for Israel. The Bible expressed, in theological terms, the effects of Baalism on the native population of Canaan by saying that the measure of their sins, by which they defiled the land, was full and that they could not hold their own against Israel—the land vomited them out (Lev. 18:24–30, 20:22–26; Deut. 9:4f.; Gen. 15:16). This was why Israel's men of God reacted so strongly against Baal. There could be no compromise between Yahweh and Baal (1 Kings 18:21). Canaan was perverse (Gen. 9:18–27, 18:20ff.; 19:36–38). The worship of Baal threatened Yahwism in its most original element and made man a piece of nature together with his cattle, his fields, and his god. The worshiper of Baal allowed himself to be carried along by the tide of the life of deified nature, in its seasons and its cycle of sowing and harvesting, death and life. Yahweh, the God of a nomadic people, could hardly compete with the settled god of the land that Israel wanted to cultivate, when this god inflicted itself upon his people.

It would seem that, in the time of the Judges, a religious syncretism came about in Israel. In their settled existence, the people of God found it difficult to shake off the influence of this syncretism, and inevitably fell back into it, whenever they succeeded in freeing themselves from it (Judges 2:11-19). Their religion was a popular Yahwism which was, in spirit and content, baalism. Although this syncretism was primitive and almost worthy in its aims in the age of the Judges, it revealed itself in the later age of the kings as a truly decadent phenomenon, affecting all of Israel's institutions.

Israel came into being as an ancient, oriental people by becoming the people of Yahweh's Covenant on a basis of the consciousness of God aroused by revelation. Thus there was in Israel a vertical power at work, lifting her out of her environment. A concrete form had to be given to the true religion by Israel's existence in a definite place at a definite time. Israel, and all that Israel was and had, was taken over by the religion of this particular revelation and was in turn made into a living witness of this revelation. This principle of the adaptation of revelation, technically known as syncatabasis, also means that there were always horizontal and leveling forces at work in Israel, threatening to equate her with her environment and period. Judged purely by its material structure, Israel's pattern of life was identical to that of the other people, a pattern of life common to all peoples at that time and place. In the case of the other peoples, however, the way of life was steeped in and entirely at the service of pagan religion. Every human religion contains within itself a tendency to become debased and degenerate, and Israel's religion was no exception. While the external forms of her religion remained in many cases consistent, the separate and Israelitic content was almost imperceptibly replaced by the pagan content of Israel's environment. The normal result of such a process is a hybrid product. Israel's degeneration can thus be termed a religious syncretism.

5. Sedentary Religion

This syncretism was nourished by and expressed in the local sanctuaries. A survey of the most important scriptural data in connection with this topic should give us a very good idea of the life of the people of Israel.

The popular sanctuary of Baal stood in an open space surrounded by a fence. This space was preferably on a hill in or near the city. The sanctuary was situated under a venerable tree or in a wood. "They offered sacrifice upon the tops of the mountains and burnt incense upon the hills: under the oak and the willow and the terebinth, because the shadow thereof was good" (Hos. 4:13). In this space stood an altar, surrounded by sacred stones (*maṣṣebhôth*). The sacred stone was sometimes some kind of memorial stone. Sometimes it represented the worshiper at the altar (*see* Chapter 2, section 6). It was even possible for it to represent the male deity, in which case it seems to have served as an image of the god. The sacred stone was often spoken of in the same breath as the sacred pole (*'ašērāh*). This above all symbolized the fertility goddess Ashtoreth—sometimes difficult to distinguish from another goddess Asherah—and there was sometimes a more or less rudimentary carving of the goddess on the pole. Almost every native settlement had its high place (*bâmāh: see* Ezek. 20:29), dedicated to its local Baal or Ashtoreth.

There was, for example, a high place of Baal at the estate of Gideon's father. The sanctuary was situated on the highest place of the city. It was fortified and contained a stone and a terebinth. With the help of ten servants, Gideon transformed it in a single night into a high place of Yahweh. Overturning the altar of Baal, he built instead an altar which he called Yahweh-shalom. On top of a pile of wood formed from the chopped up pieces of the *asherah* he placed his father's fatted calf as a burnt offering for Yahweh (Judges 6). In this way, orthodox Yahwism obtained its high places. Saul and Samuel met each for the first time in the city gate of Ramah, when Samuel was leaving the city to go up to the high place to make a public sacrifice (1 Sam. 9). Gibeah was regarded as the most prominent high place and was even known as the mountain of Yahweh (2 Sam. 21:6). Solomon offered sacrifices and burnt incense there—incidentally to the great embarrassment of the biblical historiographer—and it was there too that he had the famous dream in which he was permitted to ask what he wanted of Yahweh and asked for wisdom (1 Kings 3:2ff.). David had appointed priests to serve at Gibeah, but he did not dare to worship Yahweh there, since he had seen the avenging angel standing on Ornan's threshing floor, where the temple was to be built (1 Chron. 16:39, 21:29).

When Saul entered Gibeah, he met a band of prophets coming down from the high place in a state of ecstasy, with psalteries and timbrels, pipes and cithers (1 Sam. 10. 5). There was also a high place on Carmel, where Elijah rebuilt the destroyed altar of Yahweh (1 Kings 18:30, 19:10, 14). There must also have been many more high places which changed from one god to another and were a bone of contention between the two religions (Judges 6:25ff.). All Israel came as one man to Yahweh in Mizpah (Judges 20:1). Samuel visited this place, together with Bethel (Judges 20:18ff.), and Gilgal (Joshua 4f.), where he made sacrifices (1 Sam. 10:8), during his annual circuit, made with the purpose of judging Israel (1 Sam. 7:16). The sanctuary of Gilgal, between Jericho and the Jordan, was closely connected with the national past (Joshua 4f.). It was there that the angel of Yahweh, who redeemed Israel and accompanied the people to the promised land, had his temporary, settled abode and it was from Gilgal that the angel intervened in Israel's affairs (Judges 2:1). Samuel said to the people: "Come and let us go to Gilgal, and let us renew the kingdom there. And all the people went to Gilgal, and there they made Saul king *before the face of Yahweh in Gilgal,* and they sacrificed there victims of peace before Yahweh. And there Saul and all the men of Israel rejoiced greatly" (1 Sam. 11:14f.). At new moon, David made a family sacrifice at Bethlehem (1 Sam. 20:29; *see also* 16:5). Absalom had made a vow to Yahweh in Hebron and invited many to be present when the offerings were made. On the top of the Mount of Olives there was a spot where it was the custom to bow down in worship before God (2 Sam. 15:7ff., 32).

There were also the well-known sanctuaries at Shechem, at Nob, and above all at Shiloh. It was there that the ark to which Yahweh-Sabaoth had attached his Name stood for a long time. The girls of Shiloh danced on the yearly feast of Yahweh (Judges 21:19ff.). A good impression of what happened in that rural sanctuary, served by the priest Eli and his two sons, can be gained from the first chapters of 1 Samuel. It flourished especially during the time of Samuel, when Yahweh's word was seldom heard and visions were rare. But it was in Shiloh that Yahweh revealed himself to Samuel through his word, and Samuel's words were heard throughout the length and breadth of Israel (1 Sam. 3:1, 20f.). After the probably permanent destruction of Shiloh by the Philistines (*see* Jer. 7:12ff.), the ark eventually came to rest in Kiriath-jearim, where it was kept in the house of a private person and more or less forgotten (1 Chron. 13:3). Nob, on the other hand, rose to considerable importance—at the time of Saul there were eighty-six priests there (1 Sam. 21f.)—by coming into possession of the ephod containing the oracular stones Urim and Thummim. Gibeah similarly came into prominence, although the altar for burnt offerings was probably already there, by the possession of the sacred tabernacle.

There must have been very many high places throughout the whole of the land before the building of the temple at Jerusalem, and most of these had, in all probability, simply been taken over from baalism. This does not, however, mean that the native population stayed away from them. Wherever Israel was in the minority, too, and especially when the two population groups began to feel themselves, with the passage of time, to be one homogeneous group of city dwellers and to behave as such, the obvious course was to worship in a high place. Here, as in so many other respects, the solution may have been provided by the monarchy and its royal sanctuary, which inevitably took the lead and set the example in worship.

6. *The Acceptance by Yahwism of the Monarchy*

The monarchy was the culmination and the exponent of the settled pattern of society. But both the settled way of life and the monarchy had their light and their shadow. Although a whole set of texts comment favorably on both, it is not difficult to find another set in which the shadow can be seen. It would seem almost superfluous to go into these texts as far as the monarchy is concerned. Concerning the sedentary way of life, it should be sufficient to recall certain well-known biblical facts. On the one hand, the settled existence was an entry into Yahweh's "rest" and an inheritance of the land, both in promise and in fulfillment, a summing up of God's gifts. On the other hand, however, the Bible preserves a desert ideal. To do full justice to both aspects of the Bible's message, we may say that the possession of the land had to be experienced as God's gift and as a sign of his rest. The fact that the Bible gives both sides of the coin clearly expresses the realization that the believer as such could never lead a completely settled existence, and that he was essentially in search of the eternal city (*see* the accurate definite in Heb. 11:9f.). The risk involved in the settled way of life may be formulated as follows: settled existence in the world, if this is regarded as the ultimate meaning and content of life, means the decline of authentic religiosity. In some sense, man has to remain a nomad, for the simple reason that real security is only to be found in God, not in worldly possessions. Israel's monarchy clearly exemplifies the truth of this definition.

It is because the Bible refers to our salvation in terms created by the existence of Israel's monarchy that this monarchy was so important. Our practice of calling the new and special phenomenon which came about as a result of God's concern for man's salvation the kingdom of God is intimately connected with the fact that the community of believers expressed itself at a given moment in ancient, oriental society by taking on the form of a national kingdom. The crisis during the age of the Judges resulted eventually in a synthesis between the new religion and the objective fact of the ancient Near East itself. This synthesis was David and his kingdom. David was the ancient, oriental interpretation of a truly religious man, his kingdom was the kingdom of God in its national, ancient, oriental form. The people of God ultimately reached the average level of civilization in the ancient Near East, assimilated the pattern of society of the time and place, and then began to express itself in this pattern. The glory of this kingdom, and perhaps even more its failure, made it possible for the believer to discover Yahweh's universal kingship, and for him to express his expectation in the specific form of an expectation of the kingdom of God.

Monarchy in the ancient Near East was sacred and religious— a translation into human terms of a divine sovereignty over the people. The human king was the representative, sometimes even the incarnation of the national god, with whom he was in a living communion, with the result that divine life passed through him to the nation. Israel took over this ideology, and her king was regarded as Yahweh's anointed, and as such the lamp of Israel and the breath of life of the nation (Lam. 4:20). The sacred character of Israel's monarchy means that it could not have been a mere copy of the examples present in Israel's environment. The enormous difference between Yahweh and the other national gods must have led either to a complete transformation of the ancient, oriental pattern of monarchy or else to a disastrous degeneration in Israel's religion.

In fact, however, monarchy in the ancient Near East was nothing more than a human autocracy sanctioned by religion—it was, in a word, oriental despotism. What we said in the first chapter about the creative aspect of the mystery of Israel (section 7), has a concrete application in the case of the monarchy. In degenerate heathendom, it was not the god but man who took the initiative. The pagan gods, as misconceived products of the human mind, had no real or decisive influence on human behavior. There was no real divine power above the ancient, oriental king. He was able to indulge his lust for power quite arbitrarily, because it was reinforced rather than checked by the sacred character of his kingship. Theocratic formulae concealed and promoted an absolute autocracy. The Bible's summing up of this autocratic right of kings is justly famous because it is so true to life:

This will be the right of the king, that shall reign over you.

He will take your sons, and put them in his chariots, and will make them his horsemen, and his running footmen to run before his chariots. And he will appoint them to be his tribunes, and centurions, and to plough his fields, and to reap his corn, and to make him arms and chariots.

Your daughters also will he take to make him ointments, and to be his cooks, and bakers.

And he will take your fields, and your vineyards, and your best oliveyards, and give them to his servants.

Moreover he will take the tenth of your corn, and of the revenue of your vineyards, to give to his eunuchs and servants.

Your servants also and handmaids, your best cattle and your asses he will take away, and put them to his work. Your flocks also will he tithe, and you shall be his servants. And you shall cry out in that day from the face of the king, whom you have chosen to yourselves: and Yahweh will not hear you (1 Sam. 8:11-18).

This, then, was what Samuel had to say to the people when they expressly demanded to have a king, like all the other nations. The scriptural account of the introduction of the monarchy (1 Sam. 8–12), manifests such strange changes of front mainly because definite anti-royalist tendencies were assimilated into it. The pagan monarchy was in fact a worldly institution, and Israel, lacking faith, set her mind on having a monarchy, as well as a means of human power and a human guarantee of national well-being. The Pentateuch gives a many-sided image of the structure of the people of God, without any need for a monarchy. This is extremely significant. Israel was already complete in her constitution as the people of God and as a theocracy when monarchy came to her as a completely strange element. The whole of the history of Israel's monarchy bears distinct traces of the difficulty Israel experienced in integrating this element. Samuel, for example, argued in favor of the theocratic system and demonstrated that Israel had always managed perfectly well in the past without a king and with Yahweh alone as her savior (1 Sam. 12:6-11).

Despite all these objections, however, there were still great advantages. During the age of the Judges, Israel's organization, in the form of what may be called a democratic theocracy, seemed to lag behind the situation in which the nation was placed. Later, however, when Israel's religion had lost so much of its dynamic force, the need for some other centralized power made itself more and more strongly felt. This was, first and foremost, an urgent necessity within Israelitic society: "In those days there was no king in Israel: but every one did that which seemed right to himself" (Judges

17:6, 18:1; 19:1, 30, 12:25). At the same time, however, the situation with regard to Israel's enemies demanded a much stronger unity within Israel herself. The Philistines in particular constituted a major threat. They had invaded Canaan shortly after Israel's entry into the land, and had formed a federation of five cities which functioned extremely well, especially from the military point of view. The monarchy was the obvious answer to this challenge, especially because it had an expressly military character in primitive society.

Furthermore, the monarchy was in the direct line of Israel's development and the logical culmination of her settled existence. The ancient, tribal federation had gradually begun to feel that it had reached maturity as a settled people and had achieved a status equal to that of its neighbors. All the neighboring nations had adopted a sedentary way of life shortly before Israel, and all without exception had already been kingdoms for some time and possessed their own king and capital city. This emerges clearly from the words of the people of Israel: "Give us a king to rule over us, as all nations have." When Samuel pointed out the consequences of this, the people continued to insist: "Nay, but there shall be a king over us. And we shall be like all nations: and our king shall rule over us, and go out before us, and fight our battles for us" (1 Sam. 8:5, 19f.). The days of the Judges were of short duration and their appearance was local. Gideon was offered a hereditary crown: "Rule over us, and thy son, and thy son's son." In his answer, Gideon too pointed out the risk involved in the monarchy: "I will not rule over you, neither shall my son rule over you: but Yahweh shall rule over you" (Judges 8:22f.). There was, however, no denial here that a successful monarchy would guarantee the permanent stability of Israel's salvation as a nation.

Israel's religion could, of course, only gain by a successful monarchy. A Yahwistic king could make Israel into a Yahwistic kingdom. As a state religion, Yahwism could mark out the new, settled, national community, formed, as it had been from so many heterogeneous elements, permanently as Israel. This indeed happened in the reign of David and Solomon, and here we gain a very positive impression of the monarchy from the Bible itself.

The monarchy was, in a sense, the culminating point of the Old Testament. Apart from being historical realities, David and Solomon, Jerusalem and the Temple were also an idea and, in a very short space of time, an ideal. David, Solomon, and the holy city gave rise to a biblical theology which fully incorporated the dynastic monarchy into the Yahwistic theocracy. The classic expression of this was the Davidic covenant, which scholars have come to regard as the perpetuation and the culmination of the Covenant of Mount Sinai. The temple was the culmination of Israel's settled way of life; in the temple Yahweh, the God of a wandering people, also assumed a settled way of life and thereby guaranteed both Israel's continued existence in the land and the permanence of David's throne (2 Sam. 7). Thus, Israel formed her own ideology of the king, an ideology which was to dominate all the later writing of the Bible, although the reality of the monarchy lagged behind the ideal and was frequently dangerously close to the universal, oriental pattern.

This "baptized" ideal of the king set the tone for the biographies of the first kings. Israel's kings had to follow the example of the lives of Saul and David. The emphasis was on the unmerited vocation of both. Searching for his asses, Saul found kingship: "Am I not of the least tribe of Israel and the last among all the families of the tribe of Benjamin?" (1 Sam. 9:21; *see also* 15:17). David, the youngest and the least important son, was fetched from minding the flock, "for man seeth those things that appear; but Yahweh beholdeth the heart" (1 Sam. 16; *see also* 2 Sam. 7:8, 18; Ps. 78:70f.). The intractability of all of Israel's kings was judged in that of Saul: "because it is like the sin of witchcraft, to rebel: and like the crime of idolatry, to refuse to obey" and "Yahweh hath sought out a man according to his own heart, and him hath Yahweh commanded to be prince over his people, because thou hast not observed that which Yahweh commanded" (1 Sam. 13:14, 15:23). David, on the other hand, rose to be king after many tests and ordeals, and it was he who became the norm against which all his successors were measured.

Solomon was the example of the glory which Yahweh was, for David's sake, prepared to bestow on the dynasty. At the same time, however, the dangerous aspects of the monarchy were emphasized in Solomon. Israel's ideal of the monarchy predominated in the biblical tradition, and especially in the biographical account of Chronicles, which stressed the light and ignored the shadows. When all the facts provided in the books of Kings are considered together, however, the image of Solomon which emerges is one of a monarch who, of all the kings of Israel, most closely resembles the classic, oriental type. His priestly functions, his wealth, his harem, his merchant fleet, his buildings (and the labor force and high taxes entailed in this work), his extension, and centralization of the machinery of government and the bureaucratic system which replaced the ancient laws and local customs—there was little in any of this which was really in accordance with the Israelitic tradition. Such a king was neither a servant of Yahweh nor a servant of Yahweh's people. His reign was an example of oriental monarchy, in which both god and the people were subordinated to the personal aims of the king.

The disruption, which inevitably followed, was at the same time a punishment and a humiliation for the house of David (1 Kings 11:39; see also 2 Sam. 7:14). As a result, the monarchy, which had, during the early period, borne so many signs of its ancient, oriental origins, was given a sharp push in a more Israelitic direction, and began to acquire certain distinctly Israelitic characteristics. In some respects, it is even possible to detect a certain growth.

Monarchy in the ancient Near East was priestly. David, Solomon and Jeroboam undertook duties on many different occasions. Gradually, however, the functions became separated. In any case, the vocational priesthood sought to acquire a monopoly and, once it had achieved this, guarded it jealously and with great success. The story of the king who was stricken with leprosy because he wanted to burn incense at the altar (2 Chron. 26:16–20), is clear evidence of this. A passage such as Numbers 27:15–23 gives a clear indication of the attempt which was made to define the various functions. In the presence of all the people, Moses had to make Joshua stand in front of Eliezer, the priest, and lay his hand upon him so that Joshua might share in his glory. Joshua had, however, to appear in front of the priest, and the priest had to consult the oracle before the face of Yahweh. In accordance with the priest's decision, Joshua, together with all the Israelites and the whole community, had to go out and return. In the following passage, which is probably the most characteristic document of the integration of the monarchy into the Yahwistic system, and a perfect counterpart to the right of kings threatened by Samuel, it is possible to discern the law of kings of Israel:

When thou art come into the land, which Yahweh, thy God, will give thee, and possessest it, thou shalt say: I will set a king over me, as all nations have that are round about.

Thou shall set him whom Yahweh, thy God, shall choose out of the number of thy brethren.

Thou mayest not make any man of another nation thy king, that is not thy brother.

And he shall not multiply horses to himself, not lead back the people into Egypt, being lifted up with the number of his horsemen, especially since Yahweh hath commanded you to return no more the same way.

He shall not have many wives, that may allure his mind, nor immense sums of silver and gold.

But after he is raised to the throne of his kingdom, he shall copy out to himself this law, taking the copy of the priests of the levitical tribe. And he shall have it with him, and shall read it all the days of his life:

that he may learn to fear Yahweh, his God, and keep his words and ceremonies, that are commanded in the law: and that his heart be not lifted up with pride over his brethren, nor decline to the right or to the left: that he and his sons may reign a long time over Israel (Deut. 17: 14–20).

The king of Israel was not, like other kings in the ancient Near East, the source of law and right, but was himself subject to and bound by the Law (= Deuteronomy). He could not be an absolute monarch, but had to be a constitutional prince, because his rule had to be based on Israel's constitution, the Mosaic Law (*see* 1 Sam. 10:25).

Nonetheless, the priesthood did not act as a counterbalance to the autocracy of the kings. The priests became the king's officials and depended entirely upon his grace and favor. Saul slew the priests of Nob and only Abiathar escaped with the ephod (1 Sam. 23:6ff.). David appointed him and Zadok as priests (2 Sam. 8:17), but he was dismissed from his office by Solomon (1 Kings 2:26). King Ahaz is a perfect example of the high-handedness of Israel's kings in matters of worship (2 Kings 16:10–16). Generally speaking, the official prophets were completely at the beck and call of the kings (*see* 1 Kings 22), although the kings never succeeded in suppressing the voices of the charismatic prophets. Charismatic prophetism was a phenomenon which enabled Israel's religion to demonstrate its strength and originality in the clearest possible way and provided a balance to the oriental despotism of the kings. It was a beneficial and democratic element in Israel and an expression of the conscience of the people.

7. *The Monarchy as a Disruptive Factor*

Although it is by no means certain that the Deuteronomic law of kings had Solomon specifically in mind, it does seem to be a direct condemnation of his reign. He had, after all, 1,400 war chariots and thousands of horses—we are told of 40,000 stalls and 12,000 horsemen (1 Kings 4:26)—for which he traded all over the known world (10:28f.). He had 700 princesses and 300 concubines in his harem (11:3). His treasure houses were overflowing with gold, silver, and all kinds of rare and costly items (10:14–29). Even if such affluence could be compatible with the attitude of mind of one who felt himself to be entirely dedicated to God, the international trade relations which went hand in hand with these royal pursuits had religious consequences which went straight to the heart of Yahwism. One example of this should be sufficient. The royal residence had to be equipped for the religious needs of the foreign technicians living there and of Solomon's foreign wives. "Solomon worshipped Ashtoreth, the goddess of the Sidonians, and Moloch, the idol of the Ammonites . . . He built a temple for Kemosh, the idol of Moab, on the hill that is over against Jerusalem, and for Moloch, the idol of the Ammonites. And he did in this manner for all his wives that were strangers, who burnt incense, and offered sacrifices to their gods" (11:5–8).

If it is true that the regent's father did marry a foreign woman, then his mother would have had an influence, as mistress of the house (as queen-mother: Jer. 13:18; 19:2), which might have been disastrous for the Yahwistic religion. For what Asa, Solomon's third successor, did was exceptional—he dismissed his mother, Maacah from the position of mistress of the household, because she had made a filthy idol of Asherah (1 Kings 15:13).

(a) The Northern Kingdom of Israel and Samaria

It is always a good plan, when considering what the books of Kings have to say about the degeneration or the purification of religion, to take the political background into account as well. The division of the kingdom which occurred on the death of Solomon, for example, inevitably brought with it a religious schism. In the

Bible, this was seen from a later and typically "Jerusalem" point of view, namely that the Northern Kingdom was the renegade party and that the schism was due to the sin that Jeroboam, the son of Nebat, had made Israel commit. This is difficult to reconcile with the fact that Yahweh declared himself ready to do for Jeroboam what he had done for David (1 Kings 11:38). It is not entirely out of the question that the South had made orthodoxy unattractive by identifying it too closely with the ideas of Jerusalem, with the result that the North was driven to heterodoxy so as not to be like the South. But this situation had not yet been reached. Jeroboam was able to set up an altar in all orthodoxy. That was his right as king. He conferred the dignity of a royal temple on the ancient sanctuary of Dan and especially on that of Bethel and made them state sanctuaries, dedicated to Yahweh (Amos 7:13). Bethel, after all, had older documents than Jerusalem. The relationship between the two sanctuaries is undoubtedly characterized, at the political level, in the quarrel between the North and the South over David: "The men of Israel answered the men of Judah, and said: I have ten parts in the king more than thou; and David belongeth to me more than to thee" (2 Sam. 19:43). The "Jerusalem" point of view must have been an even greater source of annoyance:

> And he (Yahweh) rejected the tabernacle of Joseph;
>   and chose not the tribe of Ephraim.
> But he chose the tribe of Judah,
>   Mount Zion which he loved.
> And he built his sanctuary as the highest mountains,
>   as the land which he founded for ever (Ps. 77:67ff.).

The two golden calves were in no way associated with idolatry, in view of the fact that they symbolized Yahweh. They may even have had a more innocuous function, having been regarded simply as the footstool of the throne of the invisible deity. In this case, they were rather similar to Yahweh's sitting on the cherubim, although the parallel here would have been dangerously close to baalism and to Canaanite practices. From this time onwards, the Northern Kingdom celebrated the Feast of Tabernacles, which had, in Jerusalem, already taken on the character of a feast of accession to the throne (1 Kings 8:2, 65: the dedication of the temple as a consolidation of the dynasty), one month later than Judah, so as to set a seal on the break with the house of David (1 Kings 12:25–32).

Jerusalem was in any case a most important factor in the preservation of religious and political stability. The situation in the Northern Kingdom was, for the time being, relatively chaotic. As far as religion was concerned, this meant a return to the deeply rooted syncretism of the past. Omri was the first to make the Northern Kingdom a powerful state, but he was, at the same time, helped by the elements of baalism in Yahwism. The capital city which he founded did not, after all, have only a political status of its own—like its counterpart, Jerusalem, it was not tribal territory, but part of the royal estate—it also acquired its own distinctive religious status. Dan and Bethel remained the Yahwistic centers of Israel's tribes, but the population of Samaria had its own particular religious needs, since it must have been to a considerable extent made up of Canaanites and Phoenicians.

Omri sealed his relations with Phoenicia by marrying his son Ahab to Jezebel, the daughter of the Sidonian king Ethbaal of Tyre. It is clear that Jezebel had power over Ahab—the story of Naboth's vineyard illustrates this (1 Kings 21)—and that she could continue to exert an influence over Ahab's two sons Ahaziah and Jehorah in her position of "mistress" (2 Kings 10:13), and thereby have a considerable influence on the city. Ahab built a temple in Samaria for Melkart the god of Tyre (1 Kings 16:32), with the result that this "baal" became god there as well. The wife of this baal was called Asherah, a name which, even in the plural, was often mentioned together with Baal or the baals, and is often difficult to distinguish from Ashtoreth or the ashtoreths, who were similarly mentioned together with Baal. The fact that *asherah* also meant "sacred pole" makes the situation even more confused. In addition to the personnel brought in from outside to serve in the temple, there were also 450 (Phoenician) prophets of Baal-Melkart and 400 prophets of Asherah. These ate at Jezebel's table, that is to say, she provided for them (1 Kings 18:19). All the same, this Baal was angry with her son, who had been seriously injured in a fall from an upper window of his palace, that he died without Baal-zebub, the god of Ekron, whose protection he had sought, without being able to do anything about it (2 Kings 1).

Even though it was the new capital which was principally affected by all this, it also meant that there was a considerable strengthening of the Canaanite element in the political situation at home. This Canaanite element consisted mainly of those families of note in the cities that had been included in the Israelitic alliance of states since the time of David, and which probably supplied most of the personnel who were needed to take charge of the machinery of the state. It was, however, among the rural population of the Northern Kingdom that the ancient, Yahwistic federation of tribes, with its democratic structure, had its deepest roots. The state had had less hold over the people here than in the South, and there was bound to be a reaction. The contrast between the capital city and the country inevitably sharpened the antithesis between the Israelites and the Canaanites into an antithesis between Yahweh and Baal. The reaction, then, which first expressed itself in the appearance of Elijah and Elisha, was not only reflected in the attitude of the seven thousand who refused to bend the knee to Baal and to kiss his image (1 Kings 19:18). It had much wider and more far-reaching consequences, and eventually led to the blood bath of Jehu (2 Kings 9 and 10). The Phoenician Baal ceased to be the official god of Samaria, just as he had previously been driven out of the sanctuary of Carmel which, in the past, had always looked to Phoenicia rather than to Israel (1 Kings 18:20-40).

The family of Jehu, which held its own for a century, was fully occupied with the problem of Damascus. Damascus brought Israel to the verge of ruin, and it was only when Damascus became a tributary of Assyria that the Northern Kingdom was able to recover and eventually become the most powerful state in Syria and Palestine (Jeroboam II, 786-746). This new prosperity led to many abuses which were sharply criticized by Amos and Hosea. Hosea's criticism of the monarchy was particularly destructive (1:4f., 3:4, 7:3ff., 8:4, 10, 10:3, 13:1). But this history of the monarchy—a history which was above all the history of Samaria—concealed another history. Religion was at its purest and strongest, among the northern tribes, in the district of Shechem and in the remote valley of the Jordan. After the fall of Samaria, it was from these parts that the people went to Jerusalem and enriched the Judaean tradition with the heritage of the North (*see* 2 Chron. 15:9).

The death of Jeroboam II coincided with the beginning of the Assyrian advance. Revolutions accompanied the political maneuvering between Assyria and Egypt: "Ephraim is become as a dove that is decoyed, not having a heart: they called upon Egypt, they went to the Assyrians . . . Ephraim feedeth on the wind and followeth all day long the east wind . . . they made a covenant with the Assyrians and carried oil into Egypt" (Hos. 7:11, 12:1). The first deportations followed, and most of the Northern Kingdom became an Assyrian province (2 Kings 15:29). After being besieged for three years, Samaria fell (721), and the rest of Israel soon suffered the same fate (2 Kings 17:5f.). Those who were deported were replaced by new inhabitants from many different parts. Although these newcomers continued to honor the gods of their own countries, it is obvious that they could not with impunity ignore the god in whose land they were actually living. A priest of Yahweh, specially brought back from exile, settled in Bethel, and undertook to instruct the new inhabitants in the service of Yahweh (2 Kings 17:28). The final result was probably very little different from the syncretism of the age of the kings, notwithstanding the later view of the fall of Israel provided by the "deuteronomic editors," who gave a very unsympathetic account of the origin of Samaritan society (2 Kings 17:7–23).

(b) The Southern Kingdom of Judah and Jerusalem

It does not seem as if there was very much difference, in the period between Solomon's reign and the Assyrian exile, between the religious practices of the North and the South. We have already referred to the consequences of Solomon's marriages with foreign women, and there can be no doubt that these, and the results of his close relations with Phoenicia were most clearly revealed in Jerusalem itself. It was said of his successors in Judah that: "they built high places for sacrifice, and sacred columns and poles upon every high hill and under every green tree" (1 Kings 14:23). But religion could not become so chaotic here as it became in the Northern Kingdom, because Jerusalem was the city of Yahweh and the dynasty was stable. In the country, religious syncretism remained fairly consistent, even when Yahwism was sacrificed, in the capital, to politics. Jehoram's marriage with Athaliah, one of Jezebel's daughters, meant that Judah too became contaminated with Phoenician ideas and practices (2 Kings 8:18). After his death, Athaliah became "mistress" and, when her son's brief reign came to an end, she took over control of the government (842–837). Her religious aims can be divined from the fact that she attempted to extirpate the house of David and from the information that the temple fell into a ruinous condition after her death (2 Kings 12:6; see also 22:5f.). After this nightmare experience, Judah enjoyed a century of rule by kings who "walked in the ways of David their father." The only reproach which the writer leveled at these kings was the rather anachronistic one that they did not do away with the high places.

Ahaz's political independence from Assyria led, however, to a new form of syncretism—the rapidly declining influence of Phoenicia was replaced by that of the Assyrians and the Aramaeans. When Ahaz went to pay his respects to the king in Damascus, which (in 732) had been conquered by Tiglath-pileser, he saw an Assyrian altar there. He had a copy of this altar set up in Jerusalem and ordered state sacrifices to be offered regularly on it—a clear indication that his political vassaldom was expressed even in public worship (2 Kings 16:10–18). Ahaz is also the first of whom it was recorded that he made his son pass through the fire (2 Kings 16:3). This means of forcing the deity to grant a petition by child sacrifice, which apparently originated in Northern Mesopotamia, became a common practice in Jerusalem from the time of Ahaz onwards. In the valley of Ben-Hinnom or Gehenna to the south of the city, there was a spot, called Topheth, where sons or daughters were made to pass through the fire for Moloch (2 Kings 23:10).

This Mōlekh (Moloch is the spelling in the Vulgate) occurred repeatedly as *mulukh* and *malikh* in Syria and Assyria, and can be recognized in the pair Adram-melech and Anam-melech, both of whom originated in the same district (2 Kings 17:31). The original Hebrew spelling was almost certainly *melekh* (= king); the vowels of *mōlekh* were, however, taken from the word *bōšeth* (= shame, infamy). The Jewish sopherim, who did not venture to change the consonants, expressed their horror of this practice in this way. The name Astarte was similarly rendered in the Hebrew Bible by *'ašetōreth*. It is also probable that the Hebrew spelling *tōpheth* of the Greek name taphet is due to the same reason. The original example of all these changes is preserved in certain proper names, in which the element bearing the name of the god *ba'al* was replaced by *bōšeth*. This probably goes back to Hos. 2:17: "I will take away the names of Baalim out of her mouth (= Israel's mouth): and she shall no more remember their name." Saul's son was undoubtedly called *'išeba'al* (= the man of Baal; preserved in 1 Chron. 8:33, 9:39), seeing that the name *ba'al* (= "Lord") was originally applied also to Yahweh (*see also be'aleyāh* = Yahweh is Baal; 1 Chron. 12:5). This Bealiah is, however, always referred to in the books of Samuel as *'isebōšeth* (Ishbosheth, 2 Sam. 2:8, and so forth).

The fall of the Northern Kingdom (721), accompanied by the preaching of Isaiah, made the climate favorable for the purification which Ezechiah undertook, even though this was really the religious consequence of his attempt to dissociate himself from Assyria. In any case, he aimed to get rid of the symbols of Assyrian worship and to stress the distinctively Judaean and thus Yahwistic practices. "He destroyed the high places, broke the sacred columns in pieces, and cut down the sacred poles, and broke the brazen serpent, which Moses had made. For till that time the children of Israel burnt incense to it and had called its name Nehushtan" (2 Kings 18:4). Even his invitation to the northern tribes to take part in worship at Jerusalem—an invitation which was declined (2 Chron. 30:1-10)— might have had a certain political nuance. It may well have been a miracle that Jerusalem survived the Assyrian punitive expedition (701). Ezechiah had to pay a heavy tribute, but the territory that he lost did not become an Assyrian province. He had to hand it over to the loyal Philistine princes (2 Kings 18). Assyria had reached the peak of her power and, throughout the long reign of Manasseh (687–642), Judah had to pay tribute. This resulted in the reintroduction of the state religion of Assyria and the undoing of Ezechiah's reforms (2 Kings 21).

The downfall of Assyria made a national revival possible, though other factors, of course, also played a part in this. The biblical account of Josiah's purification contains many details which help us to form a vivid picture of the syncretic religion of Jerusalem (2 Kings 23). Various objects, intended to be used in the worship of Baal, Asherah, and the entire heavenly host are mentioned in this account.

There is reference to the men appointed to burn incense to Baal, the sun, the moon, the constellations, and the whole heavenly host. Mention is made, too, of the men who, as sacred prostitutes, lived in separate apartments in the temple and of the women who wove veils for Asherah. At one of the city gates, too, there was a "sanctuary of goats" (satyrs of some kind; *see also* Lev. 17:7). In the valley of Hinnom was the Topheth for the worship of Moloch and at the entrance to the temple stood the horses and the chariot dedicated to the sun. Finally, in and around the city, there was a proliferation of high places and altars, columns and sacred poles, and the sanctuaries which Solomon had erected for the worship of the Sidonian, Ashtoreth, and for Kemosh and Milkom were also apparently still in existence. Josiah extended his work of purification as far as Bethel and even as far as Samaria. For a few years, it seemed as if it were possible for the ancient kingdom of David to be restored, but this dream was suddenly shattered by the Egyptian claim to the Assyrian inheritance. Once again, Judah became a vassal state. Pharaoh Necho deposed Jehoahaz, Josiah's son and successor, and replaced him with his brother Eliakim, making it clear, by renaming him Jehoiakim, that it was only by the Pharaoh's favor that he was on the throne (2 Kings 23:34).

The political failure of Josiah's life was, however, not able to bring about the complete negation of the effects of this work in the religious sphere. It would seem that religious syncretism no longer flourished as it had done in the past in the high places, and, generally speaking, there existed a new religious and national consciousness which was later to play a very important part in the emergence of Judaism. This new consciousness, born of the needs of the time and as a result of study of the prophecies of the eighth century, which had already been recorded, derived its strength from a return to the authentic values of the national past. This renewed interest for the past was also noticeable in Egypt and in Mesopotamia. The book of Deuteronomy is the tangible proof of Israel's return to her sources. Most scholars are agreed that this book, or part of it at least, must be the book of the law found in 622 in the temple (2 Kings 22:8).

The origin of the legal material assimilated into Deuteronomy and the vital source of its characteristic sermon form are to be found in the ancient, tribal sanctuaries of the Northern Kingdom. The pagan environment of Samaria and above all the catastrophe of 721 must have led, among the priests and the prophets (insofar as these found refuge in Judah), to this reconsideration of Israel's essential being—the Mosaic federation of tribes around the one sanctuary of the one Yahweh. It is quite conceivable that the spirit that was alive in the separate circle of the "North" completely eluded the higher clergy of Jerusalem, so that it is possible to speak of a discovery in this connection. The strong, social content of the book indicates a prophetic influence. On the other hand, the priestly element is also unmistakable. To adapt Buber's description of Deuteronomy, we may say that this book led the flood of prophetic reaction into a calm, priestly channel. It was precisely because of this that this book of the law was able to serve as a practical guide in matters of day to day living in the catastrophe which was to sweep so much away.

The catastrophe came surprisingly soon. In 605, the Egyptian overlordship was replaced by that of Babylon (2 Kings 24:7). A few years later, Jehoiakim rose against Nebuchadnezzar's rule (2 Kings 24:1). The punitive expedition of 598 resulted in the deportation of Jehoiakim's successor, king Jehoiachin, and a large number of men of high rank and skilled professional men. Nebuchadnezzar appointed a new king to rule in Judah, and named him, as his vassal, Zedekiah. Acting against Jeremiah's advice (Jer. 37 and 38), Zedekiah also allowed himself to be persuaded to revolt by the Egyptian party. As a result, the temple and the city were permanently destroyed in 587 (2 Kings 25).

8. The Mutual Estrangement of the Community of Believers and the State Community

It is, to say the least, remarkable that Israel's downfall did not in fact mean the end of her religion. The catastrophe did not in any sense bring the history of Israel's religion to a close. It is more true to say that Israel's religious history really began at this point. This fact is by no means self-evident, and we are once again forced to recognize the very special quality of this national religion. What kind of a national religion was Israel's that it was able to survive the collapse of the nation? However much the religion of Israel may have been determined up to this point in her history by the national element, it is clear that this element must be understood in a different light from the part played by the national element in other national religions of the ancient Near East.

Whatever may be the secret of this, the national character of Israel's religious system is indisputable. Israel became a nation by the acceptance, on the part of more or less closely related groups of people, of Yahweh as their God. They became a nation when they became the nation of Yahweh, Yahweh's people. The national community and the "Church" coincided with one another. The monarchy made this national community into an ancient, oriental state. After a number of failures in the beginning, the monarchy gained a distinctive and even an important place in the Yahwistic system. The kingdom of God itself, which was based on Israel's redemption from Egypt, reached its Old Testament fulfillment in the monarchy. Thus, in principle, the state and the "Church" coincided also with one another. Both grew up so intimately with each other, that they cannot be conceived without each other in the given situation.

Nonetheless they did become imperceptibly estranged from each other. The state degenerated and was less and less able to be of value as the national form of authentic religion. The two kingdoms preserved their official, theoretical religion, but were only able to do this by means of syncretism. Insofar as the state and religion did succeed in remaining one, religion degenerated along with the state. As the state religion gradually lapsed into a kind of paganism, so the essential, revealed religion grew away from the state. Yahweh still remained the national God, but it was a nominal Yahwism. The Yahwism of the state religion became, by contact with so much paganism, a highly questionable alloy. It might even have been superstition rather than real faith. It is, after all, not only in Israel that man, confronted with the indisputable realities of religion, has sought, and still seeks to escape from the attitude of faith which demands the total commitment of his whole being by hiding behind certain forms of religious practice.

One of the constant themes of the preaching of the prophets was that Yahweh could not be treated like a pagan god. The prophets did not only reproach Israel with apostasy from Yahweh. They also condemned the way in which Israel believed she could approach Yahweh. A pagan attitude was revealed in the way in which Israel honored Yahweh—Israel believed that the fact that she was Yahweh's people, that there was a temple, that sacrifices were made, that splendid feasts were celebrated, and that prayers were recited in itself conferred security and special protection. The situation was really much more serious than it appeared to be from the outside. It was precisely because the official Sunday religion of Yahwism completely lacked the real content and meaning of the original religion that it lent itself so readily to explicitly pagan practices and ideas.

Thus, long before the collapse of the state, there was a wide gulf between the state and the true religion. True religion was not dead in Israel and, in the struggle for its continued existence and the preservation of its essence, it even gained inner strength. The state came less and less to be the organ of true religion in Israel. Those circles in which a truly religious awareness predominated had to hold their own against the state and to learn how to live without the state. There were several attempts to make the state, with its many possibilities for external development, into a serviceable instrument of true religion once again. But, although it was possible to eliminate certain abuses, at least for a time, by means of more or less successful attempts to purify the state religion, it was no longer possible to change the almost universal, mental attitude. Although Yahwism seemed still to be closely associated with official Israel and her institutions, the link between the true religion of Yahweh and the ancient, oriental organism within which it crystallized had already become very weak. Ancient Israel was no longer in any sense an authentic state of God. This Israel had been untrue to her own structural principle, and had thus become an outdated phenomenon, not only superfluous but also injurious. This Israel had, therefore, to disappear.

The collapse of the total fabric of the nation, which had initially protected, but in the long run had only stifled the essential religious values of Yahwism, led to the sudden liberation of these values from the past. This freedom from the past was their salvation and the way was open for a completely new line of development. It was only when the facts themselves and the situation forced men to realize it that their minds could be opened to the vision that the national character of Israel's religion was something provisional and transitory—the adaptation of divine revelation to a given, historical situation. It was, however, to be quite a long time before this truth was fully digested. The national ties were gradually loosened, but only as a result of sheer necessity and then only partially and almost unconsciously. The temptation to fall back into the state pattern of religion and to cling to this persisted until Christianity experienced its first great crisis in connection with this precise point and, like Israel, forced by the facts themselves into a clear and full realization of its own nature, made a complete and permanent break. Nothing less than the question as to whether the New Testament was really to remain new or whether it was fall back again into the Old Testament was at stake here. This question had, of course, been under discussion ever since the fall of Israel, though without the same degree of urgency—should the Old Testament believer make a virtue out of necessity and follow the path which led to the New Testament, or should he go on clinging to his lost national privilege as an imaginary ideal which might be fulfilled in the future, in an absolute form that it had never possessed in the past?

It is, then, possible to discern the gradual emergence of the traditional religion, especially during the second half of the age of the kings, into a position of clear pre-eminence, as an independent force reacting against Israel's national decadence. This reaction was given a tangible, historical form by Israel's prophets, whose appearance forms the subject of the following chapter.

VI

The Prophets of Israel

1. The Forms in Which Prophetism Appeared

By the prophets are meant, generally speaking, the men of God who appeared in Israel between the eighth and the sixth century before Christ, and whose preaching is preserved in those books of the Bible which are named after them. They played such an important part in the history of Israel's religion that the great men— Moses in particular, but also Samuel and even Abraham—who preceded these prophets tended to be modeled, in the biblical tradition, on the prophetic pattern, and to be called prophets. There are, moreover, many other facts in the Bible which establish, beyond all doubt, that the prophets who appeared at the time of Samuel only partially correspond to our generally accepted idea of a prophet. In this connection too, it is a remarkable fact that Amos (7:14), and Micah (3:8), for example, stated explicitly that they did not wish to be regarded as prophets, and that others, such as Isaiah and Jeremiah, never called themselves prophets. Jeremiah and Ezekiel in particular even went so far as to argue violently against prophetism. These facts force us to recognize that there was a form of prophetism which was firmly rooted in the earliest period of Israel's settled existence, and which persisted until the Exile. It is not possible simply to place the so-called classic prophetism in the same category as this form of prophetism, although there is undoubtedly a connection, as well as a sharp contrast, between the two.

The classic prophets did not simply originate from the ancient form of prophetism. It is far more accurate to think of them as following in the tradition of Moses and Samuel, who have themselves justly come to be called prophets, since the classic prophets took their place. That there is, however, a close connection here is sufficiently evident from the fact that Saul met Samuel at the head of a group of prophets in spiritual ecstasy (1 Sam. 19:20). The connection is also clear from the figures of Elijah and Elisha, who were, on the one hand, representatives of the ancient prophetism at its best and whose appearance was, on the other hand, a clear prelude to the reactionary prophetism of the eighth century. The biographies of Elijah and Elisha, as well as the scriptural account of the life of Samuel, are our most important sources for the knowledge that we have of the ancient form of prophetism.

This prophetism would seem to have been a constant element in Israelitic society at that time. There was a definite class of prophets, and those who belonged to it were called the sons of the prophets, in accordance with the normal Semitic usage of the word son, in the sense of one who belonged to a certain category. They were members of a sort of guild and frequently lived together as a group. Their public appearances were often made as a group. They had a leader, who was addressed as Lord or father. They accepted alms, and were recognizable by their hair shirts and leather girdles. This distinctive outward appearance, however, also went together with a special gift, the gift of prophesying. Their prophesying was accompanied by an infectious ecstasy, which was expressed in loud cries, song, gesturing, and dancing. It would seem too, as if their ecstasy was evoked by their behavior, and especially by music (2 Kings 3:15). This prophesying sometimes took the extreme form of wild movements and hysterical screaming, during which the prophets slashed their bodies, tore off their clothes, and even fainted. Such behavior might well have been excessive, and we know that such excesses were practised by the prophets of Baal (1 Kings 18:28), and forbidden by the Law (*see* Lev. 19:28; Deut. 14:1), but they were in complete accordance with all the other prophetic phenomena and those who committed them were nonetheless called prophets. This is, however, by no means all that there was to prophetism, even in its ancient form.

This striking outward behavior and appearance may be regarded as a sign that the deity had a special claim upon such men. A man became a prophet because he enjoyed a special relationship with the divine world. The people expressed their awareness of the existence of this special relationship by calling such a man a man of God or even a man of the spirit (Hos. 9:7). Such a man was seized by the spirit of God and transformed into a different person. That was why he behaved differently and was literally transported outside himself. Above all, however, he was able to see and to do things which were beyond the vision and the capabilities of ordinary mortals. In this respect, prophetism always remained quite consistent throughout the centuries. The prophet had access to God's mysteries, which were revealed to him in dreams and visions. From time immemorial, men turned to the prophet as an oracle for the future, or to learn of the outcome of any undertaking. He was the personal liaison between God and men. To comply with the wishes of other men, he would attempt to fall into a trance and thereby to learn the will of God. But in order to pass on a message from God, or to carry out a divine commission, he would come unbidden between God and men.

This essential characteristic predominated to such an extent in the case of the classic prophets that the impression which they make is a much more spiritual one. They were almost exclusively the spokesmen of God and the interpreters of his will. If any of the attendant prophetic phenomena were present in their case, these were very much in the background. At the very least, these accompanying phenomena played a part which was clearly subordinate to that of preaching. The practice of consulting the prophets is convincing proof of the fact that this essential characteristic was not entirely lacking even in the case of the earlier prophetism. The name seer is in itself also proof of this, and the following text provides a valuable insight in this connection: "Now in time past in Israel, when a man went to consult God, he spoke thus: Come, let us go to the seer. For he that is now called a prophet, in time past was called a seer" (1 Sam. 9:9). It is possible that this text is indicative of a later fusion of phenomena which were, at an earlier stage of Israel's history, distributed among different classes of men.

A very clear summary of the biblical conception of a prophet can be found in the passages depicting Moses as the greatest of the prophets. None of the prophets associated on such intimate terms with God, and none performed such great signs: "There arose no more a prophet in Israel like unto Moses, whom Yahweh knew face to face: in all the signs and wonders . . . and all the mighty hand, and great miracles, which Moses did before all Israel" (Deut. 34:10, 12). Moses corresponded exactly to the biblical idea of a prophet. He was intimate with God and a miracle worker. Jesus of Nazareth was similarly a "prophet, mighty in work and word before God and all the people" (Luke 24:19). When Jesus made it clear that he knew the secrets of her personal life, the reaction of the Samaritan woman was immediate: "Sir, I perceive that thou art a prophet." At once she wished to consult him (John 4:19). When he was asked what he thought of Jesus, the blind man whose sight had been restored to him replied without hesitation: "He is a prophet" (John 9:17). Predicting the future was not an essential element in prophecy, but it was one of the most convincing expressions of it, because the future is hidden from man and known only to God.

2. *The Function of Prophetism*

A special experience of God formed the basis of all prophecy. Moses was the greatest of all the prophets because of his intimate experience of God: "If there be among you a prophet, I will appear to him in a vision, and I will speak to him in a dream. But it is not so with my servant Moses, who is most faithful in all my house. For I speak to him mouth to mouth, and not in visions or by riddles: but he doth see the figure of Yahweh" (Num. 12:6-8). This prophetic privilege was, however, directed entirely towards preaching and bearing witness—God revealed his mysteries to the prophet in order to make his will known to men in that way.

Yahweh's word came to the prophet—Yahweh put his word into the prophet's mouth; Yahweh's hand lay (heavily) upon him; Yahweh's spirit fell upon him. The prophet was then bound to bear witness. "The lion hath roared: who will not fear? The Lord Yahweh hath spoken: who shall not prophesy"? (Amos 3:8). The prophet was bound to prophesy, even if he met with resistance and even if he encountered a wall of opposition. Jeremiah complained that Yahweh was too powerful for him, and that Yahweh's word made him a reproach and a derision every day. "Then I said: I will not make mention of him nor speak any more in his Name. And there came in my heart as a burning fire, shut up in my bones: and I was wearied, not being able to bear it" (20:7-9). The prophet was not allowed to follow his own spirit (Ezek. 13:3), and to preach a vision of his own heart (Jer. 23:16). He was to pass on Yahweh's word faithfully, and not to twist it according to the wishes of those who heard him: "They shall be turned to thee, and thou shalt not be turned to them," for "thou shalt be as my mouth" (Jer. 15:19). The prophet was called to be the interpreter and the mouthpiece— in the Bible literally the mouth—of Yahweh. As Moses' spokesman, Aaron was called his prophet (Exod. 7:1). Moses, as the one who gave Aaron his commission, was even called Aaron's god: "Thou (Moses) shalt speak to him (Aaron), and put my words in his mouth: and I will be in thy mouth and in his mouth . . . He shall speak in thy stead to the people, and shall be to thee as a mouth, and thou shalt be to him as a god" (Exod. 4:15f.).

Yahweh turned to the people through the intermediary of a prophet. Conversely, the people went to the prophet to learn Yahweh's will. Here too, Moses is an outstanding example. He was besieged from morning to night by the people, who came to him to "seek the judgment of God" (Exod. 18:13–16). At all levels, Israel turned to a prophet—for important affairs of state (1 Kings 22; 2 Kings 3), as well as for every kind of purely private matter. An incident which occurred during the time of the Maccabees provides a good illustration of the role of the prophet in the life of the people of Israel. When the temple was being cleaned, the problem of the desecrated altar of holocausts still remained. Eventually it was decided to pull it down, but "they laid up the stones in the mountain of the temple in a convenient place, till there should come a prophet and give answer concerning them" (1 Macc. 4:44–46; see also 14:41).

Prophetism, then, was the instrument through which Yahweh and Israel contacted each other since time immemorial. With the figure of Moses in view, as the ideal, Deuteronomy established a law defining why and how this instrument should function. All the nations sought contact with the divine world. The pagan nations, however, did not merely seek to know the will of their gods—they wished even more strongly to determine and to influence this will. To this end, they sacrificed children and practised all kinds of black magic, soothsaying, augury, and witchcraft and consulted subterrestrial spirits and the dead. This was abominable idolatry in the sight of Yahweh and forbidden to Israel. Israel's way was that of prophetism and had been so since the revelation on Mount Sinai. Yahweh himself had provided an authentic way by which Israel might learn his will. It was on Sinai that Yahweh had spoken directly to Israel for the first time. The people had then asked for Moses to be their intermediary and, from that time onwards, Israel was always able to come into contact with Yahweh through Moses. Even when Moses died, Israel had no need to search for other ways of knowing Yahweh's will and keeping in touch with him, for Yahweh had promised Moses: "I will raise up a prophet out of the midst of thy brethren like to thee. And I will put my words in his mouth: and he shall speak to them all that I shall command him" (Deut. 18:18). Moses was therefore not only the greatest of the prophets, he was also the first. He was the point of departure of the prophetic phenomenon, once and for all setting the standard for what can only be the pure Israelitic form of prophetism. Moses was in fact one who had received a genuine call from Yahweh, who had access to Yahweh, and who really received his words. Yahweh promised that he would always call prophets from among the people of Israel, prophets who would really hear and proclaim the word of Yahweh. Thus Deuteronomy defined the place of prophetism and its function as a permanent institution in the structure of the people of God (Deut. 18:9–22).

Prophetism shows us the distinctive character of Israel as the chosen people in a concentrated form. Israel's distinction was that she had the true God as her national God, and the distinctive aspect of Israel's prophetism was that Yahweh really spoke to her chosen men. Israel's prophetism was therefore the guarantee and the perpetuation of her election, the lasting proof and at the same time the most important instrument of Yahweh's concern of Israel: "It is I that brought you up out of the land of Egypt, and that led you forty years through the wilderness, that you might possess the land of the Amorrhites. And I raised up your sons for prophets and your young men for Nazarites" (Amos 2:11). In this passage, prophetism is referred to in the same breath as the redemption; the presence of the prophets was, then, the most certain proof that Yahweh had never abandoned his people and that his ancient will to redeem his people was still active. On the other hand, it was a sign that Yahweh had repudiated and abandoned his people, if there were no more prophets in Israel or if the prophets had to wait in vain for Yahweh's word, lacking clairvoyant vision. Jeremiah's threats were ignored, and the people felt confident of themselves: "For the law shall not perish from the priest, nor counsel from the wise, nor the word from the prophet" (Jer. 18:18). But the prophets saw vain things and foretold lies (Jer. 23; Ezek. 13), and when disaster eventually befell Israel, it was in vain that Israel would "seek a vision of the prophet: and the law shall perish from the priest and counsel from the ancients" (Ezek. 7:26).

> Behold, the days come,
> saith the Lord Yahweh,
> and I will send forth a famine into the land:
> not a famine of bread, nor a thirst of water,
> but of hearing the word of Yahweh.
> And they shall move from sea to sea
> and from north to east:
> they shall go about seeking the word of Yahweh
> and shall not find it (Amos 8:11f.; *see also* Ps. 73:9; Lam. 2:9).

3. The Development of Prophetism

The same inconsistency that we noticed at the beginning of this book occurs in the texts referred to in the preceding section. Israel's classic prophets turned against prophetism, yet, even though they did not wish to be called prophets, they were themselves prophets through and through. Israel's classic prophetism cannot be considered entirely separately from her ancient prophetism. We must look for the explanation of this strange inconsistency in the history of the rise and growth of Israel's prophetism. The data would indicate that the following reconstruction is plausible.

Israel was a unique phenomenon. Nonetheless, she never ceased to be an entirely ancient, oriental phenomenon, both in her structure and in the way in which she expressed herself. Israel's religion was in no way an exception to this, nor was her prophetism. What God seized was an ancient, oriental people, and he seized it as a whole, together with its own distinctive characteristics. In the beginning there was little to distinguish Israel from the other national communities of that period and in that environment. In the course of her development, however, Israel's ancient, oriental form seemed to become filled with a new content, and this content broke through this early form and entirely transformed it. By the time Israel's development had come to an end the Israelitic form often gives the impression of having been an original creation, a creation which was entirely a development of and an adaptation to the radically different content which Yahwism had given to it. It is only a few material details, fully integrated into the new whole, which serve to remind us of the original, ancient, oriental point of departure and seem to be in the nature of a survival from the past.

The original character of Yahwism is shown more clearly in Israel's prophetism than in any other aspect of her religious life. This is because her prophetism was so completely unique—throughout the whole of the long period when it was at its peak, it had no point of comparison with anything else in the ancient Near East. Nonetheless, it would seem to have been connected, in the remote past of Israel's origins, with a historical, religious phenomenon and an existing human manner of expression which formed one of the essential components of society at that time. The Canaanite gods and sanctuaries appear to have had their prophets. As we have said, God seized Israel in the whole of her concrete nature, with the purpose of gradually transforming her into his people. In the same way, Israel's faith in God seized hold of Israel in the whole of her ancient, oriental way of life and made this, in all its manifestations, subservient to the kingdom of God, at the same time giving it a terrestrial and national form—in other words, an historical form. Thus, the ecstatic prophetism of Canaan became, in primitive Israel, an ecstatic, Yahwistic prophetism, that is, a religious endowment peculiar to the ancient, eastern world and one that was probably even cultivated by a special professional technique, but already possessing a new content. It was then that the process of transformation began—the new inner content reshaping the outward form. The process was one in which Israel's outward form was continuously made more and more subservient to the new religious values, and was thus a process of spiritualization and purification. It would be impossible to trace the whole of this growth, but the final result speaks for itself. This was Israel's classic prophetism. Although this was a unique phenomenon with a pure religious content, it was accompanied by several sporadic attendant phenomena of purely secondary importance with characteristics reminiscent of the ancient prophetism. At the same time, this ancient prophetism appeared still to flourish, in particular among those prophets who are customarily called false, but who were probably sound enough prophets in the society of those times.

In brief, prophetism was a religious phenomenon in ancient, oriental society. The revealed religion made use of this phenomenon. But, as is the case with every human phenomenon of which God makes use, tension developed in prophetism too, between the vertical and the horizontal forces. Israel was always in danger of reverting to the general level of the ancient Near East, that of a purely pagan form of prophetism and of conforming with that level. Just as the whole of Israel's ancient, oriental structure, after having been subservient to the Kingdom of God and an expression of it, began to degenerate because a pagan content once again crept into her ancient, oriental form, so did Israel's prophetism gradually degenerate in the same way. The false prophets were nothing more or less than the authentic prophets of decadent Israel. The classic prophets, on the other hand, arose in reaction and were definitely exceptions.

The phenomena which characterized the initial stage of Israel's prophetism, when this was still very close to its ancient, oriental point of departure, can be clearly recognized in the false prophets of Israel. This reconstruction would seem to provide a satisfactory explanation of the entire, textual material and to fit best into the whole of Israel's development.

The ancient prophetism, then, developed into a professional status and a permanent institution in Israelitic society. This does not imply that personal vocations and special divine commissions were completely ruled out—we have only to think, for example, of the appearance of Nathan at the time of David, a man who was probably a professional court prophet—but the evidence of the Bible shows that this institution degenerated as Israel as a whole degenerated. It became one of the organs of Israel's decaying body—one of the organs of a Yahwism which had become infected with paganism. The prophets let themselves be used as agents between men and foreign gods (Jer. 2:8, 23:13; Deut. 13:1–5, 18:20). This, of course, is something which fits perfectly into the whole picture of Israel's apostasy from Yahweh, as does her prophets ceasing to listen any more to Yahweh's will and proclaiming, as authentic oracular utterances, only what would please the person consulting them.

4. The Factual Task of the Classic Prophets

The fact that it was above all a sense of vocation which predominated in the case of the classic prophets (Isa. 6; Jer. 1; Ezek. 2f.), is in complete accordance with the development outlined in the previous section. It is as though Yahweh had intervened outside Israel's normal institutions: "I am not a prophet, nor am I the son of a prophet: but I am a herdsman plucking wild figs. And Yahweh took me when I followed the flock, and Yahweh said to me: Go, prophesy to my people Israel" (Amos 7:14; *see also* Mic. 3:7f.). Their vocation lay outside the normal framework of prophetism because they were called to break through this framework. This, at least, was the result. The immediate object of their vocation was, however, to purify the existing framework and to make it once again a serviceable expression of the Kingdom of God. But their reaction, which at first sight seems to have been directed against Israel's degeneration—their predecessors, such as Elijah and Elisha, who were members of the ancient prophetism, also reacted in exactly the same way—extended beyond this. A consciousness of the essential inadequacy of the ancient framework began gradually to develop. The realization that the old Israel had served its purpose gained ground. Ancient Israel was played out and had to go.

It was, then, not only the international situation which led to the disappearance of ancient Israel, but also the inner, dynamic force of her prophetic sense of God. This process had, therefore, the character of a divine verdict passed on Israel because of her apostasy from Yahweh. The world events which caused not only Israel but also her neighbors to sacrifice their national independence became, in the prophetic vision, an act of God with his people and thus a divine judgment which aimed to lead the true Israel, through her national collapse, back to Yahweh. The task of the classic prophecy in the development of the history of salvation can be most accurately described by comparing it to a hinge or pivot, on which the Old Testament turned over to the New. The classic prophets had the task of proclaiming the downfall of ancient Israel. This was the prophetic message of disaster, which took the form, first of all, of threat, then of prediction, and finally of confirmation of an accomplished fact. On to this message of disaster was grafted the prophetic message of salvation, and this consisted of the proclamation of a new Israel to which only those who were converted might belong. This new Israel could, however, only be born of the downfall of the old. For this reason, even the message of salvation was a message of calamity and disaster for those in Israel who did not believe and a message of salvation only for those who would believe.

Faithful Israel was saved, but the downfall of faithless Israel was implicated in her salvation. The salvation of the new people of God was the reverse of the divine judgment passed on the ancient people of God.

Classic prophetism thus brought about the dissociation of the true, Yahwistic religion from its existing framework and the projection of this faith into the new framework. The prophets were able to say very little more about the new framework than that it was new and that full and lasting justice would be done to authentic religiosity within it. In fact, the development of this new framework was to be very gradual, and the framework was to be created by religion, in conjunction with the existing social situation in which the believers found themselves.

As an attendant phenomenon to Israel's downfall and total collapse as a state, the classic prophets in fact saved the traditional religion from the catastrophe and transplanted it among Israel's scattered remnants, where it was to find a new form of organization, not as a state, but almost as a church. Yahwism was far more deeply rooted in Israel than the state organization. Its growth together with the state had been a grave danger in Israel. The prophets broke this dangerous link, with the result that Yahwism was not dragged down with the state when the state fell, but was, on the contrary, set free again from the state. Israel's collapse was not total and absolute, because Yahwism was able to hold its own. This faith was so strong and vital, and so firmly rooted in Israel's deepest being that it was capable of maintaining itself and of preserving its distinctive character in Israel's scattered remnants and of binding these essential elements into a new and now almost exclusively religious community, cutting across all territorial and state boundaries.

In the distant past, revealed religion welded an amorphous group of servile people together into a people of God. Later, it saved the Mosaic theocracy from decline by transforming this into a Yahwistic monarchy. Now it appeared to be capable of building up, from Israel's ruins, a new religious community with, once again, a totally different social structure—world Judaism, the universal church of the Jews. This new form of organization was, of course, not that of the New Testament, but it was a transition towards it. The Jewish world was the first, provisional realization of Israel's resurrection which had been predicted, with the full certainty of faith, by the prophets. Judaism created the spiritual climate and the structure and organization in which the Christian message could be received. At the same time, however, it increasingly revealed that closed minded attitude so characteristic of the Old Testament. To a certain degree, it resulted in a restoration of the national and political framework, but this led such a precarious and sickly existence that Yahwism had ample opportunities to develop separately along the path indicated by the prophets. All the same, the New Testament message had to save what was threatened with complete inflexibility here. To do this, the New Testament went back to the prophetic message and, in going beyond it and fulfilling it, nonetheless preserved its essential and enormous attraction.

The impression which classic prophetism makes on us is one of a magnificent and homogeneous whole. The age of the prophets of course lasted for more than three centuries, and each of the prophetic books reveals a strong, individual personality with its own distinctive characteristics. Nonetheless, there is, in the Old Testament, in the words of St. Jerome, a true *corpus prophetale,* an impressive and self-contained whole. The very best of Israel's religion is concentrated in her prophecy which, more than any other literary genre in the Bible, reveals the originality of Yahwism. There is, moreover, nothing in the whole of the ancient world that can be compared with it.

When the Old Testament is considered as a whole, what strikes the reader so forcibly is the spiritual unity which underlies the entire work, despite the great variety in expression and the many divergences in mental attitude resulting from changing times and the constantly changing physical environment of the people. It is clearly the Yahwistic consciousness of God, the result of revelation, which was the one constant factor permeating and binding together everything else—the God of Revelation who was always consistent throughout the centuries. It was the first impact of revelation, strengthened and enriched by later revelation, which brought into existence the first consciousness of faith. This awareness of God and faith, constantly in touch with an immediate experience of faith, continued to expand in the living stream of the tradition of faith. The classic prophetism of Israel was itself in this stream of tradition and, because of the powerful and personal experience which the prophets had of God, was the most important general factor in extending and deepening it.

But this general factor does not completely explain the unity of classic prophetism. There was also a special factor which determined the appearance of most, if not all of the prophets and which played a most important part in the creation of the distinctive form of classic prophetism. This special factor was Israel's decadence and fall. In fact, the classic prophets provided the vocal accompaniment to Israel's downfall—they were the interpreters of decadent Israel. This was their specific function in the development of the history of salvation from the Old to the New Testament. It is thus important to bear in mind that the canonical prophets, taken as a whole, must be considered in connection with Israel's catastrophe, the Exile, which in turn should be seen as the consequence of the long prelude of Israel's decadence and in the light of the painful aftereffects of the Exile—the long sequel of Israel's existence as a remnant. The message of the prophets cannot be dissociated from the phenomenon of Israel's rejection, considered as a possible threat in the future, as a disruptive experience in the present, or even as a still disturbing recollection of an accomplished fact, the meaning of which men were still trying to fathom.

Even if it is perfectly possible, however, to situate each individual prophet quite easily within the context of the Exile, it is by no means necessary to do so, since it remains true to say that the classic prophets gained, from Israel's catastrophe, a distinctive and oracular style, which is applicable even outside this well-defined historical context. It is, after all, true of most of the styles found in the Old Testament, that, although they arose within a clearly defined situation, they afterwards led an independent life as a literary form that could be used in other situations. A striking characteristic of the Jewish period, in the early stages of the writing of the Old Testament, was that ancient, literary forms were imitated and combined, and that styles which were at one time applicable to definite, concrete situations were, at this later phase, used as literary formulae. Similarly, in the prophetic books, a good deal of literary prophecy may be found, and still existing formulae, which had been used in the past, were often preferred, as a result of later religious speculation; this prophetic style exists side by side in the Old Testament with the oracular prophetism which forms the literary expression of the historical prophetic message. It is, therefore, true to say that Israel's catastrophe is the key to the prophetic books as a whole.

5. Prophetic Themes

The strong sense of vocation that these prophets had implies that they personally experienced the divine reality. This personal experience of God underlay their entire appearance, which was, first and foremost, a testimony and a preaching of the divine reality, both in its supraterrestrial holiness and in its terrifying immanence. They fully understood the original meaning of the name Yahweh and were clearly aware of the consequences of the fact that Yahweh was Israel's God. They were also conscious of what God was really asking of man. The most important themes contained in their message can be traced back to this awareness. Yahweh was the holy and living God who had associated himself in the most intimate way with Israel. What he asked of Israel was an equally authentic and living response.

What this implied above all was that Israel was to belong entirely to Yahweh. The greatest reproach made by the prophets was that Israel had become unfaithful to Yahweh and was following strange gods. That was her greatest sin, her fundamental sin. In whatever form it manifested itself, the following of strange gods was the classic way of avoiding real duties and genuine human responsibilities. It was a breaking of the Covenant, and the prophets tried to make Israel realize the full implication of this action by referring to it as adultery (Hos. 2:4ff.; Jer. 2:2, 3:8f., 5:7, 13:22, 26f.; Ezek. 16 and 23). No other people had ever thought of being unfaithful to their national god, and these were not even gods, but Israel, the only people who belonged to the true God, had been unfaithful, and this was shameful (Jer. 2:10–13). Even animals were more faithful (Isa. 1:3; Jer. 8:7). In moving language Israel was reminded of Yahweh's faithfulness. He was the Lord of all the earth and of all nations, yet he had chosen Israel, an insignificant people, as his precious and personal possession and had caused her to prosper and to become a thriving, national community. With endless patience he had endured Israel's faithlessness from the very beginning to the present time, but the limit of his patience had been reached. If Israel would not be converted, Yahweh would reject her. This conversion included not only a recognition that Yahweh was the only God, but also a return to the original spirit of Yahwism. The belief that it was possible to satisfy Yahweh by belonging formally and officially to him was to make an idol of Yahweh. Authentic Yahwism set a standard for human behavior at all levels. This, then, was the principal theme of the prophets.

A second theme was the emphasis which the prophets placed upon social justice. To do justice to widows and orphans was to know Yahweh (Jer. 22:16; Hos. 4:1–6). Man's service of Yahweh had to be actual. A third theme was directly connected with this second theme. Worship which was accompanied by behavior which reduced this worship to the level of falsehood, and formalism was for Yahweh an abomination. So many prophetic texts express an unfavorable opinion on the subject of worship that this theme poses a certain problem.

Scarcely anyone is fortunate enough nowadays to be able to worship, in the most literal sense of the phrase, "in spirit and truth" (John 4:24). In the past this was apparently the case, and the prophets were often looked upon as the forerunners and the champions of such worshipers. Now, however, the view that the prophets did not oppose sacrificial worship as such, but rather its debasement (Hos. 8:5, 11–13; Amos 5:5, 21–23; Isa. 1:10–15, 29:13; Mic. 6:6–8; Jer. 7; Ps. 39:7–9, 49: 8–15, 68:32) is becoming more generally accepted. All that the prophets said against worship was the outcome, not of their rejection of the temple and of public worship, but of their great respect for it. The Jews, after all, were accused of this by Christ himself, and by Paul and Stephen. It is quite evident that the prophets' pronouncements against the temple were prompted by a deep awareness of the temple as the house of God. They rejected the practice of worship in Israel because this was not accompanied by a corresponding inward state and outward behavior. Moreover, those prophetic statements which appear to be an absolute repudiation of worship in Israel in fact go back to a Semitic, linguistic usage. Moses probably gave real manna in the desert, yet Christ said: "Moses gave you not bread from heaven" (John 6:32). The Mosaic law prescribed proper sacrifices, but Yahweh said: "I spoke not to your fathers and I commanded them not, in the day that I brought them out of the land of Egypt, concerning the matter of burnt-offerings and sacrifices" (Jer. 7:22). The denial in these examples served to emphasize all the more the affirmation which followed. Such a denial was not intended to be absolute. Its aim was only to draw attention to the relative and secondary nature of the one, in comparison with the importance of the other fact. In the case of the first text, then, the meaning is that it was not so much in the time of Moses, but rather in Christ that the Father gives real bread from heaven. In the case of the second, what Yahweh wished to emphasize was that he wanted true devotion, not offerings. This is clear from the parallel text of Hosea: "The knowledge of God more than holocausts" (Hos. 6:6; *see also* 1 Sam. 15:22f.). What this antithesis between denial and affirmation in fact expressed was only a difference in appreciation and priority.

Finally, the political element in the prophetic message is a fourth theme, and a further expression of the religious realism of the prophets. Politics and religion were closely interwoven everywhere in the ancient Near East, and it was simply a question as to which tipped the balance. A national religion deferred, naturally enough, to the political ambitions of the nation and affixed its seal to them. The glory of the king and the people was the glory of the national god. Early Yahwism was still inclined to yield to political aims in this way, and it was only very slowly that the true essence of the revealed religion broke through the ancient, oriental framework. The prophets demanded a course of action on the part of Israel's kings which was really determined by faith in God. They wanted a policy of trust in God, and saw, in the faith which Israel's rulers placed in horses and chariots and alliances, an apostasy from and a lack of faith in Yahweh. What the prophets demanded might well have seemed, on occasion, to be political folly and pure defeatism, but by preaching that Yahweh himself had a hand in Israel's humiliation and that he was using Israel's enemies as a rod with which to punish her, they helped to emancipate religion from politics and to make the relationship between the two more pure. Israel had to be converted. She had not to look elsewhere for her salvation. Thus the demands made by Israel's religion ran directly counter to the political aspirations of her monarchy and the national pride of her people.

6. The Theme of Disaster

Their personal experience of God enabled the prophets to see with startling clarity the enormous contrast between what God asked of man and the utterly inadequate response made by Israel. This experience of God also made the prophets deeply aware of human sinfulness in general and of the sinfulness of Israel in particular. That the Holy One of Israel, who was a consuming fire, should be dwelling among an unclean people profoundly disturbed the prophets. This was their own people, but no one seemed to be able to see what they saw. They had to speak. Yahweh's word burnt inside them and, like a flame, burst out of them (Jer. 20:9; Amos 3:4, 8). They strove to open the eyes of the people and their leaders to the divine reality and to arouse them from their lethargy. "The work of Yahweh you regard not, nor do you consider the works of your hands" (Isa. 5:12). Their faith in God enabled them to understand the signs of the times. Israel owed her existence as an independent, political unit to the fact that for centuries no single great power had been able to exert a decisive influence over the Syrian-Palestinian corridor. This situation was, however, changing. The growing strength of Assyria had already been experienced in the West. But, both in the North and in the South, a long period of peace and prosperity during the first half of the eighth century had bred a false confidence in the absolute stability of the old order. The new prosperity seemed to be a confirmation of Israel's rather pagan trust in the Covenant, and the people felt that they would automatically be exempt from calamity because of it (Jer. 8:8, 11, 14:13; Ezek. 12:22f.).

The Israelites could not believe in the downfall of their nation because they did not want to believe in it. The Israel that had been so open to those prophets who aroused false hopes and expectations until the very eve of the *coup de grâce* remained quite closed to the message of the classic prophets. Israel's stubborn blindness and deafness to the classic prophets is, of course, as classic as the prophets themselves, and is typical of the attitude of the man who will not admit defeat at God's hands. "Remember and forget not, how thou provokedst Yahweh, thy God, to wrath in the wilderness. From the day that thou camest out of the land of Egypt unto this place, thou hast always striven against Yahweh . . . You have seen all the things that Yahweh did before you . . . And Yahweh hath not given you a heart to understand, and eyes to see, and ears that may hear, unto this present day . . . For I know thy obstinacy, and thy most stiff neck. While I am yet living, and going in with you, you have always been rebellious against Yahweh. How much more when I shall be dead?" (Deut. 9:7f., 29:3, 5, 31:27). The mystery of man's hardness of heart plays a large part in the dispensation of salvation. In the Bible, it is presented in the form of the stubbornness of Israel and the Jewish world. The divine judgment and punishment of human obduracy was the prophets' message of disaster, implying, as it did, the rejection of Israel. Yahweh punished his people by striking them with stubbornness on account of their sins, just as he had previously hardened the heart of the Pharaoh. This idea of judgment and sentence is expressed most clearly in the commission to prophesy which Isaiah received when he was called:

> Go, and thou shalt say to this people:
> Hearing, hear and understand not:
> and see the vision and know it not.
> Blind the heart of this people, and make their ears heavy,
> and shut their eyes:
> lest they see with their eyes and hear with their ears and
> understand with their heart,
> and be converted and healed (Isa. 6:9f.).

Hebrew often uses the imperative form to express certainty in the future. This occurs twice in Isaiah 8:9: "Strengthen yourselves, and be overcome: gird yourselves, and be overcome." This means that the Israelites might arm themselves for war as powerfully as they liked, but they would nonetheless be defeated. The meaning of the text quoted above is probably: however much and however clearly you may have seen and heard in the past, and may see in the future, you will nonetheless not understand—however overwhelming the evidence may be, you will not admit defeat to it.

This text has many parallels. Isaiah's unwilling listeners took his prophetic message for childish prattle (*ṣaw lāṣaw ṣaw lāṣaw qaw lāqāw qaw lāqāw*). Then came the judgment: "For with the speech of lips (= in faltering language) and with another (= a strange) tongue, he will speak to this people . . . And the word of Yahweh shall be to them: *ṣaw lāṣāw ṣaw lāṣāw qaw lāqāw qāw lāqāw;* that they may go, and fall backward, and be broken, and snared, and taken" (Isa. 28:9–13). Yahweh's word had become, for Israel, a sealed book that no one could open or that had been handed to someone who could not read (Isa. 29:9–12), and in this passage we encounter again the imperative which spelt disaster: "Be astonished and wonder: waver and stagger: be drunk, and not with wine: stagger, and not with drunkenness"—a divine word by which sentence was passed: "For Yahweh hath mingled for you the spirit of a deep sleep: he will shut up your eyes: he will cover your heads."

Hardness of heart is a condition which, of its very nature, excludes conversion, because it implies, by definition, inflexibility in an attitude of unwillingness. This inflexibility is the result of free choice on the part of man. By his obstinate sinfulness man arrives at a state where every divine approach is frustrated. This inevitably leads to an increase of his own guilt. At the same time, however, this inflexibility is also a divine judgment and punishment. The mystery of divine election and rejection plays a prominent part in the inscrutable interplay between God's grace and man's freedom of choice. The Bible emphasized this mystery by ascribing an active role to Yahweh and his prophet. At the same time, the Bible made a final appeal to man's sense of responsibility through the prophets.

Isaiah's mission was positively directed towards the salvation of Israel, and the biblical account of his task of blinding Israel constituted a last, urgent invitation to be converted (*see also* Ezek. 2 and 3:1–11; 12:2; Jer. 5:21). It is always possible, at any time or place, for man to reach the limit of sin and evil. This does not, however, only mean that he thereby makes himself incapable of good. It also means that it is by God that he must be freed from evil. In this situation, something decisive, permanent, and irrevocable occurs—it is as though the shadow of eternal damnation is spread over the earth and the whole of man's existence.

The prophetic message of disaster gave a concrete form to this human situation at the Old Testament level. What was at stake was not so much the personal destiny of each individual Israelite in the life after death, but rather the worldly existence and prosperity of an entire people. The prophetic theme of disaster also includes a vivid account of how the extreme limit can be reached in the history of God and man, in the concrete form of Israel's national history. Yahweh had tried again and again to appeal to his people (Jer. 6:10, 7:24–28, 11:6–8), but now the time had come when Yahweh could no longer call Israel "my" people, but "not my people" (Hos. 1:9), "this" people (Isa. 6:9, 8:6, 28:11), and a people of Sodom and Gomorrah (Isa. 1:10; Jer. 23:14; Ezek. 16:48). The nation as a whole was delivered up to hardness of heart, and Yahweh had given it up. Israel thus lost her national privilege, the privilege of being God's people. This quite simply marked the end of the Old Testament. The Old Testament dispensation of salvation, which had been characterized by its confinement within terrestrial and national boundaries, was, in principle, finished. The God of the world and of mankind had, for a time, become the national God of Israel. That time had passed. This, then, forms the basic theme of the entire prophetic message of disaster and it is thus the hinge on which the Old Testament turned over to the New. Individual conversions were still possible, for each Israelite was free to choose this path, but the nation as a whole had been rejected. Viewed in its historical perspective, the rejection of Israel was a long process, the last collective decision occurring—perhaps only provisionally—at the time of Christ. Nonetheless, from the time of Isaiah onwards, the history of salvation was based firmly on the building up of a people of God which was in no way associated with a political and national Israel.

This radical change, this turning point in the plan of salvation, which was nothing less than the final dissolution of the Old Covenant and the beginning of the New, is a fundamental, prophetic theme, traces of which can be found in the whole of the Old Testament, especially in those sections which provide a speculative synopsis of Israel's history (Lev. 26:18ff. and the contrasting passage in Exod. 23:20ff.; Deut. 28:15-68, 29-32; Judges 2:6-23; Jer. 32; Ezek. 20; 2 Kings 17:7-20; 2 Chron. 36:12-21; Neh. 9; Dan. 9; Bar. 1:15-3:8). This theme is, however, most powerfully expressed in Isaiah 6. The New Testament quotes freely from this chapter of Isaiah, especially whenever reference is made to Israel's rejection. This in itself is a confirmation of the view that this passage cannot be interpreted as an incidental, though strongly worded penitential sermon. It must be seen as a decisive turning point and a new orientation; by rejecting Isaiah, Israel adopted an attitude which was eventually to lead to her rejection of Christ. A study of the contexts in which the New Testament quotations from Isaiah 6 occur (Matt. 13:14f.; Mark 4:12; Luke 8:10; John 12:39; Acts 28:26f.; Rom. 11:8; see also Acts 7 and Rom. 9f.), will at once reveal how parallel the situations are. The biblical writers must clearly have found Israel's rejection a most difficult problem.

If Isaiah's message is compared with the arguments of Paul and Stephen, we are bound to come to the conclusion that what Paul gives is a review of God's acts, extending this as far as the end of time, whereas Stephen, taking the attitude of the Jews in his own time as his point of departure, traces the line of development back to the beginning of Israel's history. Isaiah, however, was still in the middle of the ancient order of salvation and his principal task was thus to announce the termination of this order and to show the opposite side of the coin by pointing to the dawn of a new order of salvation, which contained a condemnation of his own faithless generation.

The rejection of Israel became a concrete fact in the Exile. The Exile was Yahweh's literal rejection of Israel from his sight. At a single stroke, the entire national Kingdom of God, built up in the past with so much care, collapsed. The Exile marked the final undoing of everything that had been promised to Abraham and everything that had become a reality in the time of Moses and David. It was a sudden and disastrous end.

7. Israel's Disaster Seen as a Purification

It follows, from the very nature of the religion of the Old Testament, that this national catastrophe must have brought an almost inconceivable religious upheaval in its wake. Israel had after all, experienced religion up to that point exclusively within the national and terrestrial framework in which it had been embodied. The total collapse of this external framework deprived Israel of all her previous security. To have everything that one has hitherto clung to taken away is a test of faith which every believer may have to face, and such crises have occurred constantly throughout the history of salvation. Israel here was subject to the law of death and resurrection, as Abraham had been, when called upon to sacrifice his son.

In accordance with the classic idea of the Old Testament, Yahweh always gave evidence of his ability and his presence by his people's prosperity. Now, however, his people might well wonder where their God was. What was Yahweh to them, and what was Yahwism, without the land, the temple, the dynasty of kings, and any kind of national existence? The disappearance of a nation from history is, by no means, an uncommon occurrence. In the Arab world, a separate place in the pantheon was allotted to such orphaned tribal and national gods. But Israel was not to disappear from history. Part of the mystery of Israel was that she could not be stamped out. The heart of this mystery is to be found in Yahweh himself. Yahweh remained, and it was simply a question of finding him in a new way, now that the old way of finding him had gone for ever. And, because Yahweh remained, Israel was to remain in one form or another. Indeed, Israel was only now to become truly Israel.

This crisis of faith was in fact a religious purification. Free of all earlier ties—ties which had become gradually more and more dangerous—the ancient Yahwism emerged from the crisis in its original and essential form. It was this naked core of Yahwism which was to form the foundation for a new community of believers, with a new social structure and a new body of religious conceptions, within which religion would be experienced in a totally new way. This new religious world necessarily took a long time to develop, and it was to a very great extent determined by the new circumstances in which Israel lived. The Kingdom of God had first of all been embodied in the Hebrew tribal federation. This embodiment was later replaced by the Israelitic monarchy. Now the Kingdom of God was to take on a third, though once more provisional form—that of the Jewish community, spread over the ancient world.

This precise form of Israel's continued existence had not been anticipated by the prophets. They were in the habit of embracing the entire future in their vision. Only the main outlines of a new religious orientation were provided by the prophets. In principle, however, they had already broken away from the still existing ancient order. They too, in their certainty that the catastrophe was inevitable, had to go through the same crisis that the people as a whole had to go through later. Their faith was already pure. They already lived in a new world of faith, a world which was, at that time, still completely inaccessible to their contemporaries. They saw the cracks in the Mosaic fabric of the ancient order of salvation. The more delapidated the old covenant became, the more clearly the prophets saw the outlines of a new covenant appear.

In accordance with their special position at the turning point of the Old and New Testaments, the prophets had to proclaim both disaster and salvation. Their message of disaster was principally concerned with the demolition of the Old Testament, whereas their message of salvation was concerned with the construction of the New. Disaster was to befall the great majority of their contemporaries, the unbelieving mass. Salvation was to come to those who believed, to those who preserved or who rediscovered their faith in the unavertable catastrophe which was to come: "The just shall live in his faith" (Hab. 2:4). Their first word had of its very nature, to be a word of disaster—Yahweh had resolved that Israel should fall. So long as Israel continued to live improvidently, disaster was bound to play the most prominent part in the prophets' message. It was only when the first heavy blows fell, demonstrating the harsh reality of this disaster, that there was a shift of emphasis in the prophetic message towards salvation. Then the prophets began to preach consolation and encouragement to those who believed that, even in disaster, Yahweh was still deeply concerned with them.

The various prophecies can, of course, be quite easily classified into prophecies of disaster and prophecies of salvation. It is, however, wrong to apply a classification of this kind to the prophets themselves—to claim, for example, that the earlier prophets were in some way prophets of disaster, and that elements of salvation present in their preaching must be interpreted as later additions. The relationship between disaster and salvation in the prophetic message is far too intimate to permit such an interpretation, which, for example, ignores the fact that the message of salvation intended for the believing Israelites at the same time contained a judgment, and thus a condemnation to disaster, of those who did not believe. Salvation was grafted on to disaster. The new Israel was to be born of the death of the old Israel. For the time being, then, even the prophets' message of salvation spelt disaster for sinful Israel. Amos expressed this in the most emphatic manner: "As if a shepherd should get out of the lion's mouth two legs or the tip of the ear, so shall the children of Israel be saved" (3:12). Salvation and disaster were two sides of the same coin, or—as it was frequently expressed at a later stage—the downfall of one nation was the salvation of all nations.

8. The Theme of the Remnant

The connection between salvation and disaster was formulated most clearly in the concept of the Remnant. The theme of the Remnant of Israel contains a summary of the entire preaching of the prophets. This theme shows that there was an essential perspective of salvation within the message of the classic prophets, but that this salvation, after having been subservient to the message of disaster for a long time, only gradually won an independent place for itself within the prophetic message, an independence which enabled it, in the long run, to predominate. It was, of course, a message of disaster for a prosperous and numerous people to have to hear that only a miserable remnant of the nation was to share in Yahweh's salvation. Nonetheless, in the whole of the later prophecy of salvation, what we find is nothing but a development of the fact that the Remnant would be saved.

Once again, it is the vision of Isaiah which provides the classic insight here. The prophet was unable to conceive that the commission which he received to preach disaster was Yahweh's final word. But the answer which Yahweh made to his question concerning the extent of the disaster stripped every illusion from those who heard Isaiah—the cities, the houses, and the fields would all be laid waste, and all the inhabitants were to go into exile. Then Israel would be like a terebinth or an oak which had been felled, and of which only a stump of the root remained standing in the ground, and "that which shall stand therein shall be a holy seed" (Isa. 6:11-13). This text comprises, in a small compass, all of Isaiah's preaching. There is factual evidence which suggests that the last sentence of this text, quoted here, was interpolated into the written prophecy in order to soften the harsh effect of the whole. It cannot, of course, be denied that this final sentence has the authentic oracular sound of Isaiah. Had it, however, formed the conclusion to the original prophecy of disaster, it would undoubtedly have weakened the forceful impact of the first part of the text containing the image of the stump of the felled tree. This part of the oracle was certainly spoken at the time of Isaiah's early appearance in Israel. The imagery of the text is particularly applicable to Israel. All around him the Israelite could find gnarled stumps, remnants of what had once been great trees, which at one time had completely dominated their surroundings, sad reminders of a glory which had been swept away at a single stroke by the violence of a sudden storm. There is little doubt that the preacher would have added nothing to this image at the time and have left his listeners with this powerful impression. Whatever the case may be, however, the text is a classic one as it stands. It does, moreover, orientate the concept of the Remnant, about the year 730, towards the expectation of salvation which was to become concentrated in the holy remnant. The text, as we now have it, provides a concise formula of the structure of the whole of the prophetic message—the prophecy of disaster, preached against the disbelief of the majority, overflowing into a prophecy of consolation and salvation for the Remnant of Israel. This is frequently true of individual oracles. It is especially true of each prophetic book as a whole.

In this passage, Israel's destruction is compared to the felling of a tree, of which only the stump remains. When the text was edited, it was, as so often happens, felt that a more hopeful perspective should be given to the harsh picture evoked by the original. The image which happened to have been chosen for the Remnant of Israel was that of a stump. This image was, however, a favorite one whenever the idea of the remnant was applied to the monarchy. It was not so much the people as a whole that came to mind, when this image was used, as the monarchy—a noble, genealogical tree with royal branches and shoots (*see* Ezek. 17; Dan. 4). The theme of the Remnant of Israel had its normal place in those oracles which were directed towards the people, but it also had a parallel in the oracles directed towards the royal house. The sinful and unbelieving dynasty was a proud cedar which was to be cut down, but whose stump and root would remain. From this root, Yahweh would cause new growth to spring forth.

The miracle of creation occurs with every new springtime. New life springs forth from the apparently dead earth. In the same way, Yahweh was to accomplish a miracle of creation in Israel, by making a new salvation, peace, and justice spring forth from her downfall (Isa. 42:9; 43:19; 58:8; *see also* Gen. 1). This miracle was to be accomplished by means of a mysterious cooperation between heaven and earth. It was to be both the bud of Yahweh and the fruit of the earth (Isa. 4:2). Dew would fall from heaven and a stream of justice would drop from the clouds, but at the same time salvation and justice would spring out of the earth (Isa. 45:8). Truth would spring out of the earth and justice would show itself from heaven, for Yahweh gave fertility and our earth yielded its fruit, thus bringing about a reconciliation between heaven and earth (the psalm of Isaiah 84:9–13). The theme of the Remnant of Israel has a close parallel here in the shoot or rod which Yahweh promised to make rise up out of the stump or root of Jesse (Isa. 11:1).

The name "Root of Jesse"—David was scornfully referred to as the "son of Jesse" by those who opposed him (1 Sam. 20:27, 30, 22:7–9, 13; 2 Sam. 20:1; 1 Kings 12:16)—evoked a memory of the time which preceded the human glory and greatness of the monarchy, when David was fetched from minding the flock. The house of David, which was defying Yahweh, was to be brought back to this state. The dynasty had to pass through judgment before it could find God again. The house of David had to be humbled, but not for ever (1 Kings 11:39). The house was to become a fallen tabernacle, but this would be built up again (Amos 9:11).

The prophecies concerning the ideal, messianic posterity of David were, like the prophecies of salvation for the remnant, charged above all with disaster for the royal house which was still standing. If this is kept in mind, a solution can probably also be found to the problem as to how the prophecy of salvation through the Emmanuel could at the same time have included a shattering message of punishment for Ahaz who had placed his hope in an Assyrian intervention rather than in Yahweh. The assurance that "God with us" was to be the only salvation was at the same time his condemnation (Isa. 7-9). Yahweh went his own improbable way and, as far as the dynasty was concerned, it is scarcely credible that the One who was to grow up as a tender plant, as a root from the thirsty ground, would silence kings (Isa. 52:13-53:2ff.).

In the same way that the Remnant of Israel in the long run became a pure messianic concept of salvation, so did the Rod of Jesse, under the name of the Branch of David (Jer. 23:5; 33:15; Zech. 3:8, 6:12). Once again, the structure of the prophetic message is revealed here—the prophecy of disaster, preached against the monarchy of that time, flowing over into the prophecy of salvation in the Branch of David. This is particularly evident in Jeremiah. His demand that the last Kings of David's line should be punished (21 and 22), and his denunciation of Israel's kings and leaders (23:1f.), finally led up to his promise that Yahweh would beget for David a Branch which was in fact just and which would therefore bear the name of "Yahweh our justice" (*yaheweh-sideqēnû*), in contrast to that of the regent Zedekiah (*sideqi-yāhû*). In this way, Jeremiah fulfilled both aspects of his commission—rooting up and pulling down, and building and planting (Jer. 11:10; *see also* 31:28). Ezekiel similarly combined his condemnation of the bad shepherds of Israel (34:1–10, 17–22), with a prophecy of the pastoral function of Yahweh (34:11–16). This would be revealed in the one ideal Shepherd, Yahweh's Servant David (34:23–31; *see also* 37:24–28).

9. The Transition from Disaster to Salvation and from the Old Order to the New

The prophets' message of disaster meant that Yahweh was to allow the old Israel to perish, but the prophecy of salvation which was so closely connected with it implied that he would gather to himself a new Israel from among the scattered remnants of the old. The old covenant was broken by the judgment and sentence which Yahweh passed on Israel, but at the same time a vision of a new covenant had been revealed. The old law had become ineffectual, but a new law was about to come. What was true of the old Israel as a whole was also true of all her institutions, since it was the whole of Israel which had become degenerate, and no part of Israel was unaffected. That is why it is possible to read oracular utterances predicting disaster for all kinds of national institutions in the prophetic books, which are accompanied by corresponding prophecies of salvation revealing the same institutions in their purified and renewed state. The monarchy of Israel is a case in point, and has been fully discussed in the preceding section. This aspect of the prophetic vision can, however, also be applied to many other phenomena in Israelitic society, and it undoubtedly provides the key to the classic prophetism of Israel. The following stages in the train of thought of the prophets as a whole are more or less explicitly revealed:

1. A recollection of what Israel ought to have been, according to the original plan that Yahweh had in mind when he called her.

2. An outline of Israel's continuous sin and faithlessness which had brought about the degeneration of the institution in question.

3. The sentence that Yahweh was in course of passing and that would lead to the abolition of the institution in question, together with the downfall of Israel as a whole, so long as Israel was not converted.

4. In certain cases, the idea of the remnant was also present. Yahweh's anger had been satisfied. What still remained of Israel in comparison with the Israel of the distant past? The miserable part of Israel which still remained aroused Yahweh's pity. In other cases, his anger was directed against Israel's enemies, whom he used to punish Israel, to judge his people and make it a remnant, but who went much too far and attributed Israel's humiliation to their own power and to their own gods who were evidently stronger than the God of Israel (Isa. 10:5-24; Mic. 4:11f.; Deut. 32:26-31). In such cases, the Name of Yahweh was desecrated by Israel's being scattered among the other nations. A situation such as this made Yahweh jealous, for he would never give his glory to another (Isa. 48:11; Ezek. 36). That is why the "zeal of Yahweh of the hosts" (Isa. 9:7; *see also* 37:32; Zech. 1:14), could not be based on Israel's downfall.

5. Yahweh once more intervened, but this time his aim was not to punish Israel: "As I have watched over them, to pluck up and throw down ... so will I watch over them, to build up and to plant them" (Jer. 31:28). He would raise his hand "a second time" (Isa. 11:11), to possess the remnant of Israel. The first time that he had raised his hand, he had done so in order to humiliate Egypt so that Israel would be redeemed. Now he proposed to humiliate the nations which were leading Israel into captivity and exile. The prophets saw, beyond Israel's disaster, the prospect of a second redemption

—another exodus, another journey through the desert, and another occupation of the promised land (Isa. 11:11-16). Yahweh's arm was still strong. He had created the heavens and he had established the earth. He had divided the waters of the Red Sea into two parts and had thereby accomplished the first redemption of his people. This same Yahweh still had power to prepare a path for his people through the Euphrates and through the desert and thus, as it were by means of a miracle of creation, to call forth a new Israel out of the downfall of the old (Isa. 40-55).

This train of thought is not only evident where Israel as a whole is concerned, but also in the case of the many different subdivisions which made up Israel. There are biblical themes which correspond to each of these. Every category or institution in the Old Testament has its parallel in the New. As we have already seen, the messianic idea of David is contrasted with the Davidic dynasty. The new people of God is set off against the old, whose God, Yahweh, promised to be the God of this new Israel, his people. The new covenant is seen against the old. Similarly, there would also be a new Jerusalem, a new Zion, a new temple, a new priesthood, a new form of sacrifice, a new land, a new family of Abraham, a new law, and a new circumcision. Everything in Israel was decadent and had to go when Israel fell, but everything would return, purified, new and recreated. There is ample material in the Bible to enable us to trace systematically the development of the various elements and institutions listed here. It is, however, important to go further than this, as the data which are explicitly given in the Bible are too fortuitous for us to permit ourselves to be limited entirely to those themes which are fully exploited in the Bible.

The categories and terms used in the Bible originated in the Old Testament. Indeed, their origin is to be found in a very early period of the Old Testament. The Jewish period was no longer productive in this respect. The language of the Bible was permanently established in the postexilic period. This means that the terminology of the Bible was originally made for and geared to the national and terrestrial Kingdom of God. The prophets created very few new means of expression. What they did was to give a new content and meaning to the various categories that were already in existence, orientating them permanently towards the content and meaning which the New Testament was later to give to the terminology of the Bible. There are very many biblical themes which developed in this way—historical terms, such as Israel, Zion, Jerusalem, Babel, and so on, and more general terms such as kingdom, land, salvation, peace, light, life, or water.

It is not difficult to situate the original, purely Old Testament point of departure here. These names and terms alluded to a clearly defined reality of a terrestrial and national nature. They had this meaning when they were introduced into the Bible, and they won for themselves a stable and permanent place in the many biblical themes. It is also not difficult to establish the ultimate point of their development in the New Testament. They occur just as frequently in the New Testament as in the Old, but their meaning and content is new. They refer to realities of a predominantly spiritual nature. They are no longer restricted to national realities. Considered as a whole, the prophets stand midway between these two extreme points and form a transition. On the one hand, they were attempting to say something new when they used this ancient language. On the other hand, however, there is no convincing evidence that they had completely dissociated themselves from the old meaning of these terms. If this is true, it is clear proof that the prophets formed the turning point of the Old and the New Testaments. The change of meaning in the old terms and categories which can be clearly distinguished in the New Testament was actually taking place at the time of the prophets.

Once the principle has been established, it should be both possible and right to supplement those themes which have not been fully worked out in the Bible. Certain links are frequently missing in the biblical data. Sometimes, for example, a theme comes to an end at a certain point in its development, for the simple reason that it does not occur in the later books or that it is forced into the background by a different theme. On the other hand, it sometimes happens that the new content of a given theme either only just reveals itself or else just fails to emerge. The expectation of a new David is, for example, quite explicit in the Old Testament, whereas that of a new Moses is far less explicit. The theme of the new Adam is only implied in the Old Testament, but fully expressed in the New. The new Eve is not named at all in the Old Testament, but only suggested, with the result that this theme soon became quite marked in the post-biblical writings. Care must be taken in this instance to distinguish, in our exegesis of the early Church, between what is merely literary performance and what is a genuine understanding of the nature of faith. What we can, however, learn from this is how to appreciate those hints and implicit suggestions which occur in Scripture and, in the freedom of true faith, to see their connection with the whole scriptural theme.

It is, therefore, of great importance to bear in mind, when considering the particular question of how the prophets really imagined that the new order of salvation would be, that a new content was already developing within the prophetic terminology. It is possible for anyone, not necessarily an exegete, who takes the trouble to familiarize himself with the various prophetic oracles on the subject of salvation and to compare them with each other, to perceive the growth of this new inner meaning, and to appreciate the fact that, if the terms used by the prophets are limited exclusively to their original Old Testament content, a grave injustice is done to the essential vision of the prophets. Bearing in mind, then, this growth of a new inner content within the outward form of the prophetic language, it should be possible to come to an understanding of the nature of the new salvation.

10. *The Prophetic Themes of Salvation*

The most striking aspect of the oracles of salvation is their thematic character—the prophets worked with a very limited and indeed stereotyped repertory. For them, the salvation which was to come was the opposite of the situation which they saw existing all around them in their own time and which they so violently opposed. The messianic kingdom and its King were, therefore, seen in contrast to the decadent kingdoms of Israel and Judah and their kings. Frequently, too, the messianic kingdom and its Ruler was contrasted in their vision with the great pagan kingdoms of this world, especially Assyria and Babylon and their rulers, with their boastful speeches, their confidence in their power and riches and their belief that might was right. The injustice and the policy of violent oppression practised by these kingdoms and Israel's apostasy from Yahweh were contrasted with the poor and the oppressed who would possess the land that would overflow with justice and knowledge of Yahweh. The force of arms and the desolation of war would be replaced with peace, rest, and prosperity. The rumble of horses and chariots would give way to the silence of faith and trust.

The prophets also depicted the messianic future as a reliving of the most perfect and ideal times of the past. This is above all represented by the paradise theme, in which the new salvation is shown as a return of the period which man spent in paradise, enjoying the miraculous fertility of the earth and living in complete harmony with his fellowmen and with the animal world. It is as the new Adam that the Messiah fits into this picture, but this particular extension of the theme did not emerge fully in the New Testament until Daniel's son of man was no longer accepted as such.

What is generally known as the desert theme also forms part of the prophetic image of the future. Israel's youthful period in the desert was idealized as a time of early marriage, when Yahweh and Israel met for the first time and Israel became Yahweh's bride.

Yahweh was to take his unfaithful bride back into the desert, and there he would speak to her heart (Hos. 2:14). This theme is to some extent related to the theme of the second exodus, during which Israel would be redeemed for a second time, by the same and indeed even greater signs and wonders (Isa. 40–55). It is also possible to consider the theme of the land—the promised land—in the same context as the themes already mentioned. In this theme, the Messiah was given the attributes of a new Moses who was to gather together those whom Yahweh had scattered and, having freed them from their captivity, to lead them as the people of a new covenant into Yahweh's rest. The New Testament enriched this theme by depicting Jesus as a new Joshua (Heb. 4:8).

By far the most important theme, however, was that of the kingdom of David, which beyond any question formed the climax of the history of the nation in the past. As in the past, during the reign of David, so in the future time of salvation, North and South would once more be united, the land would have ideal boundaries, and the capital city would be so full of inhabitants that its walls would have to be extended and the neighboring peoples would be obliged to pay tribute as subjects. Every man would be able to sit under his vine and his fig tree without fear and, under the sovereign rule of Yahweh, the people would come from far and wide to worship with one mind in the glorious sanctuary of Jerusalem. Here the Messiah is represented as the new David, in whom the characteristics of both David and Solomon (the first "son of David" on David's throne!), the prince of peace and the builder of the temple, were combined. The Messiah was visualized in this theme as a prince who was intimately associated with Yahweh and therefore a priestly prince, whose just rule would enable all men without exception, but particularly the poor and oppressed, to share in Yahweh's salvation.

In this connection, it is difficult to overestimate the importance of the Israelitic monarchy in the development of the messianic idea.

The dramatic history of the monarchy not only stimulated the nation's expectation of salvation, but also gave it a more and more clearly defined form. The monarchic ideology played a very important part in the gradual concentration of Israel's expectations of salvation, which were basically always an expectation of Yahweh, into the expectation of a savior. This in turn narrowed itself down into an almost exclusive expectation of a messianic king. The great figure of David, on the one hand, and the continued postponement of the nation's salvation during the time of David's successors on the other may well help to explain, at least partially, why the future salvation of the people was expressed in the one, short phrase, the Kingdom of God.

Israel had always expected salvation from the monarchy. A king in the ancient world was a bringer of salvation (*see* 1 Sam. 10:27 and 11:13), and in Israel he brought Yahweh's salvation. Thus Israel tended to look upon Yahweh more and more as a King, who revealed his kingship and the salvation which it brought in his anointed one, that is, in the historical king of David's lineage. After the downfall of the dynasty, and especially because the restoration of the monarchy did not come about, Israel came increasingly to realize that Yahweh was the real king (Pss. 92, 96, 98; *see also* 46f.), and to fix her entire expectation of salvation on the eventual coming of the Kingdom of God that would be revealed in the ideal Son of David. It was for this reason that the long awaited savior was ultimately called the Messiah, for the name Messiah, signifying "anointed," and thus the "anointed one of Yahweh," was the characteristic title of the king.

11. The Nature of the New Salvation

If these themes are considered with their material content in view, they can be seen to constitute the fulfillment of all the characteristic aspirations of the Old Testament. They all flow together into one great theme of national glory and material well-being and seem to continue, in the purest possible way, the line of the past into the future. The unity of God's actions is thus fully exemplified. Yahweh was faithful to the covenant and the promises which he had made to David and the Patriarchs, and intended to fulfill them in a new way. The prophets' message of salvation was thus a message of consolation and encouragement for the people in their great ordeal, for the future was to bring, in a very real sense, the restoration of Israel. Nonetheless, it was not possible for anyone who heard the prophets' message correctly to believe that the future would simply be a replica of the past. The messianic salvation was to go beyond all familiar relationships and to be something quite new. It would be a new creation, something which had as yet never been seen or heard of, and which no god, except Yahweh, who alone held the future in his hands, had ever predicted or foreseen. Even the paradise theme implied more than merely a return of the old order. The prophets had, after all, preached so emphatically against this in their theme of disaster that a restoration in that old form was unthinkable, and completely alien to the prophetic psychology.

After a long personal struggle, the prophets succeeded in breaking with the old order with which they too had grown up, and in coming to a new certainty of faith. Meditating on Yahweh's ways, they gained a deep insight into the unknown saving possibilities implicit in Yahweh—they became aware of the paradoxical nature of the Covenant. The manner in which Isaiah experienced Yahweh in the vision in which he received his vocation was, in one respect, typically national. He saw Yahweh as the God of Hosts, the King of Glory who revealed himself as the thrice holy one, sitting on the throne of the ark. But, in another respect, Isaiah's vision of Yahweh went beyond purely national limitations. The hosts surrounding Yahweh were no longer merely the hosts of Israel's army, but everything that was in heaven and on earth and under the earth. The glory that he saw was no longer restricted to Israel, but was to fill the entire earth, and the throne and the temple of his vision took on cosmic dimensions. These had all been the subjects of national sermons at one time, but now, together with the whole of sinful Israel, these sermons had become blasphemous. Isaiah, therefore, was given the task of preaching the downfall of this Israel, though he was at the same time permitted to give some inkling of the final result of the plan of salvation, the ultimate fulfillment of which God had in view (Isa. 6).

Because of Israel's sin, salvation did not come about in the Old Testament. This was a punishment, but, if it was accepted as such from Yahweh, it had a purifying effect and opened men's minds to a higher salvation. The believer who found his God by going beyond the old salvation could experience a new and more profound salvation. In this way, men were able to grow towards a deeper understanding of the essential inadequacy of a purely national and outward salvation, since this corresponded with their experience of Yahweh both as the God of the world and as the one who spoke in the deepest recesses of the human soul. It was along this and similar paths that the prophets came to certainty concerning a new salvation by means of which Yahweh would, in one way or another, fulfill his original aims. They were able to use the old terminology with such complete conviction in connection with the new salvation because they were deeply aware of Yahweh's real purposes in the ancient, worldly possessions of salvation. For them, Jerusalem was the City of God and the new community of men among whom God dwelt. When they spoke of the temple, they were referring to a central point which would enable God to become all in all. The prophets were attempting to express this certainty of faith in words and to convey it, if not to the whole people, then at least to an intimate circle to whom the mystery of the Kingdom of God had been revealed and whose members were already beginning to form a remnant in the midst of the unbelieving majority.

No one who reads the prophetic oracles of salvation can fail to be impressed by the complete certainty of the prophets in the new salvation. At the same time, however, it is clear that they were impotent to give this future a concrete form. They appear to be feeling their way towards the future. There is a dynamic power in their words and images, but there is also a certain inability to free themselves from the ancient categories and associations. They seem to find it difficult to imagine Yahweh's salvation in any other context. Those to whom they were preaching find it even more difficult— Yahweh will reveal his saving will in the future as he has revealed it in the past. The impression remains that what Yahweh aimed to do in the past will be fully realized in the future. It is evident, then, that, because they lacked better means, the prophets furnished the future with material from the past. They had no other way of expressing themselves, and no other way of making the future salvation of their vision tangible for a people which thought in concrete terms. In no other way were they able to give them real consolation. We must, therefore, conclude that the rather limited language and imagery of the prophets, drawn largely from the past and applied to the future salvation, was above all a more or less conventional means of expression, relating to the wording of their message of salvation rather than to its essential content.

On closer inspection, it is clear that the theme of national glory and material well-being was not really intended as a prediction that the good old times would return. It was rather an attendant phenomenon, a prediction of something that had up to that time never appeared in the history of Israel—a sinless Israel. What Yahweh intended to create was a new people, a people with a new heart and a new spirit, a people whose circumcision was in the heart—not a people whose external possession consisted of a law inscribed on stone tablets, but whose law was inscribed on their hearts, so that each member of this new community would keep the law spontaneously. The covenant which Yahweh proposed to make with his new people on the basis of this law was a covenant which could never be broken. It was to be a new and eternal covenant. There could be no unfaithfulness to this covenant. The false gods would disappear from the land which, in the future, would be full of the knowledge of Yahweh. The new people of God, a people which would, so to speak, be an entirely priestly people, would be permitted to approach Yahweh personally, to ascend to his holy mountain and to live with him as the first man had lived with his immanent goodness in the time of his innocence. Genesis depicted the religious situation of the first man in a most vivid way by placing him in a miraculously privileged environment. In the same way, the prophets expressed the religious renewal which was to come about in the future by situating the new people of God in a paradisal land.

Here we are confronted with a new element which is moreover the constant, latent factor in all the themes. Those elements which are apparently older must be seen as subservient to the new element. The orientation of this new element is towards the spiritual and the inner life. It is evident from the course of Israel's history, subsequent to the age of the prophets, that we are not mistaken regarding this element. Judaism was a product of prophetism, and a tendency towards the inner life was to emerge in the Jewish world, a tendency which was favorable to the New Testament, with its emphasis on the primacy of man's inward state. If this inward and spiritual element was in fact the central turning point of the prophetic message of salvation, then the external and material aspect of prophetism must have been secondary. Furthermore, the national element may also be regarded as secondary, since this is closely tied up with the external element.

The older form of salvation did not affect the individual personally and directly, because of its predominantly collective and national character. It is possible to detect a certain interaction between the prophets and the Israel of their time. The prophets were commissioned to preach the downfall of Israel as a nation, and it is perfectly consistent that they should, in this context, have felt themselves impelled to appeal to the personal faith of those who heard them and to stress personal responsibility and freedom of choice. After having appealed in vain to Israel's national conscience, they directed their appeal to the individual conscience. Although they did not use precisely these words, what they said to each individual was, in effect: "Save yourself from this perverse generation" (Acts 2:40). They were the only ones who were able to maintain their position in Israel by an individual and personal attitude. This was possible because of their personal experience of God and their divine vocation to go against the grain. They were also the first to free themselves from the security of collectivity. This collective security had degenerated little by little into a false and superstitious feeling of safety, within which Yahweh's grace and election, deprived of any vital personal and inner response on the part of those who received it, had become debased, and was barely distinguishable from the automatic salvation of the heathen world. The collapse of the national framework thus caused the personal and inward element to be stressed and this in turn opened men's eyes to the inadequacy of the national framework.

In the whole of their preaching on the subject of salvation, the prophets showed that the messianic salvation was to be completely new, both in its scope and as far as its nature was concerned. It was only comparatively rarely, however, that they stated, in so many words, that this salvation was new because it was principally spiritual and universal, that is, a salvation which would embrace all nations. Sufficient light has already been thrown on the insistence of the prophets on the intensification of the inner life in the course of this survey of Israel's prophetism, and it is difficult to overrate the value of the few explicit prophetic texts which display a conscious reaction on the part of the prophets against the purely external and national attitude towards religion. As for the universal nature of the new salvation as exemplified in the prophetic books, this tendency is clearly revealed in the whole of the book of Jonah. The prophet's vision of Yahweh was one of a God who created the world and who passed sentence on this world. The world was judged, and Israel was merely one of the nations which fell as a result of this international upheaval. Finally, their vision included the rather isolated, but for this reason all the more striking figure of the Messiah as the suffering servant of God.

The current idea of the Messiah was that of a royal Messiah, a king with the characteristics of David, and thus a king with national characteristics. The servant figure of the Messiah was not of this world. It was spirit and truth. The royal characteristics of the Servant were concealed; what was strikingly revealed was his prophetic task of bringing authentic religion to the whole world. That this was intended to correct the prevalent and mistaken idea of the Messiah is clear from an oracle such as this: "It is a small thing that thou shouldst be my Servant, to raise up the tribes of Jacob and to convert the remnants of Israel. Behold I have given thee to be the Light of the gentiles, that thou mayest be my salvation even to the farthest parts of the earth" (Isa. 49:6). This must have seemed a paradox to the Israelites. Words, too, like the following must similarly have puzzled them:

In that day, there shall be a way from Egypt to the Assyrians:
the Assyrian shall enter into Egypt, and the Egyptian to the Assyrians.
And the Egyptians shall serve Yahweh together with the Assyrian.
In that day, Israel shall be the third with the Egyptian
and the Assyrian to receive a blessing in the midst of the land.
Yahweh of the Hosts shall bless them, saying:
Blessed be the Egyptians, my people,
the Assyrians, the work of my hands,
and Israel, my inheritance (Isa. 19:23–25: *see also* 19:18–22).

There were, however, other oracles with a marked, universal tendency which must have been easier to accept, because Israel seemed still to be the central figure in them:

> Thus saith Yahweh:
> I am returned to Zion: and I will dwell in Jerusalem.
> Jerusalem shall be called the City of Truth and the mountain
> of Yahweh of the Hosts shall be called the Holy Mountain . . .
> There shall yet old men and old women dwell in the streets
> of Jerusalem, and every man with his staff in his hand
> through multitude of days.
> And the streets of the city shall be full of boys and girls,
> playing in the streets thereof . . .
> But now I will not deal with the Remnant of this people
> according to the former days . . .
> But there shall be the seed, the vine shall yield its fruit
> and the earth shall yield its increase and the heavens shall
> give their dew . . .

(Thus shall it be) until the people and the inhabitants of mighty cities come, and the inhabitants go to one another, saying: Let us go and entreat the face of Yahweh and let us seek Yahweh of the Hosts: I also will go. And many peoples and strong nations shall come to seek Yahweh of the Hosts in Jerusalem and to entreat the face of Yahweh . . . In those days, wherein ten men of all languages of the nations shall take hold and shall hold fast the skirt of one who is a Jew, saying: We will go with you, for we have heard that God is with you (Zech. 8:3–5, 11f., 20–23; *see also* Isa. 2:2–4).

In the passage quoted above, and in similar passages, Israel would certainly seem to be the central point in the new order of salvation. But what the prophets had in mind when they referred to Israel in this and in similar contexts was certainly not the old but the new Israel, thus Israel in the sense of the real people of God. It was not flesh and blood, but faith which would decide who was to belong to this people of God. As we have already shown, the name Israel was already beginning to acquire a new content by this time. In the popular expectation of salvation, a clear division was made between Israel and the other nations. The day of Yahweh—the day on which Yahweh was to intervene decisively and permanently to establish his Kingdom—would be a day of salvation for Israel and a day of disaster for Israel's enemies, both her neighbors and the great world powers. That day would mark the beginning of Israel's rule and her enemies' subordination. This appears to be borne out by numerous prophetic texts, which speak out against the nations. There is, however, an equal number of contrasting texts which prophesy impressively against Israel. Indeed, one of the first of the scriptural prophets spoke out sharply against this kind of mechanical conception of salvation:

> Woe to them that desire the day of Yahweh!
> To what end is it for you?
> The day of Yahweh is darkness and not light.
> As if a man should flee from the face of a lion, and a
> bear should meet him: or enter into the house and lean
> with his hand upon the wall, and a serpent should bite him.
> Shall not the day of Yahweh be darkness and not light:
> obscurity, and no brightness in it? (Amos 5:18–20).

Taking the inadequate and conventional nature of the prophetic terminology into account, it is possible to see the sharp division between Israel and the other nations which was frequently upheld by the prophets as a spiritual division. Israel and her classic enemies were both more than historical and national quantities. Both had an emotional value, or rather a value as signs. Israel surrounded by her neighbors was, in this sense, the faithful people of God of the future surrounded by the sinful world, the believing minority surrounded by the unbelieving majority, the men of good will, the humble and the poor whose only support was Yahweh, surrounded by the proud and the rich, who were sufficient unto themselves and who relied on their own strength. The Old Testament prophecies against the nations went beyond those particular ancient, oriental nations in their temporal and local setting, and the biblical theme of the kingdom of this world began to take shape in the prophetic books. In the same way, the prophecies concerning the new Israel were a proclamation of the City of God, even though the historical Israel was not entirely set free.

It is important, in any consideration of the prophetic oracles of salvation, to try to divine what lies behind the words. To approach these expressions of a tentative and struggling faith as though they were clear and fully worked out concepts would be to start off on quite the wrong foot. They ought, similarly, not to be taken in the limited sense, say, of the promises of well-being made on Sinai, although the language which the prophets used in connection with the future salvation was to a large extent derived from these promises. It is, on the other hand, equally undesirable to interpret the theme of national prosperity as pure imagery, as if the prophets first developed these purely spiritual notions and then later couched them in figurative language. All this is western reasoning: the whole approach is far too calculated, and cannot be reconciled to the powerful biblical feeling for the solidarity of the spiritual and the material elements in human experience, and to the biblical approach to and understanding of things in their concrete totality. The spiritual and religious elements in the Bible cannot simply be abstracted in this way—they are embodied in and expressed in the whole biblical experience of life.

The national and terrestrial elements play a very real part in the prophetic vision of the future, which was in one sense a vision of Israel's restoration made possible by a return from exile and of Israel's revival in Judaism. The symbolic interpretation of the prophetic themes bears distinct traces of an out of date spiritual approach, and even its conception of what a symbol is would seem to be outmoded. In the whole of the Bible, including the New Testament, the divine work of salvation is not seen as a concern only with man's soul, but as a recreation of the whole of man and the entire cosmos surrounding him. The effects of human sin are also seen in the Bible in this greater perspective. The prophets' vision of salvation had as its object man's total redemption from his total sin. The religious renewal of the people of God of the future occupied a central place in their vision. The renewal of the face of the earth was not simply a symbol of this; it was also a real and essential part of the whole.

VII

The Remnant of Israel

THROUGHOUT the whole of the history of salvation, the faithful community of God has always been a constant factor. The concrete embodiment of this community, however, varies according to the social situation in which it is placed. It is thus possible to divide the historical people of God of the Old Testament into several well-defined periods of approximately six hundred years each. It was by passing through these successive phases that the Old Testament community of believers, consistent in essence, developed towards the fullness of the New Testament.

An outline is given, in this chapter, of the last of these three great periods of Israel's religious history. The Israelitic state system had collapsed. An anonymous number of Israelites had remained behind, but the most vital section of the nation had to build up a new life in exile. Adapting itself to this new situation, the faithful community acquired a totally new social structure. The ancient faith had also to be thought out, experienced, and expressed in an entirely new way. In the course of time, the believing community gained a new form—the Jewish form.

1. Judaism

It is, of course, obvious that the name Judaism is connected with the name Judah. "Jew" originally meant "man of Judah." But the name Jew also has a distinctive emotive force of its own. It alludes to the new religious and social status occasioned by the Exile. Although there were, both in the Hebrew and in the Israelitic period, men of Judah—members of the tribe of Judah or subjects of the Southern Kingdom of Judah—it would certainly be an anachronism to call these Jews. They were Judaeans. This anachronistic usage does, of course, go back a long time, and is still fairly current. What is more, even the members of the ancient Hebrew federation of tribes are sometimes referred to as Jews. Nonetheless, this usage is very confusing, and it does tend to obscure an essential emphasis in the history of salvation.

In the course of time, the remnants of Israel became a separate and conspicuous phenomenon, encountered everywhere in the ancient world. It is understandable, and perfectly reasonable, that outsiders should have begun to call these people Jews. Their otherness in religion, which had led to a social otherness, made it impossible to classify them under any of the known categories. Whereas those of the ten tribes of the Northern Kingdom who were deported disappeared without a trace, the people of the old covenant maintained their religious otherness in the Southern Kingdom of Judah for a hundred and fifty years. As a result, it was the Judaean groups which preserved their religious otherness in exile, cultivated it, and finally found for it a vital expression which was closely adapted to their new predicament. Thus everything associated with this representative Judaean core—even when it was a question of the scattered elements of other tribes—became Jewish.

This Judaism was a creation of external circumstances and internal growth. A great deal of the history of the rise of Judaism is obscure. Two points, however, are quite clear. In the first place, we know the most important factors which led to the gradual rise of the new situation and, in the second place, we have a fairly clear picture of Judaism in the form in which it emerged from its period of growth. The manner in which Judaism acquired the distinctive features of total otherness in religion, and the various stages in this development, can only be filled in, in broad outline, from the two extreme points—the beginning and the end—of this growth.

2. The Former Southern Kingdom

It has been estimated that between forty and fifty thousand Judaeans went into exile. In contrast to the Assyrian practice, the Babylonian conquerors did not replace the Judaean ruling class with a foreign, governing authority, but appointed a Judaean, Gedaliah, as governor. But any hopes which this appointment had aroused of a modest, national life (Jer. 40:15b) were dashed by the assassination of the governor (2 Kings 25:25ff.). The result was a new deportation (Jer. 52:30). Judah then probably came under the jurisdiction of the Babylonian governor of the province of Samaria. This can be ascertained from the later opposition, on the part of the Samaritans, to an independent province of Judah. Samaria had already been a province of a world empire for a hundred and fifty years, with the result that she had been able to develop into a well-organized, administrative unity. The chance of exercising some degree of guardianship over Judah in her unsettled state was eagerly seized. During those first chaotic years, the land was left wide open for Ammon (Jer. 49:2; Ezek. 25:1ff.)—probably the instigator of the assassination of Gedaliah (Jer. 40:13ff.)—and Edom. It was at this time that Edom was laying the foundations for the later Idumaea (Ezek. 25:12–14, 35:5, 10, 12; Obad. 11ff.; Ps. 136:7).

The rural population, left to its own resources, undoubtedly continued in the local tradition of syncretism in worship. A characteristic expression of this was the cult of Ashtoreth, practised by the Judaeans who had fled to Egypt. These Judaeans sacrificed to the queen of heaven and baked cakes in her honor in the form of figures of Ashtoreth, "as we and our fathers have done, our kings and our princes in the cities of Judah and in the streets of Jerusalem" (Jer. 44). Some of the abominations which Ezekiel noticed in the temple, shortly before the fall of Jerusalem, were also characteristic of this syncretism. Among other things, he saw women sitting at the northern gate of the temple, loudly lamenting Tammuz, the Babylonian vegetation god who died every year and rose again with the cycle of nature (Ezek. 8). If there were, after the Exile, people in Judah who sacrificed in gardens and burnt incense on bricks and who dwelt in sepulchres and spent the night in hidden places (Isa. 65:3f.), then these practices must have crept in at an earlier stage. On the other hand, there is scriptural evidence that eighty men came, not only from Shechem and Shiloh, but also from Samaria, with their beards shaven, their clothes torn and their bodies slashed, to Jerusalem, to bring offerings and incense to the house of Yahweh (Jer. 41:5). The outward appearance of these pilgrims is, of course, similar to that of those who later made pilgrimages to the Wailing Wall of Jerusalem, but even more important, in the present context, is the proof which this text offers that the destroyed temple was still a preeminently holy place and that there were, among the population of the Northern Kingdom which had been left behind, some who had found their way back to Jerusalem (*see also* 2 Chron. 30:11, 35:18).

Although an anonymous majority was living both in the North and in the South of Palestine, and this majority formed an important ethnical continuity with the past and might have provided the foundation for a new community, the fact remains that the formative principle of this new community had to come from elsewhere. The old way of life was perpetuated in one form or another in Palestine, but it was Babylon which became the vital center of new life.

3. The Exiles

Only a radical break with the old order could make the rise of the new, Jewish world possible. This break with the past only became a fact for those who were deported. Their exile made a new pattern of life necessary, and this way of life was able to acquire a stable and lasting form because the situation which had been created by the Exile became a permanent one as a result of the Diaspora.

The first group of Judaeans were led into captivity about ten years before the fall of Jerusalem. Of these, an inner core at least was able to remain true to itself and thus to preserve the people of God. Many factors contributed to the totally different result which the Exile produced on Judah from that produced on Israel. The first Judaean exiles formed an elite group. The continued existence of the holy city kept national feelings and national hopes alive. Those who were deported from Judah were able to mix fairly freely with each other and to establish their own settlements. Finally, there was the prophetic factor, the special tradition of the prophets, from Amos and Hosea, via Micah and Isaiah, to Jeremiah. The catastrophe must have resulted in this tradition gaining considerably in authority, and the influence of Isaiah and Jeremiah, both of whom were directly concerned with the exiles, may well have been of decisive importance.

Jeremiah sent a letter from Jerusalem to "the ancients that were carried into captivity and to the priests and to the prophets and to all the people whom Nebuchadnezzar had carried away from Jerusalem to Babylon." It is evident from this list of those to whom the letter was addressed that the exiles did not consist of an amorphous mass of people without authority or leadership, but that they so to speak took their ancient, social structure with them into captivity. The prophet, in his letter, commanded the exiles, in the name of Yahweh: "Build houses and dwell in them: and plant orchards and eat the fruit of them. Take ye wives and beget sons and daughters: and take wives for your sons and give your daughters to husbands, and let them bear sons and daughters: and be ye multiplied there, and be not few in number. And seek the peace (= prosperity) of the city to which I have caused you to be carried away captives and pray to Yahweh for it: for in the peace (= prosperity) thereof shall be your peace (= happiness)" (Jer. 29). This well-known passage gives ample evidence of the possibilities that were open to the exiles. The impression gained from the whole of Jeremiah's letter is that the prophet placed all his hopes in the exiles—if the authentic Israel perished among them, then the people of God would indeed be lost. This impression is further borne out by Jeremiah's vision of the two baskets of figs. In this vision, the very good figs represent king Coniah (Jehoiachin) and the exiles. The very bad figs, on the other hand, represent those who remained behind in Jerusalem with king Zedekiah (Jer. 24).

It was probably when he was still in Jerusalem that Ezekiel also championed the cause of the exiles, of whom it was said in Judah that they were far from Yahweh, and "the land is given in possession to us" (Ezek. 11:15; *see also* 33:24ff.). After the fall of the city, however, he was certainly among the exiles. A particularly large group apparently lived on the banks of one of the many channels in southern Mesopotamia. This was the river Chebar. The exiles' settlement was called Tel-Abib (Ezek. 3:15; *see also* Ps. 136:1). The prophet also apparently had regular contact with the ancients in this settlement. These ancients were able to consult Ezekiel in a private dwelling and sit around him. This might well have been the usual auditorium for his prophecies (8:1, 14:1, 20:1). The situation is brought vividly to life in the following passage:

And thou, son of man: the children of thy people talk of thee by the walls and in the doors of the houses and speak one to another, each man to his neighbour, saying: Come and let us hear what is the word that cometh forth from Yahweh.

And they come to thee, as if a people were coming in: and my people sit before thee and hear thy words and do them not: words of love are in their mouth, but their heart goeth after their covetousness.

And thou art to them as a song of love which is sung with a sweet and agreeable voice: and they hear thy words and do them not.

And when that which was foretold shall come to pass (for, behold, it is coming), then shall they know that a prophet hath been among them (Ezek. 33:30–33).

The exiles had thus already formed their own little world, with the prophet as the central figure among them!

4. New Emphases

The land of Exile was considered to be unclean (*see* Ezek. 4:13). For this reason, there were no holy places and acts of public worship were not possible (*see* Ps. 136:4). As a result, the exiles had to cling to those religious practices which were not strictly associated with public worship and holy places or sanctuaries. The emphasis therefore shifted to a practice that was readily available—they came together. They began to do this at once. The later book of Deuteronomy was based on the prophetic and priestly admonitions which were addressed to those who visited local sanctuaries, and especially the sanctuaries of the Northern Kingdom. In just the same way, the drastically reedited book of Ezekiel may be said to be based on the preaching customary at the assemblies of the exiles. There was, after all, no shortage of priests and prophets, men who were familiar with the written and unwritten inheritance of the patriarchs. Thus, it is possible to perceive here the very beginning of something that was later to become a preeminently Jewish phenomenon—the synagogue. Several centuries were, of course, to elapse before there were buildings known as synagogues in every place where there were Jews. The name itself, however, which only later was applied to the building, indicates that the institution known as the synagogue—coming together, gathering, or assembly (*cf.* "church")—had already been in existence for a long time.

The Pentateuch frequently refers to the congregation of Yahweh. It is of importance to note that this word congregation (*qāhēl*), was reproduced more than thirty times in the Greek translation as *synagōgē*, and precisely in those cases where congregation was used purely in the sense of a worshiping community. *Synagōgē* was also the normal Greek translation of the Hebrew *'ēdāh*, meaning the tribal federation gathered around the sanctuary. This translation occurs almost a hundred and thirty times. The word synagogue is, in two respects, much more meaningful than the usual Greek translation of *qāhēl, ekklēsia* (= church), which undoubtedly has a flavor of constitutional law about it. "Synagogue" reveals, on the one hand, how conscious the Jewish world had become of itself as a great community, both united and belonging to Yahweh. On the other hand, it shows clearly how the local Jewish colonies presented themselves to the outside world, and to the civil authorities, as a synagogue, that it, as a community of believers without political claims. (This is also shown in the word ekklēsia.) Nowadays, of course, when we hear the word synagogue, we think exclusively of a building. It is, therefore, necessary to recall what the word originally meant for the Jews in exile. It will also be clear that this "synagogue" goes back to the time when the exiles became aware of themselves as a local grouping of the people of God.

While Israel was still in Canaan, the practice of the Sabbath, which was instituted at a very early date, was not given great emphasis. In Judaism, however, it was stressed to such an extent that it came to be regarded as an authentic sign of the Covenant. This too is strongly reflected in Jeremiah and Ezekiel. Jewish thought on the reason for the catastrophe is echoed, for example, in the following text from the book of Jeremiah:

And it shall come to pass, if you will hearken to me, saith Yahweh, to bring in no burdens by the gates of this city on the sabbath day, and if you will sanctify the sabbath day to do no work therein:

then shall there enter in by the gates of this city kings and princes, sitting upon the throne of David and riding in chariots and on horses, they and their princes, the men of Judah and the inhabitants of Jerusalem: and this city shall be inhabited for ever.

And they shall come from the cities of Judah and from the places round about Jerusalem and from the land of Benjamin and from the plains (the *šephēlāh*) and from the mountains and from the south (the 'Negeb'), bringing holocausts and victims and sacrifices (= offerings of food) and incense, and they shall bring in an offering (of praise) into the house of Yahweh.

But if you will not hearken to me, to sanctify the sabbath day, and not to carry burdens, and not to bring them in by the gates of Jerusalem on the sabbath day: I will kindle a fire in the gates thereof. And it shall devour the houses of Jerusalem: and it shall not be quenched (Jer. 17:24–27).

Here, as elsewhere, Ezekiel set out the Judaistic practice quite clearly, sometimes in a negative, sometimes in a positive form. As an example of the first: "Son of man, say to her (= the land): Thou art a land that is unclean and not rained upon . . . Her priests have despised my law and have defiled my sanctuaries: they have put no difference between holy and profane, nor have they distinguished between the unclean and the clean, and they have turned away their eyes from my sabbaths: and I am profaned in the midst of them" (22:24, 26). As an instance of a positive statement concerning the sabbath: "Sanctify my sabbaths, that they may be a sign between me and you, and that you may know that I am Yahweh, your God" (20:20).

One of the few ways in which the links with the past could be preserved and the mutual bonds between the people themselves could be strengthened so that this people could maintain itself and hold its own spiritually in a pagan environment was by observing the Sabbath. Another way was by the practice of circumcision. This was a universal practice in both Canaan and Egypt. In these countries, therefore, Israel had not been a conspicuous exception. The Philistines, coming from a completely different cultural environment, were the only people not to practice circumcision. For this reason, they were branded as foreigners, and referred to as the uncircumcised. In Mesopotamia, however, circumcision was not practiced. Thus circumcision was able, like the observation of the sabbath, to become a sign of the Covenant for Israel in exile, and did in fact become such a sign.

Here, then, are two points which became fundamental in the new structure and organization of the people of God, two ancient aspects of Israel's religion brought into new prominence by the predicament of exile. It is clear from the theology of Judaism—a theology which is reflected in the Bible—that the Jews in exile regarded the sabbath and circumcision as buttresses of their existence. Both were called signs of the Covenant (Gen. 17:11; Exod. 31:12–17), and both were inseparably connected with the foundations of Israel's national existence. Circumcision was linked with the name of Abraham (Gen. 17), the sabbath with that of Moses (Exod. 16). The sabbath was, moreover, intimately associated with the work of creation (Gen. 2:3).

A similar development is also discernible in the case of the laws of cleanness. These undoubtedly went back to very ancient taboos. In Judaism, however, they developed into a system of rules and regulations affecting all aspects of the day to day life of the people and protecting them against pagan influences (Ezek. 44:23; 22:26; *see also* Lev. 20:24b–26).

Although the facts concerning the Babylonian captives are so few, there is nonetheless sufficient scriptural evidence for us to be able to discern the beginning of what was later to become characteristically Jewish.

5. The New Sense of God

The growth of a new social structure was accompanied by the development of a new spiritual attitude. Chapters 40–55 of the book of Isaiah provide evidence of the difficulties attendant upon the attainment of this new attitude. This book of consolation for the exiles, in its present extant form, is undoubtedly a later edition. Nevertheless, it still bears distinct traces of the environment in which the different oracles originated. The unknown prophet, whom we call, for want of a better name, Deutero-Isaiah, was certainly entirely in the great tradition of his eminent predecessors. There is, however, a striking difference between his prophecy and the national prophecy of the eighth century—it is virtually impossible to imagine him preaching and prophesying in the streets and the public places to a great assembly of the people with nothing to do but simply to listen to him. The development to which attention has already been drawn in the case of Jeremiah and Ezekiel led, in the case of Deutero-Isaiah, to an entirely new form of prophetism— dialogue with those who listened to the prophecy.

Deutero-Isaiah was himself one of the exiles, and his book of consolation was clearly the outcome of many dialogues which took place in small, intimate gatherings. It is therefore possible to gain a fairly good idea of the exiles' attitude from these chapters of the book of Isaiah. They believed that the history of Israel as a nation had come to an end, and with it Yahweh's concern with the salvation of Israel. This began with the redemption from Egypt. The Exile, had, however, cancelled out this redemption and brought the national community to an end. The disastrous events of history, which had taken the people completely by surprise, had been followed by a deathly silence. Life went on as usual, but without Yahweh and without any kind of national existence. A whole generation had lived without any prospect of change or improvement. Everything had come to an end and Israel was dead. It was to the old things and the first things that the prophet constantly referred. The old, national history of salvation was seen as past history, as something complete in itself. Israel in exile declared: My way is hid from Yahweh, and my judgment is passed over from thy God" (40:27), and Zion maintained: "Yahweh hath forsaken me, and the Lord hath forgotten me" (49:14).

This is an example of closely reasoned logic so characteristic of the Old Testament, but the prophet had to find an answer to it. Employing every means of persuasion and every style at his disposal —consolation, satire, ridicule, reproach, prayer, canticles, the proverb form, and above all theological argument—he attempted to make his discouraged, shortsighted, and disbelieving audience view the international events and the entire world situation as Yahweh's activity with Israel. Yahweh had not forgotten his people. He was still deeply concerned with Israel. The old order had passed away, but new things were on their way. Yahweh was not only the "First"—the Creator of the world and the Redeemer of Israel—but also the "Last." He held not only the past but also the future in his hands. In brief, then, the book of consolation provides a deep insight into the activity of a great testimony of faith to lay the foundations of the future world society of Jews. The Jews were only able to be and to live as Jews by discovering their God, Yahweh, in a new way. The Jews had to learn to discover their God as the God of the world and of the whole human race. They had, therefore, to learn how to find this God everywhere.

Israel had no answer to the derisive question: "Where is thy God"? For it was precisely this question which preoccupied and troubled the exiles. The prophet had to struggle against powerful resistance to make his companions in misfortune realize that the downfall of their nation was Yahweh's action: "Hear, ye deaf, and, ye blind, behold that you may see! Who is blind, but my servant? Or deaf, but the servant of Yahweh? Who hath given Jacob for a spoil, and Israel to robbers? Hath not Yahweh himself?" (42:18f.,

24). "When thou didst pass through the waters, I was with thee: and the rivers did not cover thee. When thou walkedst in the fire, thou wast not burnt and the flames burned not in thee. For I am Yahweh, thy God, the Holy One of Israel, thy Saviour" (43:2f.). This is the voice of one who was deeply convinced of his faith and who had to come back again and again to the same themes, probably without very much visible success. Both the negative and the positive aspect of his prophetic message is summed up in the text: "Remember not former, and look not on things of old. Behold I do new things: and now they shall spring forth" (43:18f.).

These new things were clearly indicated by the prophet. He displayed all the unmistakable characteristics of classic prophetism here, by placing Israel within the context of the concrete world situation. This was changed by the swift rise of Cyrus, the founder of the Persian empire. The classic prophets had interpreted, in faith, the rise of Assyria and Babylon as activity on the part of Yahweh to bring disaster upon Israel. In the same way, Cyrus was seen as an instrument in Yahweh's hand for the purpose of fashioning a new salvation for Israel: "Thus saith Yahweh to his anointed, Cyrus, whose right hand he hath taken hold of . . . I will go before thee and will humble the great ones of the earth. I will break in pieces the gates of brass and will burst the bars of iron . . . that thou mayest know that I am Yahweh, who call thee by thy name, the God of Israel. For the sake of my servant Jacob and Israel, my elect, I have even called thee by thy name. I have given thee an honorable name: and thou has not known me" (45:1-4).

The appearance of Cyrus was an enlightenment for those who believed. The dialogue between Yahweh and Cyrus was really a clever, literary device to express this new insight into the nature of faith in words. The prophet did not intend Yahweh's words for Cyrus, but for Israel. The whole discourse is a clear formulation of the certainty of belief that the prophet wished to convey to the exiles. All the world events which were taking place at that time were aimed at God's elect. They had nothing to fear. The other nations might be thrown into a panic, but

> Thou, Israel, art my servant, Jacob, whom I have chosen,
> the seed of Abraham, my friend.
> Thou, whom I have taken from the ends of the earth,
> and from the remote parts thereof have called thee,
> and said to thee: Thou art my servant.
> I have chosen thee and have not cast thee away.
> Fear not, for I am with thee:
> turn not aside, for I am thy God.
> I have strengthened thee and have helped thee:
> and my just right hand hath upheld thee.

The prophet was aiming, therefore, to convince his hearers that Yahweh had never revoked his first love, but was still faithful to Israel. Israel had to learn to believe in this love in her national humiliation:

> For I am Yahweh, thy God, who take thee by the hand,
> and say to thee: Fear not. I have helped thee.
> Fear not, thou worm of Jacob, you that are dead of Israel!
> I have helped thee, saith Yahweh,
> and thy Redeemer is the Holy One of Israel.

For all those who would believe, the miracle would come to pass. The desert of the exiles would become a paradise.

> The needy and the poor seek for waters,
> and there are none: their tongue hath been dry with thirst.
> I, Yahweh, will hear them:
> I, the God of Israel, will not forsake them.
> I will open rivers in the high hills
> and fountains in the midst of the plains:

I will turn the desert into pools of waters,
and the impassable land into streams of waters.
I will plant in the wilderness the cedar and the thorn and
the myrtle and the olive-tree:
I will set in the desert the cypress, the plane-tree and
the fir-tree together:
that they may see and know,
and consider, and understand together,
that the hand of Yahweh hath done this,
and the Holy One of Israel hath created it (Isa. 41:8–20).

6. *The Second Temple*

Cyrus' conduct, insofar as this concerned the Jews, was fully in accordance with the whole policy of the Persians. Local customs, including religious practices, were not only taken into consideration, but even promoted and, wherever necessary, restored. The proclamation which Cyrus issued when he entered Babylon (539) is a striking monument to this policy. Among other things, this proclamation reveals that Cyrus had the images of the gods which had been taken as trophies to Babylon brought back to their cities, together with their worshipers who had been deported, and that he had both temples and houses restored. His edict in favor of the Jews (538), reported word for word in Ezra 6:3–5, ordered the rebuilding of the temple as a place of sacrifice at the king's expense, and the return of the gold and silver vessels of the temple. This Jewish edict may be regarded as an enforcement of the general, imperial edict with reference to the special situation and particular needs of the Jews. It is quite possible to imagine, in this context, a Persian ministry of religion and public worship with a large, specialized staff, including an expert qualified in Jewish religious affairs. The edict, as it appears in the Bible, should therefore not be regarded as a free biblical rendering of Cyrus' universal edict, but rather as a literal reproduction of the edict that was drawn up by the Jewish department under the control of the ministry of public worship.

The initiative for this special edict probably came from the exiles themselves. The restoration of Jerusalem as a holy place was a vital question for the scattered remnants of Israel. The restored temple could be an indisputed center for all Jews spread over the entire ancient world, something which would enable them to feel that they were once again, as they had been in the days of the amphictyony, a people of the Covenant.

A certain Sheshbazzar was given the commission and the authority to put Cyrus' edict into effect (Ezra 1:8). It would seem that he got no further with the reconstruction of the temple than the laying of its foundations (Ezra 5:16). The reason why the work stagnated is clear from Haggai 1:1-11. With the appearance of this prophet and of Zechariah, work was resumed on the temple, about the year 520. In the meantime, the Persian empire had been subdivided into satrapies, and official difficulties raised by the satrap who governed the territory to the west of the Euphrates led eventually to Darius' confirmation of Cyrus' edict. The new temple was ultimately dedicated in 515 (Ezra 6).

This was a fact of great importance for the structure of world Judaism. Since the collapse of the state, the need for a center of public worship had assumed an even greater importance. The restoration of the temple also meant that the priesthood, not the monarchy, was to play a leading role. Judaism thus acquired a new structure, that of a *world church,* under the leadership of priests. The chief priest of the restored temple was to become the leader of all Israel. As long as the monarchy remained, the priests of Jerusalem were, in their capacity as ministers of the royal sanctuary, the king's officials. This situation had in no way changed when the priests of Jerusalem, basing their claims partly on the law of Deuteronomy concerning the unity of the sanctuary, had acquired a monopoly. Now, however, the priests were the only ones available to take over the leadership. It is, therefore, no coincidence that the priestly figure of Joshua (Jeshua) occurs not only in Haggai and Zechariah, but also in the book of Ezra as a central figure in the Jerusalem society. He may be regarded as the first to fill the important new office of high priest. In addition to Joshua, the high priest, we also find the governor Zerubbabel of the Branch of David, whose person gave rise to a messianic expectation of a strongly national kind (Hagg.; Zech.). It is not clear whether Zerubbabel occupied an official position, and it is even less clear whether he had any successors.

7. The Babylonian Orthodoxy

However important these events may have been for the future of Judaism, it certainly does not look as if the true spirit of Judaism was visibly expressed in this restored congregation for a long time, although in this connection we must take into account the fact that there is a gap of almost seventy years in our information. One possible explanation is that the sense of continuity with the past was so strong in the homeland that the climate there was unfavorable for the spontaneous growth of anything so radically new. The abuses described by Malachi and Trito-Isaiah (Isa. 56–66), some of which at least were to be encountered by Nehemiah and Ezra, ought to cause us little surprise. The situation of the Exile was the point of departure for Judaism. It was only this situation, perpetuated by the diaspora, which could eventually lead to a new, stable pattern of life, a new form of the people of God.

This new pattern of life came about gradually. We can gain some idea of it from the book of Ezekiel. The material of this book must, to a very great extent, have been developed in the Babylonian diaspora. Chapters 40–48 of Ezekiel form the constitution of a thoroughly Jewish community. Both in the literary and in the spiritual sense, the preeminently priestly book of Leviticus is closely related to Ezekiel. This is also a clear indication of the fact that the priestly mentality, so well known to us from the last phase of the formation of the Bible, and so characteristically Jewish, originated in the Babylonian diaspora. What Nehemiah and Ezra actually did becomes immediately evident if the view that Judaism originated principally in Babylon is accepted. This view is at the same time emphatically confirmed by their activity.

(a) Nehemiah the Governor

When Nehemiah, who can almost be called a diaspora Jew, came to Jerusalem in 445 as governor of the Persian province of Judah, he had the task of transferring the Jewish orthodoxy, which had already reached an advanced stage of development in the Babylonian diaspora, to Jerusalem.

It is not certain whether a great procession of exiles returned to Jerusalem in 538, even if his free rendering of the edict of Cyrus was a simplification on the part of the priestly historian (Ezra 1). The list which he appended to this account is, on the other hand, undoubtedly historical, since it includes the names and numbers of those who were in Judah approximately a century after the edict. A possible explanation of the writer's simplification is that he was better able to throw light upon the full scope and wider implications of the events by reporting the departure in 538, *en bloc,* of the groups which in fact returned throughout the course of the century. The opposition of the Samaritans, which was clearly connected with the reconstruction of the city (Ezra 4:12–16), was seen by the writer as having a direct bearing on the building of the temple. He seems to have been inspired here by the religious schism which was, at the time when he was editing his book, already a fact (Ezra 4:1–3: *see also* 2 Kings 17:24–41).

The ancient capital of the Northern Kingdom, which had, for

almost a century, also given the lead to the South, realized that the rebuilding of her former rival would not only mean a considerable reduction in her influence, but also the end of her preeminence. On the other hand, the Jews of the diaspora needed the rebuilding of Jerusalem for the ultimate establishment of their own religious status. On the one hand, the city, once it had been rebuilt, would guarantee the continued existence of the central holy place which the Jews needed if they were to be aware of themselves as the community of those who worshiped Yahweh. On the other hand, a rebuilt Jerusalem would enable the Jews to form a religious community with a clearly defined and legitimate center.

This wish would, however, never be fulfilled as long as Judah remained a province dependent on Samaria. Independence from Samaria was Nehemiah's aim when he was appointed as governor. Unknown to Samaria he had the walls of the city rebuilt (Neh. 6:15), and the city itself more intensively populated (Neh. 11). He brought to an end the influence of the Samaritans and the representatives of the other neighboring provinces who had maintained relations with the ruling classes in Judah (Neh. 13). In this way, he extended the isolation which had already developed, in the diaspora, into a fixed pattern of life to Jerusalem, and established the external conditions which could lead to the rise of a strong Jewish community. He brought greater order into this new society by a redistribution in the ownership of land (Neh. 5). He also took steps leading to regular, public worship, the strict observation of the Sabbath and the prevention of mixed marriages (Neh. 13).

(b) Ezra the Scribe

As governor, Nehemiah had no authority in strictly religious matters. His power was restricted to the purely social and organizational aspect in this sphere. He did, however, create a situation within which a figure who had exceptional powers in the field of religion was able to undertake the inner restoration of the community. This figure was Ezra, a Jewish priest of the Persian province of Babylon, who was sent to Jerusalem with a special commission. Ezra's commission was implied in his title of scribe or scholar. This title was, however, something of an anachronism; in fact, it is clearly an abbreviation of the title "the scribe most learned in the law of the God of heaven" (Ezra 7:12). This full title might be rendered, in the official style of the Persian administration, as "state commissioner for Jewish religious affairs." This technical meaning was, in fact, established beyond all doubt by the discovery, in the early nineteen thirties, of the literal, biblical translation of "Ezra, the priest and scribe, learned in the words of the commandments and precepts of Yahweh for Israel" (Ezra 7:11; *see also* 7:6).

Ezra's plenary powers extended beyond Jerusalem: "Thou, Ezra, according to the wisdom of thy God, which is in thy hand, appoint judges and magistrates, that may judge all the people that is beyond the River, that is, for them who know the laws of thy God. And the ignorant teach ye freely." This royal decree made all the Jews of the Persian satrapy known as "Beyond the River" subject to the religious jurisdiction of Jerusalem. That the Jewish law was at the same time the imperial law for these Jews is clear from the rest of the text: "And whosoever will not do the law of thy God, and the law of the king diligently, (summary) justice shall be executed upon him, either unto death, or unto banishment, or to the confiscation of goods, or to prison" (Ezra 7:25f.).

No absolute certainty has, however, been reached as to the content of this law, although it may safely be assumed that it was not the law of Deuteronomy. If it was also not the whole remainder of the Pentateuch, this law must then have coincided with, or at least have been assimilated into, one or more of the great bodies of priestly laws of the Pentateuch. Of this we can be certain, since it is an established fact that the detailed formulation of those laws originated in the priestly circles of the Babylonian diaspora.

The magnificent description of the reading of the Law on the Feast of Tabernacles (Neh. 8), gives a very plausible illustration of a synagogal type of assembly. Even more than this, it also shows what Judaism was from this time forward. It gives clear evidence of the fact that the Jews were not a people restricted to one particular country, nor simply an ethnic group confined to one particular, historical period, but a people of God brought into being and kept in existence by submission to the Law. From this time onwards, the Jewish people was no longer created by divine intervention in history. It is rather as if God's historical, saving activity had ceased, after having become crystallized in the Law, this Law which became an absolute standard and a divine source of life for the worldwide congregation of the Jews. It is still possible to regard the Jewish community of this period as a theocracy, but as a theocracy which took the specific form of a monocracy.

Closely connected with this is the fact that Judaism, in contrast to the religion of the later Israel, had the nature of a religion of the book. The written Law had become, in the most complete way possible, Holy Scripture. This is a development which can already be discerned in Deuteronomy. It is quite clear, in our quest for the origin of the typically Jewish aspects of religion, that Ezra played a very special part indeed in this development. Modern research is broadly in agreement with the Jewish and Christian tradition, in ascribing such an important place to "Ezra the learned scribe" in the permanent shaping of Judaism and the Bible.

8. The Great Gap

The facts of the Hebrew bible do not extend beyond the time of Ezra and Nehemiah. The books of the Maccabees, preserved in the Greek bible, resumed the historical narrative only 175 years before the birth of Christ. This great gap of more than two centuries is fairly easy to fill in, as far as the external and political situation of

Judah is concerned, from our general knowledge of the history of the period. After the year 333, the province of Judah—the Greek name Judaea, that is, the Judaean (district), became prevalent from this time onwards—changed hands, the Persian rule being replaced by the Macedonian administration of Alexander the Great. On Alexander's death, Palestine became a bone of contention between the empires of the Diadochi, Syria, and Egypt. The conflict was eventually resolved in 301 in favor of the Ptolemies in Egypt. It was in the course of the following century that the new city of Alexandria must have developed into the most important center of the Hellenistic diaspora. Then, in 198, Palestine came permanently under the control of the Seleucids, who had their residence in the equally new city of Antioch, on the Orontes. This Antioch also became, like Alexandria, an important center for the Jews of the diaspora. The rebellion of the Maccabees took place during the rule of the Seleucids. This war for religious freedom quickly achieved its aims, but soon degenerated into a war for political freedom, and led ultimately to the rise of the Jewish kingdom in 140 (1 Macc. 14:27ff.). This precarious independence came to an end in 63 B.C. with the Roman conquest of Jerusalem.

A detailed discussion of these facts of secular, historical importance would serve no useful purpose here. The data provided by the books of the Maccabees are, however, of importance in connection with our subject, but they are historically so close to the post-biblical period of Judaism that they really fall outside the scope of this book. But, concerning the subject matter in which we are most interested here, there are hardly any facts available. The problem is what happened, between the appearance of Nehemiah and Ezra and the time of the Maccabees, within Judaism itself, and, what is even more to the point, how did the congregation of Jerusalem which they established develop? In any case, it is possible to establish certain clearly defined results which emerged in the second century B.C. as the outcome of this development. To this extent we are able to know what must have happened there in the few preceding centuries. Judaism must have already had, in the third century, the definite shape which it revealed in the second century. We saw the beginning of some of the aspects of this form in the sixth and fifth centuries. In this case, it must have been during the Persian period that this form continued to grow and to consolidate itself. We propose to go a little more deeply into three aspects of this growth and consolidation in the following three sections.

(a) The Samaritan Schism

The temple of Jerusalem was, by virtue of its origin, the royal sanctuary of the descendants of David. The Persian kings succeeded to their rights, and prayers were said for them and sacrifices were offered, at their own expense, for "the life of the king, and of his children" (Ezra 6:10). This royal privilege, this special, legal status of the Persian rulers did not, however, alter the fact that the temple was really no longer a royal or state sanctuary, but first and foremost essentially the place of worship of world Judaism—every act of public worship which took place outside Jerusalem was, in the eyes of the Jews, illegal. By definition, however, a strictly royal sanctuary was bound to leave local places of worship intact, even though it might overshadow them. With the end of the monarchy the people of God went back, at least at the ideal level, to the ancient structure, and the twelve tribes once again formed an amphictyony. This new amphictyony was, however, worldwide, and its central holy place was Jerusalem.

The Persian authorities kept a sharp eye on the wider significance of the temple of Jerusalem. In their opinion, this temple had resulted in a settlement of the religious affairs of the Jewish population of all the Persian provinces to the west of the Euphrates at least. The creation of a separate Samaritan temple was certainly not in accordance with their policy, although this must clearly have been the aim of the leading classes in Samaria since Judah had become an independent province. What arose at this time, then, was a situation very similar to that which prevailed at the time of Jeroboam I. The Samaritans obtained their own temple and, according to Flavius Josephus, it bore a close resemblance to the temple of Jerusalem. But this temple was very late in coming, and the population of the southern part of the province, the total population of which was larger than the Samaritan worshiping community, continued to go to Jerusalem. This was subsequently to lead, during the Greek period, to a change in the provincial boundary between Judah and Samaria, when it was moved to the north.

One clear fact is known to us concerning the year 168. It was in this year that Antioch IV Epiphanes replaced the worship of Yahweh at Jerusalem with that of Zeus Olympios, and the Yahwistic worship on Mount Gerizim with that of Zeus Xenios (2 Macc. 6:2). We may therefore conclude that the temple on the well-known holy mountain near Shechem was a sanctuary which had been in existence and had been fully recognized for a long time. It must have been built, either with or without the permission of the imperial government, during the disturbances which occurred towards the end of the Persian period. This is clear from the passage in which Josephus attributed the permission to build to Alexander the Great. The fact that the Samaritans recognized the Pentateuch alone as Scripture is another clear indication. About 400, however, the Elephantine colony apparently knew nothing about this sanctuary, since the colonists addressed their petition only to the governor of Samaria, the governor of Judah and the high priest of Jerusalem.

This temple set the seal on the schism that had begun to show itself during the earliest stages of Israel's history and that had, up to this point, been most clearly expressed in the division of Solomon's empire. Now, however, Samaria, a local minority, separated forever from the new Jewish unity. The Jewish state which had been created by the Maccabees, conquered Samaria and incorporated this province into itself. At this time (128), both the capital and the temple were destroyed. Samaria was rebuilt by Herod the Great, and from that time forward it became the splendid Roman city of Sebaste. The temple was never rebuilt, but Mount Gerizim has to this day been preserved as the holy place of the ever decreasing community of worshipers in the region of Shechem (*see* John 4:20ff.; Ecclus. 50:27f.; Zech. 11:14; Dan. 13:57).

(b) Scripture and Its Interpretation

Judaism was a great, united, worshiping community, with Jerusalem as its place of worship. The books of Ezekiel and Leviticus show clearly how every detail of public worship was carefully regulated and how sharply defined the hierarchy and the various functions of the ministers had become. The operation of this code of law can be seen in the account of the priestly writer. It would seem as if the entire machinery of worship was serving less and less as a religious path along which Yahweh could be sought and which could lead to a living communion with him, and more and more as an expression of a strict fulfillment of the law. This Law was the Pentateuch.

We have already referred to Judaism as a religion of the book. During the Persian period, the Pentateuch did not merely acquire its permanent scope and form. From this time onwards, what had never been true of the various parts which together constituted the Pentateuch became true of the Pentateuch as a whole—it became canonical Scripture and, in fact, identical with the Law to which Judaism knew itself to be subject and which made it Judaism as such. Deuteronomy, which in so many respects may be regarded as the link between the prophetic and the Jewish periods, prepared the way for this development. This book is, after all, our first historically tangible example of a document, written in considerable detail, which began more and more to replace direct, priestly instruction (the *tôrāh*), in the regulation of daily life (2 Kings 23:1-3; Deut. 31:9-13).

The interpretation of the Law had always been, since the very earliest times, a preeminently priestly task. At this period, however, it was the written Law which had to be interpreted. There consequently arose a group of men—initially, no doubt, within priestly circles—who specialized in the interpretation, exposition, and teaching of the written Law, in other words, in scriptural scholarship. These learned scribes, or teachers of the Law, probably formed a separate group beside the priestly class. The proper place of the priests was, at this time, the sanctuary. The priests and prophets had been the pastors of ancient Israel, with its many places of worship. After the Exile, however, the priests' functions tended more and more to be restricted to the ministry of the temple in Jerusalem, while their pastoral work in the local Jewish communities was taken over by the learned scribes who, from this time onwards, assumed an ever increasing importance as spiritual leaders of the people. The priests, then, were associated with the temple, and the interpreters of scripture with the synagogue. The name by which they became known was "rabbi." After the destruction of the temple, it was the rabbis who were to play the most decisive part in shaping post-biblical Judaism.

The prophetic history (Joshua: 2 Kings), too, must have been given its permanent, final shape in the Persian period. The prophetic, oracular literature, on the other hand, with many Jewish and, in particular, apocalyptic extensions, led to the prophetic books in the form in which we now have them.

The third group, the writings of the Hebrew bible, which takes its point of departure from the collections of psalms and proverbs and from other ancient elements, became the special literary activity of the Jewish world after the Law and the Prophets had become canonical. Wisdom, originally an international, but in particular an Egyptian, literary form, had already been taken over by ancient

Israel and been given a distinctively Yahwistic flavor. The strongly moral tone of this wisdom and its emphasis on human conduct made it particularly well suited to Judaism. As a result, this literary form continued to be very productive long after the Persian period, especially when Wisdom and the Law became identified with each other in men's minds.

(c) The Diaspora, the Elephantine Colony, and the Septuagint

It is clear that there was already a Babylonian and Persian diaspora, with Aramaean as its common language, at the time of Ezra. In this case, then, the Hellenistic diaspora must have had its origin in the second half of the Persian period. This applies particularly to the diaspora of Lower Egypt. The colony of Jewish soldiers on the Nile island of Elephantine in Upper Egypt strangely enough disappeared from the historical scene at this time as mysteriously as it had previously entered it. The Elephantine colony had its own temple, dedicated to Yahû or Yahô (= Yahweh). This temple had been destroyed about the year 410. The colonists' petition to the high priest Johanan of Jerusalem to rebuild this temple was not answered. No place of worship outside Jerusalem was permitted at that time. The letter which the colony addressed to Bagoas, the Persian governor of Judah, in 407 resulted in official permission being granted for the building of a new temple, on condition that no blood sacrifices were to be made in it. This was a compromise, by which the governor attempted to satisfy both the priests of Jerusalem and those in Egypt. As the latter regarded certain animals as sacred, the sacrificial services in the temple of Elephantine had, in their view, been idolatrous. This might also have been the reason for its destruction. It is quite clear from the Elephantine papyri that the colonists considered themselves to be completely Jewish, even though they worshiped other deities, such as Anathbethel and Eshembethel, in addition to their principal God, Yahû, in the temple. It is probable that the colonists brought this syncretism with them from their homeland—the Northern Kingdom, perhaps, or even Bethel—in which case, this small detail offers us a brief glimpse into the sort of religious practice which was rife among the people at the lowest level of society.

Egypt, once the house of bondage of the Hebrews, gradually became a place of refuge and a political asylum. Even Jeroboam I took refuge in Egypt (1 Kings 11:40). In contrast to the great powers of the eastern world, Egypt was able to offer safety, but, like a reed, its safety again and again proved deceptive (Ezek. 29:6f.; *see also* Isa. 20, 30f.; Jer. 46, 37:5–10). In 587, a group of Judaeans, acting against the advice of Jeremiah (Jer. 42–44), went to Egypt. It is not known what became of these people, but it may safely be assumed that they were able, at least partly, to maintain their Jewish identity, with the result that, in some of the cities of Egypt, Jewish quarters arose in which, to some extent, a distinctively Jewish life was able to develop. Since communications between Palestine and Egypt were busy and relatively easy, it is also possible to think of a steady flow of emigrants on a moderate scale. It is an established, historical fact that the stream of Jewish immigrants into Egypt which had begun at the time of Alexander's conquest of Egypt increased greatly during the religious persecutions of Antioch IV.

Of particular importance was the Hellenistic diaspora of the Nile Delta, the birthplace of the Greek bible, known as the Septuagint, or the translation of the Seventy. The language of Canaan (Isa. 19:18), Hebrew—called Judaean or the Jews' language in 2 Kings 18:26—was gradually ousted after the Exile by the world language of that time, Aramaic. Hebrew became the sacred language, the language of the Bible and of the learned scribes, the interpreters of scripture. The custom arose in the synagogue to follow the reading of the Law with an Aramaic translation. This was a relatively free translation and, initially at least, extempore (*baregûm*). Gradually, however, this Aramaic paraphrase acquired a fixed form and be-

came, as it were, a standard translation. The Targum of the Pentateuch, which has been preserved, is an important source for textual
criticism and above all for the most ancient history of biblical exegesis. In the west and especially in Egypt, however, Aramaic was
superseded as the world language by Greek. The Hebrew reading
of the Law in the Hellenistic synagogues was consequently followed
by a Greek paraphrase. There is general agreement at present that
the Septuagint itself, or at least the basis of the Septuagint, was in
fact a Greek targum. By 250, there was already a complete translation of the Pentateuch in existence, and by 180, a complete translation of the whole of the Hebrew bible in Greek. This is clear from
the prologue of Sirach (Ecclesiasticus), in which the Law, the
Prophets, and the other Books are mentioned three times. The
Hebrew bible was written in Aramaic characters—the Hebrew
orthography as we now know it. There were also Hebrew bibles
written with Greek letters. The extant fragments of these are extremely interesting, because they make it possible for us to test the
correctness of the Hebrew vowel system which was laid down in
the early Middle Ages.

To go more deeply into the importance of these phenomena and
of the Greek translation itself for biblical theology and textual criticism would lead us far beyond the scope of the present book. What
we are above all concerned with here is the importance of the Greek
bible for the unity and the religious aspect of world Judaism. The
careful comparison of the Hebrew and the Greek bibles is an
abundant source of knowledge concerning the religous attitude of
Judaism in the last centuries before Christ, and it is a source which
is still by no means exhausted. If we regard Judaism as the link
between ancient Israel and Christianity, we must recognize the very
special part played by the Septuagint here, in forming the link
which connects the Hebrew bible to the books of the New Testament.

9. *Judaism as a Figure of Authentic Faith*

Both the links mentioned at the end of the preceding section are of the greatest importance. The first, Judaism, was a vital link in the process of the development of the Church. The second, the Septuagint, was equally indispensable in the process of the development of Scripture. If we take the Church and Holy Scripture seriously, and accept the supernatural origin of both, then we are bound to take the Jewish period and the literary activity of this period seriously as well. There are many reasons why the Christian attitude is often inconsistent in this respect.

Those who succeeded the prophets do not always come up to our expectations. It was, after all, very difficult to follow the prophets. That the prophets should enjoy the undivided admiration of biblical scholars is quite proper. They form the indisputable climax of the Old Testament, and the Jewish world can scarcely compete with them. The literature of the Jews introduces us to another world, a world to which we cannot so readily give our consent. The result is that Judaism, at least insofar as it finds expression in the Hebrew bible, seldom receives the attention and the appreciation that it deserves, and that the Septuagint, despite the fact that it has been subjected to considerable historical scrutiny and to close textual criticism, has rarely been the object of deep, faithful understanding.

As an important link in the process of the development of the Church, that is, in the process of growth from the Old Testament to the New Testament Israel of God, however, Judaism should be approached as a work of the Spirit. Those religious and literary expressions of Judaism which are fully representative of the authentic Jewish mind must be taken in the closest possible context and similarly appreciated as a work of the Spirit, that is to say, as Scripture. The faithful Jewish community was the first to live by Scripture. It was, moreover, this community which, to a very great extent, made Scripture, by keeping the inheritance of the patriarchs alive. Whereas the community itself continued to develop, its literary expression came to an artificial end when the Hebrew language fell into disuse. This is the main reason why the form and scope of the Hebrew bible, about the year 300, were final. The three subsequent centuries were, however, not a scriptural vacuum. They formed an indispensable link in the process of scriptural development since the Jewish community continued to do, during these three centuries, what it had done throughout the past: it preserved the inheritance of the patriarchs and made it its own living possession, by expressing it in a fully contemporary manner and enriching it. The great difference between this last period of growth towards the New Testament and the earlier period was simply that the medium of expression during the last period was no longer Hebrew, but the language of the most vital and the most productive section of the community of that time, that is, Greek. With all the freedom of authentic faith, the Greek-speaking members of the Jewish community made their own Scripture for themselves, by translating the Hebrew texts that had been handed down to them according to their understanding of the nature of faith, and by extending and enriching these texts with other writings. This Septuagint was Scripture for world Judaism exactly as it was Scripture, via the New Testament, for the world Church.

The Catholic Church has always taught that the writings which were added to the Hebrew collection by the Septuagint are authentic Scripture. Speculation of a too theoretical a nature concerning inspiration, and especially concerning the relationship between the inspired, original text and its translations, has, however, led to an unfortunate situation. Current theology has almost completely lost sight of the distinctive place occupied by the Septuagint in the process of scriptural growth. This has in turn also led to the Septuagint being placed on the same level as later translations, which may, of course, be accorded scriptural authority only insofar as they reproduce in a pure form the original text. It is only in recent years that arguments have again been heard in certain quarters in favor of a reassessment of the independent, scriptural value of the Septuagint, including those places where it departs from the text of the Hebrew bible. This attitude is, of course, in complete accordance with the mind of the Early Church. The exegetical practice of consulting the Greek bible in connection with the search for the biblical message proves that here, too, nature is a good deal stronger than doctrine.

In the traditional, historical approach to the Bible, the Jewish period is invariably treated like an unwanted child. The anecdotal treatment of the material which makes the history of salvation during the preceding periods so difficult to follow and to understand is particularly intractable here. Peripheral accounts and incidents seem to be given the greatest attention, and the story of miracles and wars is carried on as usual. It is hardly ever possible to obtain a picture of this period as a whole, or to gain a convincing impression of its newness and its distinctive quality. This reproach cannot, of course, be leveled at the specialists who have rediscovered Judaism, and have devoted themselves to the study of this period, producing standard works on the subject to which the author of this outline is greatly indebted. There is no lack, in their studies, either of real understanding or of synthesis. They do, however, often seem to find it difficult to be fully sympathetic towards Judaism. Approaching the phenomenon from the rather lofty point of view of historians of comparative religion, they are frequently more disposed to judge than to teach. This attitude is bound to lead to an underestimation of Judaism. Even though the religiosity of the Jews may mean little to us, it is nonetheless a figure of authentic faith which brings into prominence aspects capable of enriching our belief. It is, in other words, essential to learn to listen to what the Jews, as believers, are really trying to convey.

An examination of the way in which the Jewish priestly mind diluted the content of the prophetic inheritance, by translating it into its own scholastic terms and interpreting it according to its legalistic conceptions, is bound to result in a totally inadequate image of Judaism. Judaism was not merely a product of prophetism. For an entire century the prophets and their disciples were at work on Judaism. The prophets occupied a central position in a great period. Their glory was that they were themselves as great as their period. Judaism was less spectacular. The Jews' special virtue was their ability to interpret the vision of the prophets and relate it to the quiet actions of everyday life. In this way, Judaism gave to the prophetic vision a practical and living form. In Buber's phrase, Judaism conducted the prophetic flood into calm, priestly channels. Judaism was rich in the religion and faith of the prophets, but this became crystallized in many different institutions and practices as it spread over the centuries.

We miss too the highly charged quality of the prophetic oracles. These new fixed forms were also, of course, accompanied by new dangers, and especially that of inflexibility. We should, however, remember in this connection that it was only a living faith which could discover these new forms. With its own special place in the Bible, the Jewish literature also has its own special way of forming and informing the believer who reads the Bible, even though this way is different from that of the prophetic books. The believer cannot always live in a state of prophetic tension. His pilgrimage on this earth should be a synthesis of prophetic dynamism and simple day to day righteousness, and this he can learn from the faithfulness of the Jews. The breadth of the cosmic vision of the Jews is borne out by the fact that both the account of the creation of the world in Genesis 1 and Daniel's apocalyptic synthesis of world history were typically Jewish. Not every Jew, perhaps, had this vision of the universe, but even so it was no mean feat to live as a member of an uprooted people, as a member of an isolated group in a pagan environment, and to be aware of the world God of the prophets in one's own private life.

It was because Judaism had lost everything that it discovered

Yahweh in an entirely new way. The prophecies were fulfilled. Yahweh had visited the old Jerusalem and had judged the men who had become fat on their lees and who said in their hearts: Yahweh will not do good, nor will he do evil. But their riches had become a booty and their houses had become as a desert . . . and neither their silver nor their gold had been able to deliver them in the day of the wrath of Yahweh (Zeph. 1:12, 13, 18).

I will take away out of the midst of thee thy proud boasters, and thou shalt no more be lifted up because of my holy mountain. And I will leave in the midst of thee *a poor and needy people,* the *Remnant of Israel* shall hope in the Name of Yahweh (Zeph. 3:11f.).

The Jews were the Remnant of Israel, the authentic Israel, Israel in the qualitative sense. A new people of God was formed within the Israel that had been deprived of everything. These were the poor of Israel—poor not only in the material sense, but also, and especially, in the religious sense. The poor of Israel had not only lost all worldly possessions and all worldly means of support; they were also no longer able to trust these. The parallelism of the text quoted above shows clearly that the prophet regarded the poor people as identical with the people that hoped and sought refuge in Yahweh. Judaism had literally become poor:

Neither is there at this time king or leader or prophet, holocaust or sacrifice or oblation or incense, or place of first-fruits before thee, that we may find thy mercy.

But, once assimilated by faith, this literal poverty led to a spiritual attitude which was to be the formative principle by which the Remnant of Israel might become the true, authentic Israel of God. This is clear from the conclusion of the above later Jewish text:

> Nevertheless in a contrite heart and humble spirit let
> us be accepted.

As in holocausts of rams and bullocks
and as in thousands of fat lambs:
so let our sacrifices be made in thy sight that day
that it may please thee (Dan. 3:38–40).

This spirituality of the poor of Israel can be regarded as the greatest glory of Judaism and, if anything can correct the one-sided judgment of Judaism so prevalent today, then it is this. It was the poor in spirit who were promised the Kingdom of Heaven. The psalmist too echoes this spirit:

For if thou hadst desired sacrifice,
I would indeed have given it:
with burnt offerings thou wilt not be delighted.
A sacrifice to God is an afflicted spirit:
a contrite and humble heart
thou wilt not despise (Ps. 50:18f.; *see also* 68:30–34; 140:2).

The wound of the national disaster continued to smart, not so much because it was humanly humiliating, but because it was a sign of divine anger. But this pain caused the Jew to admit defeat at the hands of his ancient, national God and to discover this God as the God of heaven. He knew that he was secure in this God, whom he now called the "Most High":

For thus saith the High and the Eminent,
that inhabiteth eternity,
and whose name is Holy:
I dwell in the high and holy place
and with the contrite and humble of spirit,
to revive the spirit of the humble and the heart of the contrite.
For I will not contend for ever,
neither will I be angry unto the end,
or the spirit will yield before my face,

although I have given the breath of life (Isa. 57:15f.; *see also* 66:1f.).

There was, at this period, a clear shift of emphasis from the collective to the personal. Yahweh had been close to the people as a whole because he had dwelt in the national temple. The destruction of the temple revealed that God dwelt in reality with the individual believer; his dwelling in the temple had been the sacramental sign of this. The Israelite had been borne up by the national community, of which he formed a part. The new Jewish community, scattered throughout the world, could only be sustained by the personal, religious decision of each individual.

The Jew experienced poverty and lived it in his faithfulness to the Law. This was tantamount to a complete surrender to his God. Far from acquiring a human guarantee of salvation in his strict fulfillment of the Law, he confessed by this loyalty that God himself was his only salvation. The Law was everything to him, because it showed him God's way to man and thus man's only way to his God. Even the small precepts of the Law were important, because they could be carried out with a great heart. The Jew rejoiced in the Law of Yahweh, and this was for him a rejoicing in his faith. The national downfall which had deprived him of all human sustinence and support and had made him literally poor became, through faith, an experience of God. What had been a national catastrophe was seen, in the light of faith, as a merciful judgment of the God who, by withdrawing himself in this way, had preserved a remnant of believers and had come close to it.

The Jewish literature is often too little valued because it is approached from the point of view of the rigidity which set in later and not from the point of view of the spirit in which it originated. This spirit continued to inform the religious attitude of many Jewish believers, and it was this attitude which provided the soil in which the Gospel message was later to grow.

If the Jewish books of the Bible are read according to the spirit in which they originated and not according to the spirit in which they have frequently been understood later, they will be seen to have a great deal to say to modern man in his search for a religious interpretation of his day to day existence.

The official Judaism of Christ's time had forgotten the spiritual attitude which had once characterized it and had gradually come to look for too human guarantees of salvation in all kinds of external phenomena and in false, racial beliefs. Christ withdrew from this in word and deed by fulfilling, in his own person, the ancient, prophetical, and Jewish ideal of poverty. He was himself the Poor One and the Servant of Yahweh par excellence and, anointed by the Spirit, he announced the Good News to the poor (Luke 4:17-21). The quiet religiosity of the Jews and the dynamic quality of the prophets were fulfilled and synthesized in Christ.

Bibliographical Survey

IT WAS towards the end of the sixteenth century that the religious data of the Old Testament were first studied separately from the all-embracing scheme of theology. What had hitherto been investigated, more or less at random, began at that time to emerge as a special field of study. The new science of Hebrew archaeology was, then, the creation of humanistic scholarship and the humanists' taste for ancient *realia*. Insofar as this new study was concerned with the religion of Israel— and it was sometimes exclusively concerned with this aspect of Israel, and often went into considerable detail—it limited its scope to religious institutions and followed the classic divisions of sacred places, periods, rites, and persons. There was at that time no great feeling for historical development. The biblical data were placed side by side to form a firm foundation upon which an imposing building was reconstructed. It is interesting to compare the various treatises scattered throughout the nine parts of *Critici sacri* (Amsterdam, 1698), or to glance through the thirty-four folios of Biagio Ugolini's *Thesaurus antiquitatum sacrarum* (Venice, 1744–1769). This special study has persisted up to the present day, and has produced many excellent manuals, such as:

Nötscher, F., *Biblische Altertumskunde*, Bonn, 1940
Barrois, A.-G., *Manuel d'Archéologie Biblique*, Paris, A. Picard, part I, 1939, Part II, 1953

The manual most to be recommended is:

Vaux, R. de, *Les Institutions de l'Ancien Testament*, two parts, Paris, 1958–1960

These modern manuals have, of course, a totally different character from their counterparts in the past. There are two principal reasons for this. On the one hand, the rediscovery of the historical development of the text of the Bible has led to a new insight into the historical growth of Israel's religious practices, with the result that the biblical data are now manipulated differently. On the other hand, pure imagination no longer plays such an important part as it did in the past. It has been, in fact, entirely replaced by archaeology in the modern sense of the word, that is to say, the study of the material remains of the past. This study has been powerfully stimulated by the excavations made in the last century, and has become a specialty in its own right. By breaking away from the older archaeology, it has infused new life into it. Archaeology, in the current sense, has become, together with the Bible itself, our best source of knowledge concerning the religious practices of ancient Israel. There are many books which, with the help of the knowledge gained from archaeological finds, give a very concrete picture of religious life in Israel. Among these are, for example:

Vincent, H., *Canaan d'après l'exploration récente*, Paris, 1907
Welch, A. C., *The Religion of Israel under the Kingdom*, Edinburgh, 1912
Cook, S. A., *The Religion of Ancient Palestine in the Light of Archaeology*, London, Oxford University Press, 1930
Desnoyers, L., *Histoire du peuple hébreu dès Juges à la captivité*, three parts, Paris, A. Picard, 1922–1930
Albright, W. F., *Archaeology and the Religion of Israel*, Baltimore, Johns Hopkins University Press, 1942, 4th edition, 1956
Albright, W. F., *From Stone Age to Christianity*, Baltimore, Johns Hopkins University Press, 1946, 2nd edition, 1957
Finegan, J., *Light from the Ancient Past. The Archaeological Back-*

ground of the Hebrew-Christian Religion, Princeton, Princeton University Press, 1959

Parrot, A. and others, *Cahiers d'Archéologie Biblique,* Neuchâtel and Paris, from 1954 onwards

Wright, G. E., *Biblical Archaeology,* Philadelphia, The Westminster Press, revised edition, 1963

Grollenberg, L. H., and Van Deursen, A., *Atlas van de Bijbel,* Amsterdam and Brussels, 1958; American edition, *Atlas of the Bible,* New York, Thomas Nelson & Sons, 1956

Grollenberg, L. H., *Kleine Atlas van de Bijbel,* Amsterdam and Brussels, 1960; American edition, trans. by Mary F. Hedlund, *Shorter Atlas of the Bible,* New York, Thomas Nelson & Sons, 1959

Towards the end of the eighteenth century, special interest began to be shown in the religious ideas of Israel. Although this particular study is still, at least for the time being, a part of general theology, it is already coming to be distinguished as biblical theology, as distinct from dogmatic theology. J. P. Gabler's inaugural address *Oratio de justo discrimine theologiae biblicae et dogmaticae regundisque recte utriusque finibus* (Altorf, 1787), has become a classic in this field. The problem of the place and the task of biblical theology has come up for discussion again and again and is still disputed today. One of the earliest Old Testament theologies, however, made no problem at all. This is clear from the title of this book, written by G. L. Bauer, *Theologie des Alten Testaments oder Abriss der religiösen Begriffe der alten Hebräer von der ältesten Zeit bis auf den Anfang der christlichen Epoche* (Leipzig, 1796). We have noted that it was usual to place religious *realia* side by side in the older biblical archaeology. A certain kind of biblical theology similarly tended to amass religious concepts gleaned from the Old Testament, to sort them out, and to arrange them into a system on the lines of a dogmatic theology.

This systematic form of biblical theology became, however, less and less satisfactory as biblical scholars became more and more aware of the gradual development of Scripture and began to discover the various stages in Israel's thought. Since the plan of such books is not derived from the Bible, the biblical data are always to some extent taken out of their historical and literary context. But the system has the advantage of convenience and immediate usefulness whenever a biblical text is needed to illustrate a definite point of belief or morals. The modern manuals of this kind can certainly justify their existence on this account, and all the more so if they at the same time take the historical development of Israel's religious ideas into account. Some typical examples of works of this category are:

Davidson, A. B., *The Theology of the Old Testament*, Edinburgh, 1904
Hetzenauer, M., *Theologia biblica*, Freiburg, 1908
Ceuppens, F., *Theologia biblica*, five parts, Rome, 1938–1958
Heinisch, P., *Theologie des Alten Testaments*, Bonn, 1940
Köhler, L., *Theologie des Alten Testaments*, Tübingen, 1953; American edition, *Old Testament Theology*, Philadelphia, The Westminster Press, 1958. In his preface, this author characterizes his book as "a . . . collection of those views, thoughts and concepts . . . which are, or may be edifying."
Imschoot, P. van, *Théologie de l'Ancien Testament*, part I, *Dieu*, part II, *l'Homme*, Douai, 1954–1956

Information of an archaeological and of a biblical, theological nature is also provided in many different kinds of biblical dictionaries. One of the earliest of these is Vigouroux's *Dictionnaire de la Bible* (1895–1912). The first *Supplément* to this work appeared in 1928, and further additions are still being made.

Many encyclopedias began to appear in the beginning of this century and most of those which consisted of many volumes are now complete. Beside these, other, more concise works have been published. Some of these encyclopedias confine themselves to *realia*. One among these is still quite valuable—Kurt Galling's *Biblisches Reallexikon* (Tübingen, J. C. B. Mohr, 1937). Others, such as the excellent *Vocabulaire biblique* (Neuchâtel and Paris, 1954), produced under the leadership of J.-J. von Allmen, which appeared in an American edition under the title *Companion to the Bible* (New York, Oxford University Press, 1958), only include words of importance in the sphere of biblical theology. The excellence of this book is equaled by the detailed German *Biblisch-Theologisches Handwörterbuch zur Lutherbibel und zu neueren Über-setzungen,* a dictionary produced by a team of forty experts under the leadership of E. Osterloh and H. Engelland (Göttingen, 1959)

Both realia and biblical theology proper can be found in a dictionary compiled by a large group of Dutch and Flemish scholars. This is the *Bijbels Woordenboek* (Roermond and Maaseik, 1957), an unparalleled summa of modern industry in the field of biblical theology.

There are some good books of this kind which have been compiled with the reader of the Bible more in mind:

Gispen, W. H., Grosheide, F. W., Bruijel, F. J., and Deursen, A. van, *Bijbelse Encyclopaedie,* Kampen, 1950

Corswant, W., *Dictionnaire d'Archéologie Biblique,* Neuchâtel and Paris, 1956; American edition, *Dictionary of Life in Bible Times,* New York, Oxford University Press, 1960

Miller, M. S., and Miller, J. L., *Bible Dictionary,* New York, Harper & Row, Publishers, 6th edition 1959. This book suffers from a certain oversimplification from the theological point of view, but it is full of information and, in addition, particularly easy to understand and quite entertaining.

Up to this point, no books dealing avowedly with Israel's religion have been listed. The reason for this will now be made clear.

Interest in the religions of mankind, as this is expressed in the series of which this book forms a part, began during the second half of the previous century. It was then that the study of comparative religion began to stand on its own as a separate subject. This resulted in a totally new approach to the religion of Israel—the historical approach.

Until then, theology and philosophy had only been concerned with Israel's religion as a whole. Attempts had been made to situate the natural and the supernatural in religion philosophically—deism and the Enlightenment both did this by placing them on the same level. Insofar as the religion of Israel was involved in this process, this was seen to be expressed in a cut and dried form in the Bible. Biblical archaeology and theology too, both saw Israel's religion as a static whole. Archaeology tended to make Israel's institutions the particular object of its consideration, while theology concerned itself with Israel's ideas. The historical approach to religion came as a decisive break-through here.

On the one hand, the Bible was subjected to detailed literary criticism. On the other hand, religion was examined as a universally human phenomenon. The archaeological and literary opening up of the ancient Near East coincided with the extension of the Churches' missionary activities, with the result that widespread territories of religious life became accessible for the first time from two sides at once. Religious expressions—ideas and practices—were described and listed by religious phenomenologists. Religious historians examined the origins and development of these ideas and practices and, wherever else they were met with those who specialized in comparative religion, looked for similarities and differences, interdependence and mutual influence. It would be beside the point to classify the subject in greater detail. It should be sufficient to mention some of the standard works which have shown that the historical approach can be fruitful in an understanding of Israel's religion:

Baudissin, W. W., *Studien zur semitischen Religionsgeschichte,* two parts, Leipzig, 1876–1878
Robertson Smith, W., *Lectures on the Religion of the Semites,* London, 1889 and 1927
Lagrange, M.-J., *Etudes sur les religions sémitiques,* Paris, 1905

The spirit of the times and the influence of the history of religion can be sampled at first hand from the Dutch series *De voornaamste godsdiensten,* in which Abraham Kuenen devoted more than a dozen large pages to the religion of Israel, under the title of *De godsdienst van Israël* (Haarlem, 1869). Kuenen was, of course, a biblical scholar of international repute, and people learned Dutch in order to read him. At the invitation of the Hibbert Foundation, he delivered five lectures on *Volksgodsdienst en Wereldgodsdienst* (The Religion of the People and of the World). These lectures, published in Leiden in 1882, had as their aim the "spread of Christianity in its simplest and most easily understandable form" and the "unrestricted exercise of private judgement in matters of religion."

What had, up to that time, been called "Old Testament theology" became known as the "history of Israel's religion," and even though the former name was preserved, it was frequently mixed with fairly large doses of the "history of Israel's literature." A. Kayser's posthumously published *Theologie des Alten Testaments* (1886), subsequent editions of which were edited by K. Marti, were called, after 1897, *Geschichte der Israelitischen Religion.* On the other hand, E. Kautzsch's outline, which appeared in James Hastings' *A Dictionary of the Bible* (New York, Charles Scribner's Sons, 1927), under the title of *Religion of Israel,* was published in German as *Biblische Theologie des Alten Testaments* (Tübingen, 1911). Theology, then, was hardly to be found in most of the biblical theologies of that time. The unrest that began to be felt on this account by more and more scholars especially since the first world war led, in the twenties, to a more precise definition. Lively discussion went on in learned journals, and the titles of the most important articles are so characteristic that they should be mentioned:

Staerk, W., "Religionsgeschichte und Religionsphilosophie in ihrer Bedeutung für die biblische Theologie des Alten Testaments," *Zeitschrift für Theologie und Kirche,* Neue Folge, 4, 1924, pp. 289–300

and in *Zeitschrift für Alttestamentliche Wissenschaft:*

Steuernagel, C., "Alttestamentliche Theologie und alttestamentliche Religionsgeschichte," Beiheft 41, Marti-Festschrift, 1925, pp. 266–273
Eissfeldt, O., "Israelitisch-jüdische Religionsgeschichte und alttestamentliche Theologie," Beiheft 44, 1926, pp. 1–12
Eichrodt, W., "Hat die alttestamentliche Theologie noch selbständige Bedeutung innerhalb der alttestamentlichen Wissenschaft?" Beiheft 47, 1929, pp. 83–91

Some scholars wanted a division between theology and the history of religion, similar to the division between faith and science which had been advocated by them. Others wanted the two to be connected, but did not perceive with any clarity how this was either theoretically or practically possible. Many authors tried to avoid the problem by writing two books or one book in two parts, thus providing a historical and a systematic outline side by side. This was the case with the biblical theology which has already been mentioned—that of Hetzenauer. Procksch used the same technique in his work, following the three hundred pages of *Die Geschichtswelt* by another three hundred pages of *Die Gedankenwelt*. E. König wrote, in addition to his comprehensive history, *Geschichte der Alttestamentlichen Religion* (Gütersloh, 1924), a *Theologie des Alten Testaments* (Stuttgart, 1923), a book which polemicizes so strongly against real or imagined rationalists that it can no longer be read with pleasure, but which nonetheless deserves to rank as a courageous achievement. E. Sellin's *Israelitisch-jüdische Religionsgeschichte* also appeared in the same year as his *Theologie des Alten Testaments* (Leipzig, 1933).

The above mentioned article by Eichrodt is still worth reading. In the first place, he refers to history, which had in any case already gone far beyond the ideal of purely objective history and considers a subjective a priori as indispensable for the authentic writing of history. In the second place, he shows how the Christian and theological vision, or rather, an attitude of faith which is in tune with the evidence of the Bible, is in the nature of things an a priori in any historical description of Israel's religion. Eichrodt not only brought about a synthesis between the theological and the historical approach to the Bible in theory. He also did this in practice.

Old Testament theology has emerged rejuvenated from this lengthy debate. Not only has it regained its strictly theological character but it has also retained, from its untheological rival, the history of religion, which had suppressed it for half a century, a sense of historical development. Biblical theology has flourished as never before during the past twenty-five years. This period began with the publication of a work which almost at once became standard: W. Eichrodt's *Theologie des*

Alten Testaments, part I, *Gott und Volk* (Leipzig, 1933, Stuttgart and Göttingen, 1957), part II, *Gott und Welt* (1935, 1961), part III, *Gott und Mensch* (1939, 1961). An American edition of volume I appeared under the title *Theology of the Old Testament* and was translated by John Baker (Philadelphia, The Westminster Press, 1961). The culminating point was reached with the appearance of Gerhard von Rad's monumental *Theologie des Alten Testaments,* part I, *Die Theologie der geschichtlichen Überlieferung Israels* (Munich, 1957), part II, *Die Theologie der profetischen Überlieferung Israels* (1960). The American edition appeared under the title *Old Testament Theology* (New York, Harper & Row, Publishers, 1962).

In between the appearance of these two, literally epoch-making works several very stimulating books were produced. In addition to the work of Köhler, T. C. Vriezen's *Hoofdlijnen der Theologie van het Oude Testament* (Wageningen, 1960), American edition, *Outline of Old Testament Theology* (Newton Centre, Charles T. Branford Company), E. Jacob's *Théologie de l'Ancien Testament* (Neuchâtel and Paris, 1955), American edition, *Theology of the Old Testament* (New York, Harper & Row, Publishers, 1958), Gerhard von Rad's edition of O. Procksch's *Theologie des Alten Testaments* (Gütersloh, 1950) and the two above mentioned parts of E. Sellin's work, published under the one title of *Alttestamentliche Theologie auf religionsgeschichtlicher Grundlage* are worthy of mention.

Many books dealing with specific themes in the Bible have also appeared during this period. Among the most outstanding are:

Snaith, N. H., *The Distinctive Ideas of the Old Testament,* London, 1944; American edition, New York, Schocken Books, Inc.

Gelin, A., *Les idées maîtresses de l'Ancien Testament,* Paris, 1948; American edition, *Key Concepts of the Old Testament,* Glen Rock, N.J., The Paulist Press.

Guillet, J., *Thèmes bibliques,* Paris, 1950; American edition, *Themes of the Bible,* Notre Dame, Fides Publishers, Inc.

Rowley, H. H., *The Faith of Israel. Aspects of Old Testament Thought,* London, 1956.

Robinson, H. W., *The Religious Ideas of the Old Testament*, London, 1913, reprinted five times during this period; American edition revised by L. H. Brockington, Naperville, Illinois, Alec R. Allenson, Inc., 1956.

Johannes Pedersen's highly original and unusually stimulating work, *Israel. Its Life and Culture* (London and New York, Oxford University Press, parts I and II, 1926, parts III and IV, 1940), deserves to be mentioned here, although it is less of a theological than a psychological and sociological study, since it played a part in the renewal of exegetical thought together with the books listed above.

A century of detailed work in the philological and literary and the critical and historical spheres has resulted in a period of synthesis and integration. The newly gained insights have at last become integrated in a living human reality; first in the present-day feeling for life in the ancient Near East, then, on a basis of this, in a vital conviction concerning the individual believer and the believing community of that time, and finally in the life of the Church today and of the believing Christian of today. All this begins to resemble theology, that is, a scientific speculation which allows the Bible to function as the Bible, in other words, as a standard for the life of faith. What is recognized in Scripture is the voice of convinced faith, from which the present-day community of faith must live and which it must make its own in order to find new life. Exegesis, we now realize, has done its work properly when it allows Scripture to speak in such a way that the reader is aroused to faith and is thus able to make Scripture a living book, his Scripture. Very slowly we are approaching an answer to the question, the great question, why and how the Old Testament is a Christian book with a message for us today. In providing a partial answer to this question in his book, *Das Christuszeugnis des Alten Testaments* (in two parts, Zurich, 1934–1942), W. Vischer forced many others to think seriously along these lines:

Dodd, C. H., *The Authority of the Bible,* London, 1938; American edition, New York, Harper & Row, Publishers, 1958

Robinson, H. W., *Redemption and Revelation in the Actuality of History*, London, 1942

Robinson, H. W., *Inspiration and Revelation in the Old Testament*, London and New York, Oxford University Press, 1946

Dodd, C. H., *The Bible Today*, New York, Cambridge University Press, 1946

North, C. R., *The Old Testament Interpretation of History*, London, 1946

Charlier, C., *La lecture chrétienne de la Bible*, Maredsous, 1949; American edition, *Christian Approach to the Bible*, Westminster, Maryland, Newman Press, 1958

Danielou, J., *Sacramentum futuri. Les origines de la typologie biblique*, Paris, 1950

Lubac, H. de, *Histoire et Esprit. L'intelligence de l'Ecriture d'après Origène*, Paris, 1950

Schildenberger, J., *Vom Geheimnis des Gotteswortes*, Heidelberg, 1950

Wright, G. E., *God Who Acts. Biblical Theology as a Recital*, London, 1952; American edition, Naperville, Illinois, Alec R. Allenson, Inc., 1958

Bright, J., *The Kingdom of God in Bible and Church*, London, 1955; American edition, Nashville, Abingdon Press, 1953

A general survey of the discussions is provided in:

Baumgärtel, F., "Erwägungen zur Darstellung der Theologie des Alten Testaments," in *Theologische Literaturzeitung*, 1951, cols. 257–272

Porteous, N. W., "Old Testament Theology," in Rowley, *The Old Testament and Modern Study*, London, 1951, 1961, New York, 1952, Oxford University Press

Bleeker, L. H. K., *Hermeneutiek van het Oude Testament*, pp. 190–222 (*Christologische exegese? "Theologische" exegese*), Haarlem, 1948, *Probleme alttestamentlicher Hermeneutik, Aufsätze zum Verstehen des AT von 1950–1960*, collected by C. Westermann, Munich, 1960

Although there has been an abundance of theological literature on the Bible, the historical aspect of Israel's religion, has to a very great extent, been dealt with untheologically. The classic example of this is R. Smend's *Lehrbuch der alttestamentlichen Religionsgeschichte* (Freiburg, 1899). It is a remarkable fact that very few really comprehensive works have been produced in the last forty years, and even fewer of lasting importance. The period opened with the appearance of three outlines—now for various reasons no longer useful—by R. Kittel (Leipzig, 1921), G. Hölscher (Giessen, 1922), and R. Kreglinger (Brussels, 1922). The three most important books to appear during this period came out in 1930. The first of these was a work in two volumes by the Dutch scholar B. D. Eerdmans (Huis ter Heide; second edition in English, Leiden, 1947). This was followed by a book by A. Lods, *Israël dès origines au milieu du VIIIe siècle* (Paris, 1930), American edition, *Israel* (New York, Alfred A. Knopf, Inc., 1932), in which some three hundred pages were devoted to Israel's religion, and by the first edition of an outstanding book, *Hebrew Religion,* by W. O. E. Oesterley and T. H. Robinson (London, 1930), American second edition (New York, The Seabury Press, Inc., 1937). Apart from A. Loisy's erudite revision (Paris, 1933) of two earlier outlines (1901 and 1908) and a few books which never succeeded in attracting much attention, such as those by the Danish scholar F. F. Hvidberg (1944) and the English scholar W. L. Wardle (1936), there is little that is worthy of mention. Recently, however, two new books appeared:

Penna, A., *La Religione di Israele,* Brescia, 1958
Kaufmann, Y., *The Religion of Israel,* London, 1960–1961, a condensed
   English translation of a Hebrew work in seven volumes (Tel Aviv,
   1937–1948). An American edition of this work was translated by
Moshe Greenberg (Chicago, University of Chicago Press, 1960). Neither of these two works, however, appear to fulfill the expectations that many had of them, insofar as both tend to revert, in their approach to the subject, to conservative positions. They provide, therefore, an unsatisfactory answer to current biblical questions. What is still needed is a book which displays some sensitivity towards the relative aspects of the

biblical framework, but which at the same time retains the biblical vision of faith in its intact state and perhaps even allows this vision to come completely into its own.

Although there are so few books on the subject, there is a large number of outlines in books consisting of contributions by various authors. The first three listed below appeared more or less simultaneously. Excellent of their kind, they all illustrate well the apologetic approach:

Peters, N., in Esser and Mausbach, *Religion Christentum Kirche,* Munich, 1911

Touzard, J., in J. Bricourt, *Où en est l'histoire des religions?* Paris, 1911

Nikel, J., in Huby, Christus, *Manuel d'histoire des religions,* Paris, 1911

The last mentioned was recently reprinted, and is still more impressive that E. Magnin, in Brillant and Nédoncelle, *Apologétique,* Paris, 1937. A brief review is provided by

Vaux, R. de, in Robert, A., and Tricot, A., *Initiation biblique,* Paris 1954; American edition, *Guide to the Bible,* New York, Desclee Co., Inc., 2 vols., 1960

Barrois, A., in Gorce and Mortier, *Histoire genérale des Religions,* part I, Paris, 1948

Sutcliffe, F. F., in *A Catholic Commentary on Holy Scripture,* London, 1953; American edition, New York, Thomas Nelson & Sons

Vincent, A., in Brillant and Aigrain, *Histoire des religions,* part IV, Paris, 1956

The following provides a more detailed treatment of the subject:

Heinisch, P., in Huby and Bellon, *Christus. Handboek van de geschiedenis der godsdiensten,* Utrecht and Brussels, 1950

Among these more detailed outlines, the following are outstanding by reason of their synthetic vision:

Buber, M., in G. van der Leeuw, *De Godsdiensten der wereld*, Amsterdam, 1948

Schildenberger, J., in F. Fönig, *Christus und die Religionen der Erde,* part I, Vienna, 1951

Eichrodt, W., in F. Valtjavee, *Historia mundi,* part II, Munich, 1953

Renckens, H., "De Godsdienst van het Oude Testament," in *De Wereld van de Bijbel,* Utrecht and Antwerp, 1957

A great deal of indispensable data can also be found in the following types of manual:

A. Introduction to Holy Scripture

In addition to the classic works of O. Eissfeldt (Tübingen, 1956), Artur Weiser (Göttingen, 1957), Aage Bentzen (Copenhagen, 1958), and R. H. Pfeiffer (London, 1952), the following deserve special mention:

Robert, A., and Tricot, A., *Initiation biblique,* Paris, 1954; American edition, *Guide to the Bible,* New York, Desclee Co., Inc., 2 vols., 1960

Cools, *De Wereld van de Bijbel,* Utrecht and Antwerp, 1957

Robert and Feuillet, *Introduction à la Bible,* part I, *l'Ancien Testament,* Douai, 1959

B. Histories of Old Testament Literature

Three classic examples of this category are:

Kuenen, A., *Historisch-kritisch onderzoek naar het ontstaan en de verzameling van de boeken des Ouden Verbonds,* in three parts, Leiden, 1861-1865

Wildeboer, G., *De letterkunde des Ouden Verbonds naar de tijdsorde van haar ontstaan,* Groningen, 1893

Driver, S. R., *An Introduction to the Literature of the Old Testament,* Edinburgh, 1891

Without any trace of scholasticism and unequaled as history of art is the splendidly produced book by J. Hempel, *Die althebräische Literatur und ihr Hellenistisch-jüdisches Nachleben* (Wildpark and Potsdam, 1930). The standard French work is by A. Lods, *Histoire de la Littérature hébraïque et juive* (Paris, 1950). The three following outlines, though short, are thorough and comprehensive in their treatment:

Robinson, H. W., *The Old Testament. Its Making and Meaning,* London, 1937

Vriezen, T. C., *Oud-Israëlietische Geschriften,* The Hague, 1948; American edition, *Outline of Old Testament Theology,* Newton Centre, Charles T. Branford Co. This work was recently re-issued in an amplified edition as *De literatuur van Oud-Israël,* Servire pocket edition 50/51, 1961.

Rowley, H. H., *The Growth of the Old Testament,* London, 1950; American edition, New York, Harper & Row, Publishers

Particularly helpful to the understanding of the history of salvation is the deeply religious work by G. Auzou *La tradition biblique. Histoire des écrits sacrés du peuple de Dieu,* Paris, 1957; American edition, *Formation of the Bible. History of the Sacred Writings of the People of God,* New York, Herder & Herder, Inc., 1963.

C. Histories of Old Testament Piety

Hempel, J., *Gott und Mensch im Alten Testament,* Stuttgart, 1926

Hempel, J., *Das Ethos des Alten Testaments,* Berlin, 1938

Baumgärtel, F., *Die Eigenart der alttestamentlichen Frommigkeit,* Schwerin, 1932

Hänel, J., *Die Religion der Heiligkeit,* Gütersloh, 1931

Gelin, A., *l'Ame d'Israël dans le livre* in the series *Je sais-Je crois 65,* Paris, 1958

D. Histories of Israel or Biblical Histories of the Old Testament

The following are standard works:

Kittel, R., *Geschichte des Volkes Israel*, parts I and II, Stuttgart, 1932, part III, 1927

Oesterley, W. O. E., and Robinson, T. H., *A History of Israel*, two parts, London and New York, Oxford University Press, 1932

Ricciotti, G., *Storia d'Israele*, Turin, 1934; American edition, *History of Israel*, St. Paul, Bruce Publishing Company, 1955

Heinisch, P., *Geschichte des Alten Testaments*, Bonn, 1950

The special nature of the following book is fairly obvious from its title, but it does at the same time provide an outstanding synthesis of the course of the people of God through history:

Causse, A., *Du groupe ethnique à la communauté religieuse. Le problème sociologique de la religion d'Israël*, Paris, 1937

Among those books intended for a wider circle of readers, the following are valuable: Daniel-Rops, *Histoire sainte. Le peuple de la Bible* (Paris, 1943), and the six volume series by J. Eyckeler, *Uit het Boek der boeken* (Haarlem, 1948–1953).

Deliberately limiting himself to a reconstruction of the course of events, M. A. Beek has made a successful attempt to incorporate the recent data in his *Geschiedenis van Israël van Abraham tot Bar Kochba. Een poging*, published in De Haan's *Academische Bibliotheek* (Antwerp, 1960), American edition, *Concise History of Israel* (New York, Harper & Row, Publishers, 1964). E. H. Ehrlich's book, *Geschichte Israels* (Göschen collection 231/231a, Berlin, 1958), is an outstanding work of this category.

Equally well informed are the following two works, both of which attempt to make the recent data subservient to an understanding of the facts as history of salvation:

Bright, J., *A History of Israel*, Philadelphia, The Westminster Press, 1959, and London, 1960

Anderson, B. W., *Understanding the Old Testament*, Englewood Cliffs, Prentice-Hall, Inc., 1957

Martin Noth's book, *Geschichte Israels* (Göttingen, 1950), American edition, *History of Israel* (New York, Harper & Row, Publishers, 1960), is so important, that we must consider it at somewhat greater length.

Noth's vision, and that of the school to which he belongs, has been critically assimilated into this present book, though without any expressly polemical aim. The most recent advances in the field of Old Testament history have been brilliantly assimilated into Noth's work, which was written as a manual for students. In particular, he has made use of the findings of A. Alt. He has, however, at the same time also incorporated a very large number of dubious findings, of the kind that originate in special schools of thought. A manual must be a rounded whole and achieve a definite result. A certain line of investigation, in which there is much that is valuable, does seem to lead, in Noth's book, to a conclusion that bears a close resemblance to the dead end of a system.

Gerhard von Rad especially has made present-day exegetes very sensitive towards the constant, yet varied a priori standpoint from which the faithful community have tended to see the facts of the past throughout the centuries. According to Noth, it is precisely this a priori standpoint which has made the way in which the facts came about in detail so very obscure, to such an extent that it is impossible to deduce anything certain from the Bible any more concerning Israel's origin and fortunes in history. Noth reduces the historical content of the biblical account to small fragments, but he fails to give a satisfactory explanation as to how these isolated fragments were able to become such a coherent, living whole. He is unable to do so because he is so taken up with the reconstruction of Israel as an empirical and political quantity that he overlooks the most important fact of all: he does not enquire where the biblical fact a priori come from, and as a result he does not observe the real quantity which is the source of this biblical fact. He forgets that what appeared in the historically accessible Israel was a believing community which must have originated and developed from a long time previously. Israel did not construct for herself a creed from all kinds of heterogeneous elements. On the contrary, a definite creed made Israel. What escapes Noth is that an a priori standpoint in faith could bring about a book, after having first brought about a people among whom that book was able to develop and grow.

Using the current, literary analysis of the books of the Bible as a basis, von Rad, and after him Noth, went on to establish the most ancient form of Israel's creed. Their most important writings in this connection are:

Rad, Gerhard von, *Das formgeschichtliche Problem des Hexateuch,* 1938; reprinted in *Gesammelte Studien,* Theologische Bücherei 8, Munich, 1958

Noth, M., *Die Gesetze im Pentateuch,* 1940; reprinted in *Gesammelte Studien,* Theologische Bücherei 6, Munich, 1957

Noth, M., *Überlieferungsgeschichtliche Studien. Die sammelnden und bearbeitenden Geschichtswerke im Alten Testament,* 1943; reprinted Tübingen, 1957

Noth, M., *Überlieferungsgeschichte des Pentateuch,* Stuttgart, 1948; reprinted 1960

In these studies, the authors distinguish the themes and motives from which Israel's creed was constructed. The origin and the fortunes of each of these thematic elements are traced. The principal elements are the promise made to the patriarchs, the deliverance from Egypt, the journey through the desert, the experience on Mount Sinai, the figure of Moses, the name of Yahweh, and the conquest of Canaan. Israel's creed thus appears to be historical in the sense that each theme is ultimately based on a fact experienced by one or another human grouping. Just as Israel, seen from the ethnological point of view, was the final result of a process in which all kinds of heterogeneous ethnic groups grew together to form a single whole, so was the content of Israel's creed a tangle of traditional material belonging to each of these various groups. Group traditions became the traditions of all Israel. This is in no way satisfactorily established, since there is a lack of any binding and vitally assimilative principle, and all the more so since the elements of the creed already formed a unity before what Noth calls "Israel" existed. The various themes grew towards each other in a living space which is nowhere apparent in Noth. They formed structures and crucial complexes, around which many different kinds of elements, often of a "secondary" nature, tended to cling. The last stages of this process can occasionally be conjectured in literary shaping of Scripture (*Formgeschichte*). Noth and von Rad, however, have attempted to trace the process far into the pre-literary, oral stage (*Traditionsgeschichte*).

They observed a phenomenon which undoubtedly did occur, but Noth certainly goes too far if he believes that everything can be explained by this phenomenon. Von Rad is right in characterizing the Hexateuch as a gigantic accumulation and bringing together of the most widely diverse materials under a single and relatively simple, basic idea. It may well be true that the Bible as we have it today was filled out with traditional material from many different sources, but our real concern is the basic idea. For von Rad this incorporated the essential facts of salvation which formed the constant content of Israel's creed. For Noth, on the other hand, this basic idea lost all its binding and assimilative power because it took its origin from a chance combination.

Although Noth's book was very favorably received, his professional colleagues displayed a certain reserve with regard to his conclusions and their practical application to Israel's most ancient history. One fundamental criticism, the merit of which is that it was voiced so soon, may be indicated here. In *Bijdragen* (13, 1952, pp. 436–438), I wrote: "Noth may to some extent be right in believing that the people of Israel originated from elements coming from fairly heterogeneous sources. His view, that Israel's repository of faith was also constructed from heterogeneous elements is, however, untenable. If the salt should lose its savour . . . , if the principle itself which formed Israel is heterogeneous, how are we to explain the strikingly homogeneous phenomenon of Israel"? Towards the end of this article, I went on: "If a confession of faith derives its formative and binding power from a collective, historical experience, then this does not, in Noth's view, explain the origin of Israel as a people set apart and so completely orientated towards past experiences. If Noth is correct in his conclusions, several different peoples should have come about—a mosaic people, stemming from the group that experienced Moses, a Yahwistic people, coming from the group whose own God was Yahweh, a people delivered from Egypt, and so on, and each of these peoples would have had its own ethnic origin and, above all, its own repository of faith."

The great defect in Noth's book seems to me to be traceable to the fact that Noth acts as if there was nothing at all when Israel was not there as something historically tangible. In this respect, my outline of Israel's religion puts forward a more or less opposite view. I have tried to understand the historically ascertainable Israel as an empirical form of the true Israel of God, that is, of a community of believers. My book aims to show how Israel gradually proceeded from religious otherness and separation, to social and finally to national otherness. Indeed, it was only this separate, national phenomenon which was known as Israel. But this Israel, known to history, had a pre-history, which was above all the history of Israel's religion. Noth shows altogether too little interest in this, and this constitutes an essential deficiency in a book which sets out to give an outline of Israel's history, since, in the case of Israel, faith and history were inseparably linked. Noth has no comment to make when the political and national Israel is not tangibly present. Scripture, on the other hand, even where it fills out the past with facts from later or from alien sources, is always concerned with the nucleus of believers which is already present.

Many views similar to that of Noth have been put forward in recent years. In his Einleitung, mentioned above, A. Weiser maintains that the vital question—unanswered by Noth—is in which spiritual place did the great edifice of the pentateuchal tradition originate and develop. On the basis of this, Weiser has provided an impressive and positively constructive "literary" and "traditional" criticism (Chapter 13, *Das Problem der Entstehung der Pentateuchquellen*).

Both fundamental and technical objections are discussed in John Bright's study, *Early Israel in Recent History Writing,* Studies in Biblical Theology 19 (London, 1960), American edition (Naperville, Illinois, Alec R. Allenson, Inc., 1956).

G. A. F. Knight, in his *Christelijke theologie van het Oude Testament* (Aula pocket edition 63, pp. 124–133), American edition, *Christian Theology* of the Old Testament (Richmond, John Knox Press, 1959), reveals in a most intelligent way the incongruity of Noth's reconstruction within the plan of salvation. A. S. van der Woude, in the address which he made on his taking up office on November 8th, 1960—*Uittocht en Sinai* (Nijkerk, 1961)—devoted himself exclusively to this question, as did J. A. Soggin in his article "Alttestamentliche Glaubenszeugnisse und geschichtliche Wirklichkeit," *Theologische Zeitschrift* 17 (1961, pp. 385–398).

Special Bibliography

In MAKING the following selection of books and articles, my aim has been to mention at least one classic work and one good, modern book in which further bibliographical references can be found. Other books and articles have been mentioned, either because they are readily available or because I have taken them into account in my argument, or simply because they give some indication of the direction in which scholars are moving or have moved in the past.

Abbreviations

GS   *Gesammelte Studien zum AT* (in the series Theologische Bücherei, Munich) by M. Noth (no. 6, 1957) and G. von Rad (no. 8, 1958)

KS   *Kleine Schriften zur Geschichte des Volkes Israel* by A. Alt, part I–II, Munich (1953), part III (1959)

OM   *Opera Minora: Studies en bijdragen op Assyriologisch en Oudtestamentisch terrein* by F. M. Th. de Liagre Böhl, Groningen and Djakarta (1953)

OTS   *Oudtestamentische Studiën*, part I–XII, Leiden (1942–58)

SP   *Sacra Pagina: Handelingen van het Intern. Kath. Bijbel-congres Brussel-Leuven 1958*, part I, Paris and Gembloux (1959)

SVT   *Supplements to Vetus Testamentum*, part I–VIII, Leiden (1953–61)

ZAW   *Zeitschrift für die Alttestamentliche Wissenschaft*

Chapter I

Cools, J., et al., *Het mysterie van Israël*, Utrecht Antwerp, 1957. These studies were undertaken on the initiative of the Catholic Council for Israel of the Netherlands and its Committee for the Study of Israel (Katholieke Raad en Studiecommissie voor Israël).

Kraus, H.-J., *Geschichte der historisch-kritischen Erforschung des Alten Testaments von der Reformation bis zur Gegenwart*, Neukirchen, 1956

Baroni, V., *La Contre-Réforme devant la Bible*: *La Question Biblique*, Lausanne, 1943, with a supplement, *Aperçu sommaire de la question biblique dans L'Eglise romaine après la Contre-Réforme*

Reid, J. K. S., *The Authority of Scripture*: *A Study of the Reformation and Post-Reformation Understanding of the Bible*, London, 1957

The first of these three books completely overlooks modern Catholic exegesis, with the exception of an incidental reference to M.-J. Lagrange —as J. Langrange!—as the author of a book. The other two books are not entirely free from sectarianism, although they do incorporate the available data.

Lagrange, M.-J., *La méthode historique surtout à propos de l'Ancien Testament*, Paris, 1903

Coppens, J., *Histoire critique des livres de l'Ancien Testament*, Desclée De Brouwer, 1942; *De Geschiedkundige Ontwikkelingsgang van de Oudtestamentische Exegese vanaf de Renaissance tot en met de Aufklärung*, Antwerp and Utrecht, 1943

A competent and well documented outline of the origin and growth of the new exegesis can be found in:

Levie, J., *La Bible*: *Parole humaine et message de Dieu*, Paris and Louvain, 1958, and especially in the first part of this work: Progrès historique et exégèse biblique. A travers un siècle de recherche exégétique: de 1850 à nos jours, pp. 3–226; American edition, *The Bible*: *Word of God in Words of Men*, translated by Roger Capel, New York, P. J. Kenedy & Sons

A most illuminating survey of the entire history of biblical exegesis has been included in the second impression of the following book which is intended for the reader of the Bible:

Auzou, G., *La Parole de Dieu: Approches du mystère des Saintes Ecritures*, Paris, 1960, chapter 6: La Bible dans l'Eglise en marche, pp. 217–391; American edition *Word of God*, New York, Herder & Herder, Inc., 1960

Alt, A., *Der Rhythmus der Geschichte Syriens und Palästinas im Altertum*, 1944; reprinted in *KS*, part III, pp. 1–19

Hehn, J., *Die biblische und die babylonische Gottesidee: Die israelitische Gottesauffassung im Lichte der altorientalischen Religionsegeschichte*, Leipzig, 1913

Balscheit, B., *Alter und Aufkommen des Monotheismus in der israelitischen Religion*, Berlin, 1938

A most useful summary can be found in:

Hamp, V., "Monotheismus im Alten Testament," *SP*, pp. 516–21

The following provides a broad survey together with an extensive bibliography:

Rowley, H. H., "Moses und der Monotheismus," *ZAW* 69, 1957, pp. 1–21. What I say on page 8f. of my book should be compared with the following statement by Rowley: "Religion should be judged by the character, and not by the number of the gods, and monotheism in the Bible is more than the belief that God is one" (page 4). According to Rowley, Moses' work resulted not so much in the doctrine that Yahweh was one as in the doctrine that he was unique (page 8). His reference to S. A. Cook, *The "Truth" of the Bible* (1938), is also very pertinent: "In the interests of progressive religion we must insist that those monotheistic or monotheizing beliefs or tendencies of which we have information are not to be mentioned in the same breath with that lofty spiritual teaching which is Israel's permanent contribution to mankind" (page 21). Durr, L., *Ursprung und Ausbau der israelitisch-jüdischen Heilandserwartung*, Berlin, 1925. In order to make a contrast between the faith of the Bible and the philosophy of the Greeks, B. A. Groningen says: "The gods have no leading role notwithstanding their power; they merely manifest themselves. There is no law aiming at a final purpose, but one which determines that everything happens as it does," from *In the Grip of the Past: Essay on an Aspect of Greek Thought* (1953, page 120). This amounts to the same thing as a testimony from a very different quarter: "The historical facts, as we read them, are that, whereas India experimented with God, God experimented with Israel," from H. C. E. Zacharias, *Human Personality: Its historical emergence in India, China and Israel* (London, 1950, page 13).

Jacob, E., *La tradition historique en Israël*, Montpellier, 1946

Östborn, G., *Yahweh's Words and Deeds: A Preliminary Study into the Old Testament Presentation of History*, Uppsala and Wiesbaden, 1951

Rad, Gerhard von, *Der Anfang der Geschichtsschreibung im alten Israel*, 1944; reprinted in *GS*, pp. 148–88

Seeligmann, I. L., "Phasen uit de geschiedenis van het Joods historische bewustzijn," *Kernmomenten der antieke beschaving en haar moderne beleving*, Leiden, 1947, pp. 49–73; *Geschiedenis: Een bundel Studien over de zin der Geschiedenis*, Assen, 1944

Ridderbos, H. N., "Het Oude Testament en de Geschiedenis," *Gereformeerd Theol. Tijdschrift* 57, 1957, pp. 112–20; 58, 1958, pp. 1–9

J. Danielou frequently deals with the relationship between general and particular revelation, for example in the following books, all of which have been published in Paris: *Le mystère du salut des nations* (1946); American edition, *Salvation of the Nations* (Notre Dame, University of Notre Dame Press, 1962); *Le mystère de l'Avent* (1948); *Essai sur le mystère de l'histoire* (1953); *Les saints "païens" de l'AT* (1956). A clear synthesis can be found in *Le Problème Théologique des Religions non chrétiennes* (Rome, 1956); originally printed in *Archivio di Filosofia*. E. Schillebeeckx is also worth reading in this connection, especially: *Christus, Sacrament van de Godsontmoeting* (Bilthoven, 1959, pp. 13–22 et passim); American edition, *Christ the Sacrament of the Encounter with God* (London and New York, Sheed & Ward, 1963); "Heilige Schrift," *Theologisch Woordenboek* (Roermond and Maaseik, 1958, part III, pp. 4294–99); *Op zoek naar de levende God* (Utrecht and Nijmegen, 1958); "God en de Mens," *Theologische Week over de Mens* (Nijmegen, 1959); "God op de helling," *Tijdschrift voor Geestelijk Leven* 15 (1959, pp. 397–409); finally, a carefully formulated synthesis is provided in "De betekenis van het niet-godsdienstig humanisme voor het hedendaagse katholicisme," *Modern niet-godsdienstig humanisme* (Nijmegen, 1961).

Rahner, K., "Het christendom en de niet-christelijke godsdiensten," *Kerk en Ruimte,* Hilversum, 1961

A detailed review of the problem and its history will be found in:

Benz, E., *Ideen zu einer Theologie der Religionsgeschichte* (Akad. Wissensch. u. Literatur, Abh. geostes- u. sozialwissensch. Klasse 1960, 5), Mainz and Wiesbaden, 1961, pp. 423–96.

Koopmans, J. J., "Beknopt overzicht van de cultuur van het Oude Nabije Oosten als achtergrond van de Bijbel," *Gereformeerd Theol. Tijdschrift* 59 (1959, pp. 1–35). This article includes a detailed bibliography.

Wright, J. E., *The Old Testament against its Envirmonment,* London, 1950

Moscati, S., *Die altsemitischen Kulturen* (Urban-Rucher 3), Stuttgart, 1960

Fichtner, J., "Die Bewältigung heidnischer Vorstellung und Praktiken in der Welt des Alten Testaments," *Baumgärtel-Festschrift,* Erlangen, 1959, pp. 24–40

Pinard de la Boullaye, H., "La thèse de la condescendence," *L'étude comparée des religions,* Paris, 1929, part I, pp. 552–71; "Les infiltrations païennes dans l'Ancienne Loi, d'après les Pères de l'Eglise," *Recherches de Science Religieuse* 9, 1920, pp. 197–221. This important article goes back to a simply written, more broadly based study by H. Pinard, "Infiltrations païennes dans le culte juif et dans le culte chrétien," *La Revue Apologétique,* Brussels, 1908–9, pp. 465–507, 611–57.

Chapter II

Tichelen, Th. van, *In den patriarkentijd,* Louvain, 1923; "an outline of the situation and civilization of Canaan at the time of the great patriarchs"

Ridderbos, J., *Abraham de vriend Gods,* Kampen, 1928

Edelkoort, A. H., *Pioniers van het Geloof: Het Leven der Aartsvaders,* Amsterdam, 1948

Trigt, F. van, *De Verhalen over de Aartsvaders*, Tielt and The Hague, 1961

Dhorme, E., *L'évolution religieuse d'Israel*, part I, *La religion des Hébreux nomades*, Brussels, 1937

Vaux, R. de, "Les Patriarchs hébreux et les découvertes modernes," *Revue Biblique*, 1946–49. This series of articles has been published in book form in a German translation under the title: *Die hebräischen Patriarchen und die modernen Entdeckungen*, Düsseldorf, 1959

Böhl, F. M. Th. de Liagre, *Das Zeitalter Abrahams*, 1930; adapted and augmented in *OM*, pp. 26–49

Schneider, N., "Die religiöse Umwelt Abrahams in Mesopotamien," *Miscellanea biblica B. Ubach*, Montserrat, 1953, pp. 49–67

Beek, M. A., "Das Problem des Aramäischen Stammvaters (Deut. XXVI 5)," *OTS* VIII, pp. 193–212

Alt, A., *Der Gott der Väter*, 1929; reprinted in *KS*, part I, pp. 1–78

Gemser, B., *Vragen rondom de Patriarchenreligie* (speech), Groningen, 1958

Keller, C. A., "Über einige alttle. Heiligtumslegenden," *ZAW* 67, 1955, pp. 141–68; 68, 1956, pp. 85–97

Rad, Gerhard von, "Verheissenes Land und Jahwes Land," *Hexateuch*, 1943; reprinted in *GS*, pp. 87–100; *Es ist noch eine Ruhe vorhanden dem Volke Gottes*, 1933; reprinted in *GS*, pp. 101–8

Hoftijzer, J., *Die Verheissungen an die drei Erzväter*, Leiden, 1956

Junker, H., "Segen als heilsgeschichtliches Motivwort im AT," *SP*, pp. 548–58

Schreiner, J., "Segen für die Völker in der Verheissung an die Väter," *Biblische Zeitschrift*, Neue Folge 6, 1962, pp. 1–31; "Abraham, Père des Croyants," *Cahiers Sioniens* 5, 1951, pp. 93–232; see also *Bible et Vie Chrétienne* 10, 1955, pp. 57–86

Lecuyer, J., *Abraham notre père*, Paris, 1956

Keller, C. A., "Grundsätzliches zur Auslegung der Abraham-Überlieforung in der Genesis," *Theologische Zeitschrift* (Bâle) 12, 1956, pp. 425–45

George, A., "Le sacrifice d'Abraham," *Études de Critique et d'Histoire Religieuses* (Mélanges Vaganay), Lyons, 1948, pp. 99–110

Henninger, J., "Was bedeutet die rituelle Teilung eines Tieres in zwei Hälften?" *Biblica* 34, 1953, pp. 244–53

Snijders, L. A., "The Covenant with Abraham," *OTS* XII, pp. 261–79

Schildenberger, J., "Jakobs nächtlicher Kampf mit dem Elohim am Jabok," *Miscellanea biblica B. Ubach,* Montserrat, 1953, pp. 69–96

Trigt, F. van, "La signification de la lutte de Jacob près du Yabbok," *OTS* XII, pp. 280–309

Chapter III

Buck, A. de, "De Hebreën in Egypte," *Varia Historica,* Assen, 1954, pp. 1–16

Vergote, J., *Joseph en Egypte: Genèse chap. 37–50 à la lumière des études égyptologiques récentes,* Louvain, 1959

Montet, P., *L'Egypte et la Bible,* Neuchâtel, 1959

Janssen, J. M. A., *Ramses III: Proeve van een historisch beeld zijner regering,* Leiden, 1948. An attractive and informative little book, giving a lively outline of the situation at the time. *Het Boek der Wijsheid van Amen-em-ope, den zoon van Kanecht,* translated from the Egyptian by W. D. van Wijngaarden, Santpoort, 1930

Rad, Gerhard von, "Josephgeschichte und ältere Chokma," *SVT* I, pp. 120–7; reprinted in *GS,* pp. 272–80

Böhl, F. M. Th. de Liagre, *Wortspiele im AT,* 1926; reprinted in *OM,* pp. 11–25; *Die fünfzig Namen des Marduk,* 1937; reprinted and augmented in *OM,* pp. 282–312

Noth, M., *Die israelitischen Personennamen in Rahmen der gemeinsemitischen Namengebung,* Stuttgart, 1928

Oosterhoff, B. J., *Israëlitische Persoonsnamen,* Delft, 1953

Grether, O., *Name und Wort Gottes im Alten Testament,* Giessen, 1934

Dürr, L., *Die Wertung des göttlichen Wortes im Alten Testament und im antiken Orient,* Leipzig, 1938

Johnson, A. R., *The One and the Many in the Israelite Conception of God,* Cardiff, 1942

Baudissin, W. W., *Kurios als Gottesname im Judentum und seine Stelle in der Religionsgeschichte,* 4 parts, Giessen, 1929

Eerdsmans, B. D., "The Name Jahu," *OTS* V, pp. 1–29

Thierry, G. J., "The Pronunciation of the Tetragrammaton," *OTS* V, pp. 30–42

Alfrink, B., "La prononciation 'Jehova' du tétragramme," *OTS* V, pp. 43–62

Vriezen, Th. C., "'Ehje 'ašer 'ehje," *Festschrift A. Bertholet*, Tübingen, 1950, pp. 498–512

Dhorme, E., "Le nom du Dieu d'Israël," *Revue de l'histoire des religions* 141, 1952, pp. 5–18

Dubarle, A.-M., "La signification du nom de Jahweh," *Revue des sciences phil, et théol.* 35, 1951, pp. 3–21

Lambert, G., "Que signifie le nom divin YHWH?" *Nouvelle Revue Théol.* 74, 1952, pp. 897–915

Zimmerli, W., "Ich bin Jahwe," *Geschichte und Altes Testament* (*Alt-Festschrift*), Tübingen, 1953, pp. 179–209

Mayer, R., "Der Gottesname Jahwe im Lichte der neueren Forschung," *Biblische Zeitschrift*, Neue Folge 2, 1958, pp. 26–53

Chapter IV

Vaux, R. de, "A propos du second centenaire d'Astruc: Réflection sur l'état actuel de la critique du Pentateuque," *SVT* I, pp. 182–98

Cazelles, H., "A propos du Pentateuque," *Biblica* 35, 1954, pp. 279–98

Kuschke, A., "Die Lagervorstellung der priesterschriftlichen Erzählung," *ZAW* 63, 1951, pp. 75–105

Rad, Gerhard von, *Das Geschichtsbild des chronistischen Werkes*, Stuttgart, 1930

Parrot, A., *The Temple of Jerusalem*, London, 1957

Kristensen, W. B., *De Ark van Jahwe*, 1933; reprinted in *Verzamelde Bijdragen tot kennis der antieke godsdiensten*, Amsterdam, 1947, pp. 169–99

Brouwer, C., *De ark*, Baarn, 1955

Gressmann, H., *Die Lade Jahves und das Allerheiligste des salomonischen Tempels*, Berlin, 1920

Zapletal, V., *Alttestamentliches*, Freiburg, 1903, IV: *Das Ephod*, pp. 55–77

Rad, Gerhard von, *Zelt und Lade*, 1931; reprinted in *GS*, pp. 109–29

Morgenstern, J., *The Ark, the Ephod and the "Tent of Meeting,"* Cincinnati, 1945

Eissfeldt, O., "Lade und Stierbild," *ZAW* 58, 1940–1, pp. 190–215

Danielou, J., *Le signe du temple ou la Présence de Dieu,* Paris, 1942; American edition, *Presence of God,* translated by Walter Roberts, New York, Taplinger Publishing Co., Inc., 1959

Schmidt, M., *Prophet und Tempel: Eine Studie zum Problem der Gottesnähe im Alten Testament,* Zollikon and Zürich, 1948

Congar, Y., *Le mystère du Temple ou l'Economie de la Présence de Dieu à sa créature de la Genèse à l'Apocalypse,* Paris, 1958; American edition, *Mystery of the Temple,* New York, The Newman Press, Westminster, Maryland, 1962

Grollenberg, L., "Over Gods women in zijn tempel te Jerusalem," *Tijdschrift voor Theologie* 1, 1961, pp. 91–108

Lefevre, A., "Lévitique (organization)," Vigouroux' *Dictionnaire de la Bible,* Supplement V, pp. 389–97

Eberharter, A., "Der israelitische Levitismus in der vorexilischen Zeit," *Zeitschrift für kath. Theologie* 52, 1928, pp. 492–518

Mohlenbrink, K., "Die levitischen Uberlieferung des Alten Testaments," *ZAW* 52, 1954, pp. 184–230

Dussaud, R., *Les origines cananéennes du sacrifice israélite,* Paris, 1941

Medebielle, A., *L'expiation dans l'Ancien et le Nouveau Testament,* Rome, 1924, pp. 9–165

Moraldi, L., *Espiazione sacrificiale e riti espiatori nell'ambiente biblico,* Rome, 1956

Stamm, J. J., *Erlösen und Vergeben im Alten Testament: Eine begriffsgeschichtliche Untersuchung,* Diss. Basel, Berne, 1940

Duller, J., *Die Reinheits- und Speisegesetze des Alten Testaments,* Munster i. W., 1917

Gispen, W. H., *De levietische wet op de melaatsheid* (speech), Kampen, 1945; "The Distinction between Clean and Unclean," *OTS* V, pp. 190–6

Maertens, Th., *C'est fete en l'honneur de Yahvé,* Desclée De Brouwer, 1961

Ten Boom, W., *De drie hoofdfeesten van het Oude Testament en hun symboliek,* The Hague, 1940

Auerbach, E., "Die Feste im Alten Israel," *Vetus Testamentum* 8, 1958, pp. 1–18

Haag, H., "Ursprung und Sinn der alttestamentlichen Paschafeier," *Luzerner Theol. Studien* 1, 1954, pp. 17–46

Kraus, H.-J., "Zur Geschichte des Passah-Massot-Festes im Alten Testament," *Evangelische Theologie* 18, 1958, pp. 47–67

Kutsch, E., "Erwägungen zur Geschichte der Passahfeier und des Massotfestes," *Zeitschrift für Theologie und Kirche* 55, 1958, pp. 1–35

Lohse, E., "Pentekoste," *Theologisches Wörterbuch zum Neuen Testament,* part VI, pp. 44–53

Kraus, H.-J., *Gottesdienst im Alten Israel: Studien zur Geschichte des Laubhüttenfestes,* Munich, 1954; American edition, *People of God in the Old Testament,* New York, Association Press, 1958

Danielou, J., "Les Quatre-Temps de septembre et la Fête des Tabernacles," *La Maison Dieu* 46, 1956, pp. 114–37; "Le symbolisme eschatologique de la Fête des Tabernacles," *Irénikon* 31, 1958, pp. 19–40

Tur-Sinai, N. H., "Sabbat und Woche," *Bibliotheca Orientalis* 8, 1951, pp. 14–24

Botterweck, G., "Der Sabbat im Alten Testament," *Theologische Quartalschrift* 134, 1954, pp. 134–47, 448–57

Jenni, E., *Die theologische Begründung des Sabbatgebotes im Alten Testament,* Zollikon and Zürich, 1956

This outstanding publication refers, on page 14, note 25, to W. Eichrodt's article: "Gottes ewiges Reich und seine Wirklichkeit in der Geschichte nach alttestlicher Offenbarung," Theologische Studien und Kritiken 108, 1937, pp. 19f. The following quotation is probably the best summary of the interpretation of Israel's worship advocated in my book: "No matter from what roots Israel's various acts of worship may originally have sprung—and comparative religion places a great deal of emphasis on the relationship of these acts with pagan customs—they preserve their unity by serving as impressive symbols of God's dominion and by being contained with increasing consistency within this principal idea. Everything in Israel—space and time, possessions and life itself—belonged to Yahweh and was sustained by his blessing. This fact was bound to be expressed in the content of the law of worship. Israel's feasts and sacrifices, her rites of cleanness, and her cultic ceremonies all served to acknowledge God's unbounded power to dispose over and to bless man. In all this the Israelite was reminded that his entire life was dedicated to God and was given its meaning by its external representation of the character of the people of Yahweh's personal possession."

Galling, K., *Die Erwählungstraditionen Israels nach dem Alten Testament*, Giessen, 1928

Rowley, H. H., *The Biblical Doctrine of Election*, London, 1950

Vriezen, Th. C., *Die Erwählung Israels nach dem Alten Testament*, Zürich, 1953

Wildberger, H., *Jahwes Eigentumsvolk: Eine Studie zur Traditionsgeschichte und Theologie der Erwählungsgedanken*, Zürich, 1960

Rost, L., *Die vorstufen von Kirche und Synagoge im Alten Testament*, Stuttgart, 1938

Lods, A., "Les antécedents de la notion d'Eglise en Israël et dans le Judaisme," *Origine et nature de l'Eglise (Conférences prononcées à la Faculté libre de Théologie protestante)*, Paris, 1939, pp. 7–50

Aalders, G. Ch., *Het Verbond Gods*, Kampen, 1939

Kritzinger, J., *Qehal Jahweh: Wat dit is en wie daaraan behoort* (essay), Kampen, 1957

Hulst, A. R., "Der Name 'Israel' im Deuteronomium," *OTS* IX, pp. 65–106

Zimmerli, W., "Israel im Buche Ezechiel," *Vetus Testamentum* 8, 1958, pp. 75–90

Alt, A., *Die Ursprünge des israelitischen Rechts*, 1934; reprinted in *KS*, part I, pp. 278–332

Cazelles, H., *Etudes sur le Code de l'Alliance*, Paris, 1946

Brongers, H. A., *Hammurabi*, The Hague, 1949

David, M., "The Codex Hammurabi and its Relation to the Provisions of Law in Exodus," *OTS* VII, pp. 149–78

Aalders, J. G., *De verhouding tussen het Verbondsboek van Mozes en de Codex Hammurabi*, The Hague, 1957

Stamm, J. J., *Der Dekalog im Lichte der neueren Forschung*, Berne, 1958; French translation, *Le Décalogue*, etc., Neuchâtel, 1959

Kraus, H.-J., *Die prophetische Verkündigung des Rechts in Israel*, Zollikon, 1957

Mendenhall, G. E., *Recht und Bund in Israel und dem Alten Vordern Orient*, Zürich, 1960

Würthwein, E., "Der Sinn des Gesetzes im Alten Testament," *Zeitschrift für Theologie und Kirche* 55, 1958, pp. 255–70

Buber, M., *Moses*, Oxford, 1947; American edition, *Moses: The Revelation and the Covenant*, New York, Harper & Row, Publishers, 1958

Auerbach, E., *Moses*, Amsterdam, 1953

"Moïse, l'homme de l'Alliance," *Cahiers Sioniens* VIII, 1954, pp. 2–4; reprinted Paris, 1955. The figure of Moses in history and in the tradition of the Old Testament, Judaism, Christianity, Islam, and the liturgy.

Cazelles, H., "Moïse," Vigouroux' *Dictionnaire de la Bible, Supplément* V, pp. 1308–37

Neher, A., *Moïse et la vocation juive*, Paris, 1957; American edition, *Moses and the Vocation of the Jewish People*, New York, Harper & Row, Publishers, 1959

Rad, Gerhard von *Moses* (in the series World Christian Books, no. 32), London, 1960

Smend, R., *Das Mosebild von Heinrich Ewald bis Martin Noth*, Tübingen, 1959

Chapter V

Rowley, H. H., *From Joseph to Joshua*, London, 1950

Rad, Gerhard von, *Die deuteronomische Geschichtstheologie in den Königsbüchern*, 1947; reprinted in *GS*, pp. 189–204

Vriezen, Th. C., "De compositie van de Samuël-boeken,"*Orientalia Neerlandica*, Leiden, 1948, pp. 167–87

Buber, M., "Die Erzählung von Sauls Königswahl," *Vetus Testamentum* 6, 1956, pp. 113–73

Wildberger, H., "Samuel und die Entstehung des israelitischen Königtums," *Theologische Zeitschrift* 13, 1957, pp. 442–69

Weiser, A., "Samuel und die Vorgeschichte des israelitischen Königtums," *Zeitschrift für Theologie und Kirche* 57, 1960, pp. 141–61

Noth, M., *Das System der zwölf Stämme Israels*, Stuttgart, 1930

Hoftijzer, J., "Enige opmerkingen rond het Israëlitische 12-stammensysteem," *Nederlandse Theologische Tijdschrift* 14, 1959–60, pp. 241–63

Alt, A., *Die Landnahme der Israeliten in Palästina*, 1925; reprinted in *KS*, part I, pp. 89–125; *Josua*, 1936; reprinted in *KS*, part I, pp. 176–92; *Erwägungen über die Landnahme der Israeliten in Palästina*, 1939; reprinted in *KS*, part I, pp. 126–75

Simons, J., " 'Landnahme' en 'Landesausbau' in de Israëlitische traditie," *Bijdragen Ned. Jez.* 4, 1941, pp. 201–23

Galling, K., *Die israelitische Staatsverfassung in ihrer vororientalischen Umwelt*, Leipzig, 1929

Alt, A., *Die Staatenbildung der Israeliten in Palästina*, 1930; reprinted in *KS*, part II, pp. 1–65; *Das Grossreich Davids*, 1950; reprinted in *KS*, part II, pp. 66–75; *Israels Gaue unter Salomo*, 1913; reprinted in *KS*, part II, pp. 76–89; *Jerusalems Aufstieg*, 1925; reprinted in *KS*, part III, pp. 243–57; "Der Anteil des Königtums an der sozialen Entwicklung in den Reichen Israel und Juda," 1955; printed for the first time in *KS*, part III, pp. 348–72

Fohrer, G., "Der Vertrag zwischen König und Volk in Israel," *ZAW* 71, 1959, pp. 1–22

Noth, M., *Amt und Berufung im Alten Testament* (speech), Bonn, 1958

Lagrange, M.-J., "Le Règne de Dieu dans l'Ancien Testament," *Revue Biblique* 17, 1908, pp. 36–61

Mowinckel, S., *Psalmenstudien*, part II, *Das Thronbesteigungsfest Jahwäs und der Ursprung der Eschatologie*, 1920; reprinted in Amsterdam, 1961; American edition, *Psalms in Israel's Worship*, translated by D. R. Ap-Thomas, Nashville, Abington Press, 1962

Böhl, F. M. Th. de Liagre, *Nieuwjaarsfeest en Koningsdag in Babylon en Israël*, 1927; reprinted in *OM*, pp. 263–81.

Noth, M., *Gott, König, Volk im Alten Testament*, 1950; reprinted in *GS*, pp. 188–229

Alt, A., *Gedanken über das Königtum Jahwes*, 1945; reprinted in *KS*, part I, pp. 345–57

Buber, M., *Königtum Gottes*, Heidelberg, 1956

Feuillet, A., "Les Psaumes eschatologiques du Règne de Yahvé," *Nouv. Revue Theol.* 73, 1951, pp. 244–60, 352–63

Kraus, H.-J., *Die Königsherrschaft Gottes im Alten Testament: Untersuchungen zu den Liedern von Jahwes Thronbesteigung*, Tübingen, 1951

North, C. R., "The Religious Aspect of Hebrew Kingship," *ZAW* 50, 1932, pp. 8–38

Boer, P. A. H. de, *Het Koningschap in Oud-Israël* (speech), Amsterdam, 1938

Fraine, J. de, *L'aspect religieux de la royauté israélite: L'institution monarchique dans l'AT et dans les textes Mésopotamiens*, Rome, 1954

Johnson, A. R., *Sacral Kingship in Ancient Israel*, Cardiff, 1955

Koolhaas, A. A., *Theocratie en Monarchie in Israël* (essay), Wageningen, 1957

Hooke, S. H. et al., *Myth, Ritual and Kingship: Essays on the Theory and Practice of Kingship in the Ancient Near East and in Israel*, Oxford and New York, Oxford University Press, 1958

Bernhardt, K.-H., "Das Problem der altorientalischen Königsideologie im AT unter besonderer Berücksichtigung der Geschichte der Psalmenexegese dargestellt und kritisch gewürdigt," *SVT*, part VIII

Simons, J., *Opgravingen in Palestina*, Roermond and Maaseik, 1936; chapter XI: Godsdienst en Doodenzork, pp. 358–86

Vincent, L.-H., "La notion biblique de haut lieu," *Revue Biblique* 55, 1948, pp. 245–78, 438–45

Albright, W. F., "The High Place in Ancient Palestine," *SVT* IV, pp. 242–58

Kraus, H.-J., "Gilgal: Ein Beitrag zur Kultusgeschichte Israels," *Vetus Testamentum* 1, 1951, pp. 181–99

Ridderbos, J., *Israël en de Baäls: Afval of ontwikkeling*, Nijverdal, 1915

Wendel, A., *Säkularisierung in Israels Kultur*, Gutersloh, 1934

Nyberg, H. S., "Studien zum Religionskampf im Alten Testament," *Archiv für Religionswissenschaft* 35, 1938, pp. 329–87

Ostborn, K., *Yahweh und Baal,* Lund, 1956

Balscheit, B., *Gottesbund und Staat,* Zollikon and Zürich, 1940

Nystrom, S., *Beduinentum und Jahwismus,* Lund, 1946. A study of the "desert ideal."

Rost, L., "Sinaibund und Davidsbund," *Theol. Literaturzeitung* 72, 1947, pp. 129–34

Van den Bussche, H., "Le texte de la prophétie de Nathan sur la dynastie davidique (II Sam. VII, I Chron. XVII)," *Ephemerides Theol. Lovan.* 24, 1948, pp. 354–94

Simon, M., "La prophétie de Nathan et le Temple (Remarques sur II Sam. 7)," *Revue d'hist. et phil. religieuses* 32, 1952, pp. 41–58

Noth, M., "Jerusalem und die israelitische Tradition," *OTS* VIII, pp. 28–46; reprinted in *GS,* pp. 172–87

Schmidt, H., "Jahwe und die Kulttradition von Jerusalem," *ZAW* 67, 1955, pp. 168–97

Vaux, R. de, "Le schisme religieux de Jeroboam Ier," *Angelicum* 20, 1943, *Biblica et Orientalia R. P. Vosté dicata,* pp. 77–91

Talmon, S., "Divergences in Calendar-Reckoning in Ephraim and Juda," *Vetus Testamentum* 8, 1958, pp. 48–74

Alt, A., *Das Königtum in den Reichen Israel und Juda,* 1951; reprinted in *KS,* part II, pp. 116–34; *Der Stadtstaat Samaria,* 1954; reprinted in *KS,* part III, pp. 258–302

Vriezen, Th. C., *Hosea: Profeet en cultuur,* Groningen, 1941; "La tradition de Jacob dans Osée XII," *OTS* I, pp. 64–78

Wolff, H. W., "Hoseas geistige Heimat," *Theol. Literaturzeitung* 81, 1956, 83–94

Rad, Gerhard von, *Deuteronomium-Studien,* Göttingen, 1947; American edition, *Studies in Deuteronomy,* Naperville, Ill., Alec R. Allenson, Inc., 1950

Alt, A., "Die Heimat des Deuteronomiums," 1953, *KS,* part II, pp. 250–75

Dumermuth, F., "Zur deuteronomischen Kulttheologie und ihre Voraussetzungen," *ZAW* 70, 1958, pp. 59–98

Rowley, H. H., "The Prophet Jeremiah and the Book of Deuteronomy," *Studies in Old Testament Prophecy (presented to T. H. Robinson),*

Edinburgh, 1950, pp. 157–74; American edition, Naperville, Ill., Alec R. Allenson, Inc., 1957

Böhl, F. M. Th. de Liagre, *Nebukadnezar en Jojachin*, 1942; reprinted in *OM*, pp. 423–9

Chapter VI

Robinson, T. H., "Neuere Phopheten-Forschung," *Theol. Rundschau* 3, 1931, pp. 75–103

Porteous, N. W., "Prophecy," H. W. Robinson, *Record and Revelation*, Oxford, 1938, pp. 216–49

Eissfeldt O., "The Prophetic Literature," H. H. Rowley, *The Old Testament and Modern Study*, Oxford and New York, Oxford University Press, 1951, pp. 115–61

Fohrer, G., "Neuere Literatur zur alttestamentlichen Prophetie," *Theol. Rundschau* 19, 1951, pp. 277–346; 20, 1952, pp. 193–271, 295–361

Rowley, H. H., "The Nature of Prophecy in the Light of Recent Study," *Harvard Theological Review* 38, 1945, pp. 1–38; adapted and reprinted in his *The Servant of the Lord and Other Essays on the Old Testament*, London, 1952, pp. 91–128

Dürr, L., *Wellen und Wirken der alttestamentlichen Propheten*, Düsseldorf, 1926

Junker, H., *Prophet und Seher*, Trier, 1927

Volz, P., *Prophetengestalten des Alten Testaments*, Stuttgart, 1938

Neher, A., *L'essence du prophétisme*, Paris, 1955

Renckens, H., *De Profeet van de Nabijheid Gods*, Tielt and The Hague, 1961

Rowley, H. H. et al., *Studies in Old Testament Prophecy*, Edinburgh, 1950; American edition, Naperville, Ill., Alec R. Allenson, Inc., 1957

Van den Oudenrijn, M. A., "Extatische verschijnselen bij de oudtestamentische profeten," *Studia Catholica* 1, 1924, pp. 351–83

Ridderbos, J., "Profetie en Ekstase, Aalten (n.d.)," *Gereformeerd Theol. Tijdschrift* 41, 1940

Edelkoort, A. H., "Prophet and Prophet," *OTS* V, pp. 179–89

Ridderbos, H. N., *Israëls Profetie en "Profetie" buiten Israël*, Delft, 1955

Rad, Gerhard von, "Die falschen Propheten," *ZAW* 51, 1933, pp. 109–20

Quell, G., *Wahre und falsche Propheten: Versuch einer Interpretation*, Gütersloh, 1952

Van den Born, A., *Profetie metterdaad: Een studie over de symbolische handelingen der Profeten*, Roermond and Maaseik, 1947

Fohrer, G., *Die symbolischen Handlungen der Propheten*, Zürich, 1953

Lattey, C., "The Prophets and Sacrifice: A Study in Biblical Relativity," *Journal of Theol. Studies* 42, 1941, pp. 155–65

Hentschke, R., *Die Stellung der vorexilischen Schriftpropheten zum Kultus*, Berlin, 1957

Roubos, K., *Profetie en cultus in Israël* (essay), Wageningen, 1956

Kraus, J.-J., *Prophetie und Politik*, Munich, 1952

Jenni, E., *Die politischen Voraussagen der Propheten*, Zürich, 1956

Hesse, F., *Das Verstockungsproblem im Alten Testament*, Berlin, 1955

Vaux, R. de, "Le 'Reste d'Israël' d'après les Prophètes," *Revue Biblique* 42, 1933, pp. 526–39

Muller, W. E., *Die Vorstellung vom Rest im Alten Testament*, Leipzig, 1939

Garofalo, S., *La nozione profetica del "Resto d'Israele,"* Rome, 1942

Dreyfus, F., "La doctrine du reste d'Israël chez le prophète Isaïe," *Revue des sciences phil. et théol.* 39, 1955, pp. 361–86

Delorme, J., "Conversion et pardon selon le prophète Ezéchiel," *Mémorial J. Chaine*, Lyons, 1950, pp. 115–44

Edelkoort, A. H., *De Christusverwachting in het OT*, Wageningen, 1941

Heinisch, P., *Christus der Erlöser im Alten Testament*, Graz, 1955

Mowinckel, S., *He that cometh*, Oxford, 1956; American edition, translated by G. W. Anderson, Nashville, Abington Press, 1956

Leeuw, V. de, *De Ebed Jahweh-Profetieën* (essay), Assen, 1956

Bentzen, A., *Messias, Moses redivivus, Menschensohn*, Zürich, 1948

Fohrer, G., *Messiasfrage und Bibelverständnis*, Tubingen, 1957

Kahmann, J., "Die Heilszukunft in ihrer Beziehung zur Heilsgeschichte nach Isaias 40–55," *Biblica* 32, 1951, pp. 65–89, 141–72

Brongers, H. A., *De Scheppingstradities bij de Profeten* (essay), Amsterdam, 1945

Vriezen, Th. C., "Prophecy and Eschatology," *SVT* I, pp. 199–229

Gross, H., *Weltherrschaft als religiöse Idee im Alten Testament*, Bonn, 1953

Lagrange, M.-J., "Pascal et les Prophéties messianiques," *Revue Biblique* 15, 1906, pp. 533–60

Vaccari, A., "La 'theoria' nella scuola esegetica di Antiochia," *Biblica* 1, 1920, pp. 3–36

Peters, N., "Sache und Bild in den messianischen Weissagungen," *Theol. Quartelschrift* 112, 1931, pp. 451–89

Coppens, J., "Les particularités du style prophétique," *Nouvelle Revue Théologique* 59, 1932, pp. 673–93

Schildenberger, J., "Weissagung und Erfüllung," *Biblica* 24, 1943, pp. 107–24, 205–30

Van der Ploeg, J., "Profetie en Vervulling," *Studia Catholica*, 28, 1953, pp. 81–93

Gross, H., *Die Idee des ewigen und allgemeinen Weltfriedens im Alten Orient und im Alten Testament*, Trier, 1956

This last mentioned book comes to a very subtly and purely formulated viewpoint with regard to the "terrestrial and material" data with which the prophets filled out the future of salvation: "One remarkable fact emerges from a review of such promises based on the history of revelation. It would seem that the images were completely absorbed in external realities in the early period and direct man's gaze to a higher reality behind these external realities only by way of allusion. At a later stage, however, although the original reality did not in any sense disappear from the message of the prophets, the images became much more transparent, and were chiefly oriented towards the other, higher reality, so that it was essentially expressed" (page 160). This view, which is the answer given by Gross to the question of "image and matter in Israel's hope of peace," would appear to be in accordance with what I have tried to say in my book on pages 83–90 and 249–65.

This smooth shift in conceptual content Gross calls "Motivtransposition." He discusses it again in his essay entitled " 'Motivtransposition' als Überlieferungsgeschichtliches Prinzip im Alten Testament," *SP*, pp. 325–34. See also his article "Zum Problem Verheissung und Erfüllung," *Biblische Zeitschrift*, Neue Folge 3 (1959), pp. 3–17.

Chapter VII

Lods, A., *Les prophètes d'Israël et les debuts du Judaïsme*, Paris, 1935; American edition, *Prophets and the Rise of Judaism*, translated by S. H. Hooke, New York, E. P. Dutton & Co., Inc., 1937

Lagrange, M.-J., *Le Judaïsme avant Jésus-Christ*, Paris, 1931; *Le Messianisme chez les Juifs*, Paris, 1909

Welch, A. C., *The Work of the Chronicler: Its Purpose and Date*, London, 1939

Van den Bussche, H., *Het probleem van Kronieken*, Louvain, 1950

Brunet, A.-M., "Le Chroniste et ses sources," *Revue Biblique* 60, 1953, pp. 481–508; 61, 1954, pp. 349–86; "La Théologie du Chroniste: Théocratie et Messianisme," *SP*, pp. 384–97

Noth, M., "La catastrophe de Jérusalem en l'an 587 avant J.-Chr. et sa signification pour Israël," *Revue d'hist. et phil. religieuses* 33, 1953, pp. 81–102

Beek, M. A., *Aan Babylons stromen*, Amsterdam and Antwerp, 1951

Böhl, F. M. Th. de Liagre, "Babylon de Heilige Stad," *Jaarboek Ex Oriente Lux* III, 10, 1948, pp. 491–525; abbreviated and reprinted in *OM*, pp. 430–62

Janssen, E., *Juda in der Exilszeit: Ein Beitrag zur Frage der Entstehung des Judentums*, Göttingen, 1956

Snijders, L. A., "Het 'volk des lands' in Juda," *Ned. Theol. Tijdschrift* 12, 1957–8, pp. 241–56

Causse, A., *Les dispersés d'Israël: Les origines de la Diaspora et son rôle dans la formation du Judaïsme*, Paris, 1929

Vaux, R. de, "Les décrets de Cyrus et de Darius sur la réconstruction du temple," *Revue Biblique* 46, 1937, pp. 29–57

Grosheide, H. H., "Twee edicten van Cyrus ten gunste van de Joden," *Gereformeerd Theol. Tijdschrift* 54, 1954, pp. 1–12; *De terugkeer uit de ballingschap*, The Hague, 1957

Chary, T., *Les Prophètes et le Culte à partir de l'exil: Autour du second temple: L'ideal cultuel des prophètes exiliens et postexiliens*, Douai, 1955

Zarb, M., "De Synagogarum Origine," *Angelicum* 5, 1928, pp. 259–72

Schaeder, H. H., *Esra der Schreiber*, Tübingen, 1930

Cazelles, H., "La mission d'Esdras," *Vetus Testamentum* 4, 1954, pp. 113–40

Pavlovsky, V., "Die Chronologie der Tätigkeit Esdras," *Biblica* 38, 1957, pp. 275–305, 428–56

Rowley, H. H., "Nehemiah's Mission and its Background," *Bulletin J. Rylands Library* 37, 195, pp. 528–61

Fraine, J. de, "Esdras en Nehemias: Uit de grendtekst vertaald en uitgelegd," *De Boeken van het Oude Testament*, Roermond and Masseik, 1961

Alt, A., *Die Rolle Samarias bei der Entstehung des Judentums*, 1934; reprinted in *KS*, part II, pp. 317–37; *Zur Geschichte der Grenze zwischen Judäa und Samaria*, 1935; reprinted in *KS*, part II, pp. 346–62

Rowley, H. H., "Sanballat et le temple Samaritain," *L'AT et l'Orient* (*Journées Bibliques de Louvain 1954*), Louvain, 1957, pp. 175–91

Wagenaar, C. G., *De Joodse kolonie van Jeb-Syene in de 5de eeuw v. Chr.*, Groningen, 1928

Vincent, A., *La religion des Judéo-Araméens d'Elephantine*, Paris, 1937

Beek, M. A., "Relations entre Jérusalem et la diaspora égyptienne au 2e siècle avant J.-C.," *OTS* II, pp. 119–43

Dodd, C. H., *The Bible and the Greeks*, London, 1935 and 1954; American edition, Naperville, Ill., Alec R. Allenson, Inc., 1954

Seeligmann, I. L., *The Septuagint Version of Isaiah*, Leiden, 1948; see especially chapter 4: The Translation as a document of Jewish-Alexandrian Theology, pp. 95–121

Prijs, L., *Jüdische Tradition in der Septuaginta*, Leiden, 1948

Gehman, H. S., "The Theological Approach of the Greek Translator of Job 1–15," *Journal of Biblical Literature* 68, 1949, pp. 231–40

Wevers, J. W., "Exegetical Principles Underlying the Septuaginta Text of 1 Kings II 12- XXI 43," *OTS* VIII, pp. 300–22

Bertram, G., "Praeparatio evangelica in der Septuaginta," *Vetus Testamentum* 7, 1957, pp. 225–49

Benoit, P., "La Septante est-elle inspirée?" *Vom Wort des Lebens* (*Meinertz-Festschrift*), Münster, 1951, pp. 41–9; reprinted in *Exégèse et Théologie*, Paris, 1961, part I, pp. 3–12

Auvray, P., "Comment se pose le problème de l'inspiration des Sep-
tante," *Revue Biblique* 59, 1952, pp. 321–36
Coste, J., "Le texte grec d'Isaïe 25. 1-5," *Revue Biblique* 61, 1954, pp.
36–66; "La première expérience de tradition biblique: la Septante,"
La Maison Dieu 53, 1958, pp. 56–88. A very well orientated article
with an excellent bibliography.
Joussard, G., "Requête d'un patrologue aux biblistes touchant les
Septante," *Studia Patristica,* Vol. I (*Texte und Untersuchungen,* Band
63), pp. 307–27
Gelin, A., "La question des 'relectures' bibliques à l'intérieur d'une
tradition vivante," *SP,* pp. 303–15
Lemonnyer, A., "Le messianisme des 'Béatitudes,'" *Revue des sciences
phil. et théol.* 11, 1922, pp. 373–89
Birkeland, H., *'Ani und 'Anaw in den Psalmen,* Oslo, 1933
Van der Ploeg, J., "Les Pauvres d'Israël et leur piété," *OTS* VII, pp.
236–70
Gelin, A., *Les pauvres de Yahvé,* Paris, 1953
Brongers, H. A., "De Chasidim in het boek der Psalmen," *Nederlandse
Theol. Tijdschrift* 8, 1953-4, pp. 279–97
Leeuwen, C. van, "God, de koning en de armen in Psalm 72," *Neder-
landse Theol. Tijdschrift* 12, 1957-8, pp. 16–31
The purport of the whole of this section has the unexpected support of
a scholar of the importance of R. Smend. The author of the classic work
Lehrbuch der alttestamentlichen Religionsgeschichte wrote, in the
apparently forgotten preface to the first edition of this book (March 15,
1893): "In my opinion, a much clearer distinction than is usually made
must be drawn between the earlier and the later periods of Judaism,
that is, between the pre-maccabaean and the post-maccabaean Jewish
world. Insofar as the prehistory of Christianity is historically known to
us (excluding what we know of this from the New Testament itself),
its positive preparation is to be found in the pre-maccabaean period. The
post-maccabaean period, on the other hand, has essentially only a negative significance in this early history. The latter is more or less universally acknowledged, whereas the positive importance of pre-maccabaean Judaism has been greatly underestimated. This earlier Judaism in

no way corresponds to what is usually understood as the Jewish religion of the Law. The psalms testify to the vitality of the religion of the prophets, at least in the special form prepared for it by the Second Isaiah, in the early Jewish world. In all the happiness and misfortune that he encountered, the Jew of this period experienced the grace and the greatness as well as the gravity of his God. This undoubtedly counterbalanced the Law, which, on the evidence of the Book of Job, the Proverbs, and Ecclesiasticus, had essentially moral implications for the Jew in pre-maccabaean times. Observance of the Law and the worship prescribed by the Law were certainly of the greatest importance in the rise of the post-exilic community and in its external organisation in the hierocracy."

The emphasis on "morality" may well be characteristic of the age in which the author was writing, but this in no way invalidates what he is saying.

Index of
Principal Biblical Citations

357

Index